Women Politicking Politely

Women in American Political History

Series Editors: Pam Parry and David R. Davies

Advisory Board: Maurine Beasley, Barbara G. Friedman, Karla K. Gower, Janice Hume, Margot Opdycke Lamme, and Jane Marcellus

Women in American Political History focuses on influential women throughout the history of American politics. From the Colonial period through the Founding up to the present, women often have played significant and meaningful roles in politics, both directly and indirectly. Many of their contributions have been overlooked. This interdisciplinary series seeks to advance the dialogue concerning the role of women in politics in America and highlight their various contributions, including women who were elected and appointed to office and those who have wielded political power behind the scenes, such as first ladies, journalists, activists, and public relations practitioners. The series welcomes contributions from all methodologies and disciplines across the social sciences and humanities.

Recent Titles

Press Portrayals of Women Politicians, 1870s–2000s: From "Lunatic" Woodhull to "Polarizing" Palin, by Teri Finneman, 2015

Gendered Politics: Campaign Strategies of California Women Candidates, 1912–1970, by Linda Van Ingen, 2017

Ruby A. Black: Eleanor Roosevelt, Puerto Rico, and Political Journalism in Washington, by Maurine H. Beasley, 2017

Women Politicking Politely: Advancing Feminism in the 1960s and 1970s, by Kimberly Wilmot Voss, 2017

Women Politicking Politely

Advancing Feminism in the 1960s and 1970s

Kimberly Wilmot Voss

LEXINGTON BOOKS
Lanham • Boulder • New York • London

Published by Lexington Books
An imprint of The Rowman & Littlefield Publishing Group, Inc.
4501 Forbes Boulevard, Suite 200, Lanham, Maryland 20706
www.rowman.com

Unit A, Whitacre Mews, 26-34 Stannary Street, London SE11 4AB

Copyright © 2017 by Lexington Books

All rights reserved. No part of this book may be reproduced in any form or by any electronic or mechanical means, including information storage and retrieval systems, without written permission from the publisher, except by a reviewer who may quote passages in a review.

British Library Cataloguing in Publication Information Available

Library of Congress Cataloging-in-Publication Data

Library of Congress Control Number: 2017936855
ISBN: 978-1-4985-2229-8 (cloth : alk. paper)
ISBN: 978-1-4985-2230-4 (electronic)

∞™ The paper used in this publication meets the minimum requirements of American National Standard for Information Sciences Permanence of Paper for Printed Library Materials, ANSI/NISO Z39.48-1992.

Printed in the United States of America

This book is dedicated to my husband, Lance Speere, and my children, Curtis and Paul.

It is also dedicated to all of the important, well-behaved women who still need to be part of the historical record.

Contents

Acknowledgments		ix
1	Meeting the Well-Behaved Women Who Made a Difference	1
2	World War II, Women's Pages, and Women's Clubs	29
3	Women's Journalism Organizations, Women's Political Writing, and Offbeat Washington	49
4	Washington Press Club, Fundraising Cookbooks, and Glaser's Years as Head of Washington Press Club	67
5	Questions of Feminism, the 1969 Press Conference, and the President's Task Force on Women's Rights and Responsibilities	79
6	Kathryn Clarenbach, Continuing Education Programs, and Helping Traditional Women	93
7	*Xilonen*, the 1975 United Nations Women's Year Conference in Mexico City, and the 1977 International Women's Year Meeting in Houston	111
Afterword: What Happened in the Post-Houston Years		127
Bibliography		139
Index		149
About the Author		157

Acknowledgments

The story of the women described in this book was more than a decade in the making. I first learned and wrote about Dorothy Jurney and Marjorie Paxson when I wrote my dissertation at the University of Maryland about women's page journalists. I had been introduced to them through the Washington Press Club Foundation's Women in Journalism oral history project. Their stories ran counter to the stereotype that women's pages contained insignificant content and that the editors lacked power. (Marie Anderson was also chosen for the project but her Alzheimer's disease made her oral history transcript problematic. Luckily her papers and clips filled in the details of her life, as did the oral histories of her friends and colleagues.)

The material for this book came from the personal papers and oral histories of several women who worked together in various media, clubs, and governmental agencies. I examined the papers of journalist Helen Muir at the University of Miami and lawmaker Martha Griffiths' papers at the University of Michigan. There were additional mentions about the women in numerous books, journal articles, and government reports.

I also went through the papers of feminist activist Robin Morgan at Duke University and later was able to interview Morgan in 2016 about *New York Times* journalist Charlotte Curtis who covered the 1968 Miss America protest. I appreciate funding to go through Morgan's papers from the Mary Lily Research Grant from the Sallie Bingham Center for Women's History and Culture.

The seeds for this book were set at the Schlesinger Library Summer Seminar on Gender History in the summer of 2007. The theme, "Writing Past Lives: Biography as History," reinforced the need for the stories of women's lives to be told—especially women whose narratives have not been part of the historical record.

I would like to thank the University of Wyoming's American Heritage Center for a grant to go through the papers of Vera Glaser. Material about Glaser came from several places. She has papers at the National Women & Media Collection, which is housed at the State Historical Society of Missouri at the University of Missouri and extensive papers at the University of Wyoming—which were unindexed at the time of my research trip. Glaser took part in two oral histories. One was located at Penn State University and was part of the "A Few Good Women" presentation about working with the Nixon administration. Another was with the National Press Club. Her interview with the Press Club was especially helpful as I was able to actually hear Glaser's voice. Some of her stories and talks were read into the *Congressional Record*.

I appreciate a travel grant from the Schlesinger Library in the Radcliffe Institute for Advanced Study at Harvard University for a grant to go through the papers of Catherine East. Her letters were the key to understanding the unique relationship between government and the press when it came to women's roles.

The University of Central Florida provided funding to travel to the University of Wisconsin to go through Kathryn "Kay" Clarenbach's papers in 2009. An oral history with Clarenbach is also located at the University of Wisconsin and available online. There were also several articles about Clarenbach, in which she was quoted, that were available online thanks to the Google News archive scanning of the *Milwaukee Journal*. (This resource has since been removed.)

Catherine East's papers are at the Schlesinger Library at Harvard University; I went through her papers on two visits in 2005 and 2007. I appreciate the travel funding, which was provided by the Schlesinger Library for the first visit. An extensive, transcribed oral history of East was also located at the Schlesinger Library, which the UCF's ILL librarians tracked down; I went through the history twice.

Dorothy Jurney's papers are at the National Women & Media Collection which is now housed at the State Historical Society of Missouri at the University of Missiouri. She kept numerous letters, photos, and memos. She was also part of the previously mentioned oral history project. Her extensive memory helped to detail many moments from women's liberation history.

Marjorie Paxson's papers are at the National Women & Media Collection which is housed at the State Historical Society of Missouri at the University of Missiouri. I went through her papers in the early 2000s. She gave more papers in later years, and I appreciate the archivists who indexed the new materials. I was also able to speak to Paxson by phone several years ago and was on a panel at the University of Missouri when the collection celebrated its twentieth anniversary in 2007.

Marie Anderson's papers are also located at the National Women & Media Collection. She kept everything, and I was able to go through her unindexed papers in 2000. Her papers now include a detailed finding guide.

Numerous sources were also drawn from the research I have conducted during the past decade about women journalists and the women's liberation movement. Both in media mentions and personal letters, these women shared a bond. These women were connected both personally and professionally as they fought to help women at a time when much of society was conflicted about women's roles.

They are a white, educated, and middle-class group of women. Yet, they were keenly aware of issues of racial and class discrimination. They worked to help the lives of all women although, overall, they were late to the issues of lesbians and some reproductive issues. Some women in this group were quick to support birth control and other women came to understand these issues a few years later.

These women made a significant difference in the lives of other women, even if they were largely forgotten by many historians. Luckily they left behind primary sources and mediated accounts, which allow their stories to be told. I appreciate the UCF librarians who helped me track down books, magazines, and newspaper articles that helped verify the facts in this book. They went above and beyond to help me.

Thank you to Pam Parry and David Davies who inspired me to write this proposal and then book. The three peer-reviewers provided important feedback and helped me look at some issues differently. Also, thank you to editor Kathryn Tafelski and her assistant Madhu Koduvalli who made the writing and editing process enjoyable.

Lastly, I thank my husband, Lance Speere, for assisting me with going through these papers and the endless discussions about these important women over the past decade. Also, thanks to my young children Curtis and Paulie who were so well behaved while their mother wrote this book.

Chapter One

Meeting the Well-Behaved Women Who Made a Difference

In 1971, longtime government employee Catherine East and journalist Vera Glaser gathered a list of women lawyers and judges. Their goal was to find women qualified to become the first female member of the Supreme Court. First Lady Pat Nixon wanted to see a woman named during her husband's administration and sought names. Letters between East and Glaser show their excitement in helping a woman be named to the nation's highest court—and that the woman would never know. That did not happen, of course. It would take another decade for a woman to be named when President Reagan named Sandra Day O'Connor. The dashed hope of a female first was a disappointment that many women felt when Hillary Clinton was not elected president in 2016. Both examples demonstrate that hopeful progress for women does not always come to fruition, although at least there was improvement for female candidates in the case of the Supreme Court.

When 2016 presidential candidate Donald Trump called fellow candidate Clinton a "nasty woman" during a debate, her supporters embraced the term. Yet, it was a term that was a far cry from the world that many women in the public sphere could afford to abide by decades earlier. Clinton—then Rodham—attended the all-female Wellesley College from 1965 to 1969. The book, *Rebels in White Gloves*, explains the stories of Clinton's classmates at Wellesley. As the title suggests, it was still a time when being a lady was the center of women's roles. As the author wrote: "For girls so deeply ingrained with the feminine habits of silence and docility, the audacity of Hillary Rodham's speech on graduation day was unimaginably liberating."[1]

After years of fighting formally and informally for women's rights, it truly became a national, public conversation in 1977—about a decade after Clinton's speech. The meeting began after a flaming torch, emulating the ceremony of the Olympic torch, had been carried by different women more than 2,600 miles. It traveled from Seneca Falls, New York—home of the first women's rights convention in 1848—to Houston to open the National Women's Conference. It was attended by a diverse two thousand delegates from across the country. One member said the goal of the meeting was to establish "a more perfect union for all womankind, whether they want it or not."[2] This was a reminder that not all women wanted change—especially those who enjoyed a privileged position. That International Women's Year meeting in Houston was a significant moment for women in American history. Many women were formally seeking space in the public sphere—a place that was not welcoming both by law and practice.

For several of the women leading the Conference, this was the moment they had long waited for. They had worked within the system and by mediated pressure to create regulations that would address the many inequities against women. Years before, the President's Commission on the Status of Women had begun to document women's roles in the early 1960s and each state created its own commission during that decade. These groups laid the foundation for what would happen in Houston. By the time the United Nations established the 1975 meeting in Mexico City and then asked for each country to take action, many American women were ready to advocate for a new role. For decades, women in various fields—especially government and journalism—had been fighting for better opportunities for women.

One example of this advocacy would be longtime government employee Catherine East and journalist Vera Glaser, had been working together since 1969 when Glaser asked President Nixon when he was going to name women to his cabinet; separately they had been working for women much earlier. Later, the women would join journalists Marjorie Paxson and Dorothy Jurney in creating portions of the 1976 governmental report *To Form a More Perfect Union*, which addressed many injustices American women faced. The document laid the groundwork for the 1977 International Women's Year meeting in Houston that brought together more than twenty thousand women from across the country. The documentary *Step By Step* includes the story of the landmark Houston meeting and explained "the political side of the women's movement grew out of the labor movement, not the elite."[3] This is especially true if the work of the Women's Bureau in the Labor Department and East are included.

The Houston meeting drew media attention for the several First Ladies who attended and the firing of Congresswomen Bella Abzug from the National Advisory Committee on Women. It was the beginning of a growing conservative group against increasing rights for women, including the Equal Rights Amendment, led by Phyllis Schlafly. (In the media, Schlafly predicted that the Houston meeting would be the "death knell for women's liberation movement."[4]) What is less known is the story of Kathryn "Kay" Clarenbach who spent decades helping women, and who was the initial Chair of the Board of the National Organization for Women, and the deputy director of the IWY meeting. One of the staff members of the meeting described Clarenbach and the daunting task she faced: "You could tell it wasn't her favorite thing in the world to have to direct this motley crew. It was really like herding cats, all these different people and we're all so young. But she did it well. She had a good attitude about it."[5] Clarenbach was recommended for the position by East. They were bonded by their ability to make a difference for women quietly while also keeping their government jobs safe.

Historians were late to uncover the stories of many of these largely behind-the-scene women. Those who were included in the historical record were typically the women who were significant because of the men they married or the children they produced. As the history of women began to be documented, it was the First Ladies and various "firsts" who were initially highlighted. Then, it was those who took a stand for women's issues, such as suffragists or later women's liberation movement leaders who garnered media attention. It led to the oft quoted "well-behaved women seldom make history."[6] Yet, to truly document a complete history, well-behaved women should also be included. Many of them worked to make a difference, although often behind the scenes, particularly in the 1960s and 1970s. As one scholar wrote: "The 1960s would mark a period of social change. A women's movement that had been fragmented and class bound would begin to take on a popular form. In Washington, the nature of politics was undergoing a transformation."[7] It is also worth noting that while these women may have not made headlines, they were, at times, considered radical for even questioning inequities.

This book includes the relatively unknown stories of two female political operatives who worked behind the scenes along with four female journalists who also occasionally worked within government to advance women's rights during the 1950s through the 1970s. Much of it centers on Washington, DC, as well as the more unlikely cities of Madison, Wisconsin, and Miami, Florida. It includes the story of a women's page journalist who published an official government report in her newspaper section when the White House refused to release it. This book documents the stories of women who organized to help gain employment for other women and also worked to raise the stature of homemakers. Numerous other issues for women were also addressed. The fight for equality became more visible in the 1960s although the foundation had been laid as early as the 1950s, fueled by the post-World War II era. Change was initiated by a mix of women in government (among others) and women in the news media—at times going back and forth in those positions. These particular women were chosen because of their interactions with each other as they rallied around a common cause and because their names were overshadowed by other women's liberation leaders. It is not meant to be an exhaustive story of the fight for women's rights but rather an addition to the great memoirs and scholarship that already exist about women in the 1950s, 1960s, and 1970s.

Several women's liberation leaders, including Gloria Steinem, Bella Abzug, and Betty Friedan were household names and regularly covered by the media. Furthermore, some leaders such as Friedan, *The Feminine Mystique* author and National Organization for Women's first president, were portrayed as having a divisive personality[8] and too removed from "typical women" to represent their views. Friedan said to a reporter: "I'm nasty, I'm bitchy, I get mad, but by God, I'm absorbed in what I am doing."[9] A review of feminist history devoted a chapter to what was described as "The Battle of Betty."[10] Of course, to make a difference, one often needed to be forceful. Consider feminist Susan Brownmiller's statement about Friedan: "Visionaries by nature are difficult, impatient people."[11] Also, as historian Carolyn G. Heilbrun has written: "To denounce women for shrillness and stridency is another way of denying them any right to power."[12] Initially, the women had a rocky start in NOW as Clarenbach's children used to screen calls from Friedan, but over time they developed a strong working relationship. According to Clarenbach, "I developed one of the best working relationships that anyone had with her. We did come to respect each other."[13]

While there were disagreements among women in the women's movement, this is not to imply the gendered catfight stereotype. The media's use of the catfight framework or women-against-women presentation has marginalized the concept of feminism and is also a part of how some journalists covered advocates—one woman pitted against another. It was a common model used in news story—Betty Friedan on one side and Phyllis Schafly on another side, for example. That woman-against-woman media focus has created an odd space for women in the public sphere. As popular culture historian Susan Douglas has written,

> The media referees insist on putting feminism in one corner and antifeminism in the other, as if feminism could never be in the middle, but what they fail to recognize is that feminism *is* the middle ground. It may be filled with ambivalence and compromise, tradition and rebellion, but the space between the two cats—the space where we, the girls are—is what feminism is all about.[14]

According to Douglas, the mediated images of women were dominated by the catfight frame. She wrote that the image served "as a metaphor for the struggle between feminism and antifeminism, the catfight provided a symbolic catharsis of women's internal conflict between the desire for liberation and the longing for security."[15] Of course, this does not mean that all women get along nor that they would all agree on political goals. The six women in this book did not agree with many of the more radical approaches to women's rights. In some ways, it was because they had experienced success by working within the system. It was also about their personalities. They were not as assertive in their styles as Friedan or Abzug. It may have also explained their friendships.

Clarenbach was one of many women from the Midwest who are sometimes left out of women's political history. Many of the founders of NOW and the National Women's Political Caucus came from the middle of the country. Renowned historian Gerda Lerner created an oral history project in 1992 to celebrate these women. As she wrote in an article about the project:

> Without in any way wanting to diminish the importance of Betty Friedan's book and her organizing energy, nor discounting the burst of initiative and creative energy of young women out of the civil rights movement (disenchanted with that movement's sexism) and the breakthrough of theoretical insights and organizing genius of lesbians and others involved in the sexual revolutions, I would argue that up to now we have insufficiently recognized the contributions to the movement made by other groups of women.[16]

The women described in this book made a difference because they worked behind the scenes. Much less is known about East, for example, because she helped those women who made the headlines or she encouraged journalists to write those headlines. She avoided attention and worked to connect people in unofficial ways. For the most part, she was not covered by the media but she planted stories in newspapers through reporters, including Glaser. Likewise, outside of Wisconsin, there is little mention of Clarenbach despite her leadership of the National Organization for Women. It was Freidan who received most of the recognition for the initiation of the organization. Similarly, Clarenbach's role as executive director of the 1977 Women's Conference in Houston was overshadowed by Abzug's controversial role as presiding officer.[17] In another example of the friendship of the women at the center of this book, East had been the one to recommend Clarenbach for the position.

The women in this book were chosen because of the ways in which their lives intersected as they fought for women's rights in often more subtle ways than liberation leaders of the time. (Glaser's reporting would be an exception although rarely do "official" stories of the women's liberation movement include her syndicated five-part series on women's rights in 1969 or her presidential press conference questions about women.) Proof of their activism was found in their papers, news reports, and in oral histories. These women worked primarily behind the scenes. Their stories deserve to come out from the shadows.

Friedan described East as "the midwife to the contemporary women's movement."[18] This was an appropriate description. While a midwife has the power to help bring a life into the world, she typically does not get the same respect as a doctor. East, too, has not gotten the recognition for all that she did to help women. Yet, this is how she operated: low key, private letters, and anonymous contributions. In the role, she made sure action was taken without risking her significant government position. East's governmental experience provided invaluable data and her progressive thinking helped advance women's positions in society.

In a *New York Times* article about Clarenbach, Ellen Chesler, senior fellow at the Roosevelt Institute, wrote: "Friedan had moxie, but no practical skills to organize a broadly based political movement. Kay Clarenbach had the establishment credentials and genial manner that made her an ideal partner for the more truculent Friedan. She had the presence of mind to collect twenty-seven contributions of five dollars each—NOW's first treasury. She became the organization's most trustworthy doer." In a book about the Women's Movement, Clarenbach was described as "cool-headed Kay Clarenbach" and "the tall, dignified Wisconsin women's leader."[19] (Clarenbach said that Friedan viewed her as "slow-witted Midwesterner."[20] Historian Marcia Cohen wrote: Clarenbach's "prestige far outweighed Friedan's media-oriented flamboyance."[21]) In a letter to Clarenbach, East contributed five dollars to the new organization but explained that the contribution could not be in her name due to her government position. (That letter was found in Clarenbach's extensive papers at the University of Wisconsin.) In another example of Clarenbach's marginalization, Chesler noted: "Clarenbach's death in March went almost unnoticed outside her home state. Historian Lerner said at Clarenbach's memorial service: 'Kay was the foremost organizer of the modern women's movement, recognized as such by all who worked with her . . . the reliable, sustaining force without which there is no social change.'"[22]

Glaser has also been largely overlooked although in many ways she is at the center of these stories. She was friendly with all of the women in this book. As was noted in the *Washington Post* after Glaser's death, "She made a significant difference in the coverage of the women's liberation movement." Women like her "worked behind the scenes. Their names might not be well known, but they laid the groundwork, and she was on the forefront of writing about the women's movement."[23] She continuously interviewed government officials and asked tough questions about women's roles. Glaser not only raised questions about the government's treatment of women but held politicians accountable for their promises with the follow-up stories she wrote. East described Glaser as "one of our unsung heroines" for the women's movement.[24] Glaser also questioned her own industry, which had a history of discriminating against women employees. She spoke out about the topic during a 1971 speech before the Minnesota Newspaper Association. The provocative speech (for the time) questioned why more women were not in positions of power at newspapers, and it was not received well by what was likely a mostly male audience. Rather than accept such treatment, she had the speech read into the *Congressional Record* so her words would have a wider audience.[25]

In many ways, the ability to use primary sources for this book is thanks to Paxson who created the National Women & Media Collection thanks to a retirement policy at Gannett, initially located at the University of Missouri, and then encouraged her friends to donate their papers. Paxson had worked with Jurney and Anderson during the important women's page years of the 1960s. Two decades later, Paxson became the fourth female publisher in Gannett newspaper chain—and one of the first women in that position. Ultimately, Paxson did not consider the role of publisher to be her most significant accomplishment. Instead, she cited her work as editor of *Xilonen*, the eight-page daily newspaper published for the United Nations World Conference for International Women's Year held in Mexico City in 1975 as her most important work. Yet, her work and actions of women at the conference had little voice. For example, the US media did not cover the issues at the Conference and instead focused on brief moments of conflict. When Paxson returned to America, she wrote a series of articles about what really happened and sold the series to several newspapers.

Several of these women shared roles in both journalism and government work over the years. Glaser, for example, worked as a press agent for a politician and then a political party before returning to being a journalist and later served on a White House task force. Jurney and Paxson worked under government contracts while taking breaks from journalism. This book addresses their political roles as they found that feminism often trumped objectivity when it came to women's rights. Glaser mentioned the challenge in an oral history:

> I have felt that my participation in the women's movement was a very pivotal point in my life. I am so happy I did it. I had qualms at the beginning. I had qualms as a journalist about asking the President the kind of question (about women) that I did. And yet in simple justice, you had to ask it. But I sometimes felt that I was conflicted between journalism and trying very, very hard not to be partisan for a cause. You have to be very even handed in our business.[26]

These women were surrounded by other powerful women, often in governmental positions. One of those women had connections both in government and journalism: Oveta Culp Hobby. She had a significant impact on Paxson, then women's page editor of the *Houston Post*. Hobby earned a law degree from the University of Texas Law School in 1925. After graduation she became parliamentarian for the Texas House of Representatives, and assistant city attorney in Houston. In 1931 she married William P. Hobby, the former governor of Texas and publisher of the newspaper, the *Houston Post*.

She helped her husband run the *Post*, until 1941, when Mrs. Hobby went to Washington, DC, to head the War Department's Women's Interest Section. From 1942 to 1945, she served as director of the newly created Women's Army Auxiliary Corps. Following World War II, Hobby returned to Houston and the *Post*. In 1953, President Dwight D. Eisenhower named her head of the Federal Security Agency, which, later that year, was elevated to a cabinet position and renamed the Department of Health, Education, and Welfare with Hobby becoming its first secretary, a position she held until 1955 when she resigned.[27]

One of the staples of any newspaper women's section was stories about local brides. Several progressive women's page editors in the 1950s and 1960s were looking to reduce and change wedding news. Paxson was the women's page editor in 1951 when she decided to fight to get brides off the front pages of the Sunday section so that more important news could be covered. After speaking with her newspaper management, Paxson was told that she could move the photos inside. Two weeks after the change, an important family in the city had a wedding and the father of the bride called the governor to ask for an exception to the new policy. Paxson told Governor Hobby that she would stick to her policy. He spoke to his wife and Mrs. Hobby backed up Paxson's decision. Paxson said in an oral history interview: "That was my first lesson in management: That when you delegate authority, you better back your people up."[28] Like Hobby, there were several women in the federal government who achieved top billing. Although they are few and far between, historians have begun to document the stories of women in the federal government in the post-World War II era. In 2009, the life and legacy of Frances Perkins, titled *The Woman behind the New Deal*, was published.[29]

While these women have existed, there has not necessarily been a recording of the relationship between some of the women leaders of the federal government and journalists. Letters, newspaper clippings, and oral histories show the friendships and the professional partnerships of these women. The women chosen for this book all had at least two friendships in common—although usually more. Some were personal friends such as Anderson and Jurney who travelled together quite a bit in later life. Other women had relationships that were more professional in nature, such as East and Clarenbach—although they considered each other friends. Much of what they accomplished was based on their partnerships, both personally and professionally.

The stories of these women are important additions to the historical record. It builds on the work of scholars like Lee Ann Banaszak who examined women who worked with the Federal Government for change, especially the Equal Employment Opportunity Commission and the Women's Bureau.[30] Stephanie Gilmore explored the creation of the National Organization for Women and the grassroots feminist activism in the post-World War II years.[31] Esther Peterson and other female labor leaders were documented in *Rocking the Boat: Union Women's Voices, 1915–1975*.[32] *The Rebirth of Feminism* documented the many parts of the Women's Liberation Movement by 1971.[33]

Sociologist Alice S. Rossi documented the background and stories of the First National Women's Conference.[34] As scholars in the book *No Permanent Waves: Recasting Histories of U.S. Feminism* pointed out, a lot happened between the so-called waves: "in reality, such movements overlapped and intertwined across U.S. history."[35] Further, in *Deans of Women and the Feminist Movement*, East and Clarenbach are mentioned in the challenge against the "dual waves" theory of women's history.[36]

Backgrounds of the Women

Vera Glaser

Vera Glaser was born in 1916 and was raised in St. Louis, Missouri. She was interested in journalism while in high school and on the weekends she visited the newsrooms of her local newspapers, the *St. Louis Post-Dispatch* and *St. Louis Globe-Democrat*. She graduated from high school first in her class, a position that typically meant a scholarship to Washington University. Instead, that year the honor went to a male who had been at the school for less than a year. Decades later, she recalled the snub, writing that her high school experience, plus some workplace discrimination, turned her into "a fighting feminist." She took undergraduate classes in the evenings at Washington University in St. Louis and then at the local George Washington University and American University in Washington, DC. She stopped attending just prior to completing a bachelor's degree.[37]

She married Herbert Glaser, an administrative officer in the National Labor Relations Board. They had a daughter who was born in 1947. She began her career in magazine, newspaper, and radio journalism before turning to governmental public relations work in the 1950s, including overseeing the women's division for the Republican National Committee. Glaser became a Washington, DC-based reporter for the North American Newspaper Alliance in the 1960s. Then she became the Washington Bureau Chief for the Alliance in the 1960s. Her articles typically ran in the women's pages. (She joined the Washington Bureau staff of Knight Newspapers in the 1970s.) During those years, her work ran in the women's pages of the Miami and Detroit newspapers—especially when there was news about women coming out of Washington, DC. For example, when a Women's Bureau event was coming up, Anderson would ask Glaser to cover the meeting. Glaser agreed to cover the conference and signed the letter with "warm regards."[38] Anderson later requested that Glaser focus on the inequities faced by women in various fields.[39] Glaser played a significant role, although often overlooked, in early coverage of the movement. These stories were written prior to Glaser becoming friendly with East. For example, in 1963, she wrote a wire story about discrimination against women. In it, she noted a "simmering resentment over the relatively few women in top appointive and career posts."[40]

Glaser was one of the first women to be a Washington bureau chief. She was an occasional guest on the television program *Meet the Press*. She recalled her appearance on the program on October 8, 1967, when she asked pointed questions of President Lyndon Johnson's consumer affairs advisor Betty Furness who appeared caught off guard. According to a transcript of the program, Glaser asked pointed questions about consumer credit, inflation, and price controls. Glaser later recalled: "One of my questions was so tough that it tripped her up and LBJ was furious. Before we got out of the studio, he was on the phone telling her how she should have answered me."[41]

Glaser was a member of President Nixon's Task Force on Women's Rights and Responsibilities from 1969 to 1970. This appointment followed the previously mentioned press conference question to Nixon about the lack of women in government that received national exposure. It led to an emphasis on women's liberation news, which she covered in addition to her regular news beat. The feminist group KNOW, Inc. included Glaser on a short list of "Reporters You Can Trust."[42]

In 1971, Glaser was elected the president of the Washington Press Club, a social and professional organization for journalists. (The Washington Press Club was created in 1919 by women journalists and was then known as the Women's Press Club, as women were not allowed to be members of the National Press Club. Women were not allowed to become members of the NPC until 1971.[43]) She was the first president to oversee the club after men were allowed to become members. Within the first year, a new male member wrote Glaser a letter complaining that there were too many women officers in the formerly all-female club.[44] The two journalism clubs merged in 1985 with the Washington Press Club becoming a foundation that would later produce the oral history project Women in Journalism. Anderson, Jurney, and Paxson were interviewed as part of the project—three of the only four women's page editors included in the project. Their stories demonstrated the foundation that was being laid for the women's liberation movement in the 1950s and 1960s.

Catherine East

Catherine Shipe was born in 1916 in the small town of Barboursville, near Huntington, West Virginia. Her parents were Ulysses Grant Shipe, a bank president and mayor of the town, and Bertha Woody Shipe, a homemaker who suffered from mental illness. Growing up, Catherine wanted to be a lawyer. It was a goal that her mother and grandmother supported. Her father viewed a career as something for her to fall back on if her future husband became ill. When she was eleven years old, her mother had a mental breakdown. In 1931, when she was fifteen years old, her father lost his business in the Great Depression and committed suicide. In her oral history, she noted that her mother suffered by not having a career outside the home. She said that her mother's lack of career helped her understand the need for paid employment.

Her father left her one thousand dollars in his will, and she used it to pay her college tuition. She attended Marshall University (then Marshall College) from 1932 to 1935. She majored in English and math before leaving school with eleven hours left to complete. She was unable to pay the tuition and took the civil service exam beginning her career in government. She completed her coursework at George Washington University at night and earned her degree from Marshall in 1941. From 1942 to 1944, she studied law at GWU, completing eighteen hours of study. She has at times been incorrectly labeled as an attorney. She later noted of her legal expertise, "I learned enough about legal research to find out what I needed to know."[45] She demonstrated this in various legal arguments for women policy experts and lawmakers—including Mary Eastwood and Martha Griffiths.

She married Charles D. East, a parts expert for the Defense Department, on July 2, 1937. The couple had two daughters. She noted that the couple began to grow apart during World War II as she began to grow more independent and he grew more dependent.[46] They divorced in 1956 when her daughters were four and eleven. She largely raised her children as a single mother, often using a housekeeper and babysitters for child care when she was at work. Her recognition of the struggles of women who work outside the home would later be reflected in the official reports that she oversaw. The need for quality child care was a common request from the federal and state governments during the 1960s and 1970s. While attempts for government-sponsored child care were made, nothing was ever passed.

Over the years, East worked her way up the government career ladder. This was a common path for many Washington, DC, career women of the time. Other notable government women of that time included lawyer Marguerite Rawalt,[47] Eastwood and, later, Barbara Hackman Franklin.[48] East came to Washington, DC, in 1939 and began work as a clerk at the Civil Service Commission, which became the Office of Personnel Management. She rose through the ranks of government to serve as executive secretary of the Committee on Federal Employment in President John F. Kennedy's administration, the Interdepartmental Committee on the Status of Women, and the Citizen's Advisory Council on the Status of Women. She held senior posts with every presidential advisory commission on the status of women from 1962 to 1977. East was also one of the architects of the strategy, along with Pauli Murray and Martha Griffiths, to bring the Equal Rights Amendment out of committee and to passage in the House of Representatives.[49] (The ERA was first introduced into Congress in 1923; Griffiths' battle was a significant legislative victory at the time. Ultimately, not enough states ratified the amendment for it to be added to the Constitution; the legislation and strategies to ratify are still being debated today. Many of the fear tactics—such as gay marriage—are now legal.)

One of her early visible roles was serving on the Presidential Commission on the Status of Women. (She learned of the commission in the women's pages of her newspaper.) Esther Peterson, director of the Women's Bureau, knew of East's previous work and named her as a staff member to the commission. It was Bureau Director Libby Koontz who finally allowed East to be more open about her work with women's groups. East's last governmental position was as coordinator of policies and plans for the International Women's Year secretariat. She resigned a year later after her own health issues and differences with Congresswoman Bella Abzug. In her retirement, she would work on a project with Jurney documenting the media's coverage of women's issues. She also worked for passage of the ERA in Virginia and as women's issues coordinator for the John Anderson presidential campaign.

Kathryn Clarenbach

Kathryn "Kay" Clarenbach was born in the small town of Sparta, Wisconsin, in 1920. She was an active high school student including playing the lead in the school play. She earned a bachelor's degree in political science in 1941 from the University of Wisconsin–Madison. During her studies, she was not allowed into the all-male Rathskeller pub in the student union. The snub made an impression on her. (Decades later, NOW would challenge the restaurant and bar policies that excluded women.) She went on to earn a master's degree in political science in 1942.

She passed the federal civil service exam and worked in Washington, DC, during World War II. From 1942 to 1944, Clarenbach worked as an administrative analyst for the War Production Board in Washington, DC. She then moved back to Madison to earn her doctoral degree in political science. While there, she was introduced to fellow student Henry "Hank" Clarenbach. They married in 1946—the same year that she earned her doctoral degree in political science. They remained married until his death in 1987. She said of their relationship: "We had as close to an egalitarian marriage and household as any I know. Both in-the-home and outside activities were never divided along gender lines at all but according to whoever was good at it."[50]

She taught political science at Purdue University before taking a few years off professionally to raise her three young children—born in 1949,

1953, and 1957. During this period she did volunteer work and became a Missouri state board member of the League of Women Voters. In 1961, Clarenbach took a teaching position at Edgewood College in Madison, Wisconsin. She was elected to the board of trustees at Alverno College—an all-women's school. She was energized by the idea of an all-women college and believed strongly in its mission. In 1962, the focus of Clarenbach's work became women's issues when she was asked to devise a program for continuing education for women through the University of Wisconsin–Extension. Clarenbach could not find child care when she took the job so her husband rescheduled his real estate work so he could be at home when the children got off the bus. During a statewide conference she organized, Clarenbach's life was changed when the idea of a state-wide Governor's Commission on the Status of Women was unanimously recommended.

The following year, Clarenbach was hired to develop a program in continuing education for women at the University of Wisconsin-Extension. She initiated extension courses for women who sought higher education and training for employment outside the home. At a 1963 conference on professional opportunities for women, she met Esther Peterson, the director of the Women's Bureau in the US Department of Labor, who had helped persuade President Kennedy to establish the President's Commission on the Status of Women in 1961. Clarenbach then worked with Peterson and state women's organizations to persuade Governor John Reynolds to approve the Wisconsin Commission on the Status of Women. Several cities and universities also established commissions.

In July 1963, Clarenbach planned the first women's conference in Wisconsin that took place in January 1964. She went to chair the commission for many years. Throughout the 1960s, Clarenbach began to champion changes in her state's laws. For example, in 1965, she asked the governor to change a law that prevented mothers from signing the form that allowed their minor children to get a driver's license. The request was overruled by the head of the motor vehicles department who responded that only fathers were the heads of a household.

In her later, most visible roles, she was an initial founder of the National Organization for Women. Mary Jean Collins helped found the Milwaukee chapter of NOW and was an early member of NOW in Chicago. When asked who influenced her in the early years of the movement, she pointed to Clarenbach for "helping hold the organization together when it was a fragile flower."[51] She was also an early member of National Women's Political Caucus and coordinator of the historic 1977 Houston National Women's Conference. Her honed administrative skills and calm demeanor made her the perfect person to mediate the sometimes strident voices that also championed women's causes in the 1960s and 1970s. As the *New York Times* noted in 1995, "Clarenbach had the establishment credentials and genial manner that made her an ideal partner for the more truculent Friedan."[52] According to former Wisconsin US Senator Russ Feingold: "Clarenbach was credited by many of her early colleagues for providing the organizational glue that held the women's movement together and allowed it to move forward."[53]

Dorothy Jurney

Dorothy Misener Jurney said she was raised "to believe that a woman with a brain should have a career."[54] She was born Dorothy Misener in Michigan City, Indiana, in 1909. Her very first role as a journalist was in her childhood when she edited the "Dick-Dot Newspaper" she created with her brother Dick Misener.[55] Her father ran the local newspaper, the *Michigan City News*, and Jurney learned every aspect of journalism at the newspaper, from selling subscriptions to editing to layout to recognizing press type. Her mother, Mary Hershey Misener, was a graduate of the Kings School of Oratory in Pittsburgh. She was active in the suffrage movement and was one of the first women elected to the Indiana legislature.[56] While in office, she sponsored and fought for Indiana's first voter registration law.[57] Many of Jurney's beliefs about women's roles in society were based on her mother's activism. She said, "I guess I was always a feminist. My mother was a feminist, certainly. I was not as outspoken about it, but it was part of my values."[58] Over the years, her acts as a feminist became more obvious and combined with her news judgment to expand the definition of women's news.

After high school, Jurney attended Western College for Women in Oxford, Ohio, now part of Miami University, for two years. She completed her junior and senior years at Northwestern University with a major in journalism and an emphasis in economics. Jurney had every intention of pursuing a professional career, like many of her female classmates, when she graduated in 1930. She said: "My friends were career minded, there was that impetus that we should all be working—we should be working women and have careers. But nobody ever pointed out, or we were not smart enough to realize, that the horizons were not very high."[59]

Jurney said she was frustrated by women who were not using their educations outside of the home. She said, "I was very disappointed when I found that the women who were in college around the time of World War II were not career-minded. They were marriage and family and children minded. And that struck me as regression for women."[60] This may have been a common feeling for the numerous women coming out of journalism programs during this period. All newspapers had a women's section that provided journalism employment for women, as well as women's magazines.

She graduated from Northwestern University in 1930 and began working as a reporter at her father's newspaper.[61] During her career from 1930 until her retirement in 1975, Jurney was a journalist at numerous newspapers. It was not until the end of her career that she reached newspaper management. In her retirement, she continued working on having more women in newspaper management. That included surveying newspapers for the industry group ASNE (American Society of News Editors) and creating her own recruitment firm for women in newspaper management.

Jurney was a founder of New Directions for News and was the first female board member of Associated Press Managing Editors. Along with Paxson and East, she worked on the report for the third presidential Status of Women Commission. Jurney served as media specialist to the Women's Study Program and Policy Center at George Washington University on a project that analyzed newspaper reporting of issues and events of importance to women, and published the findings in a report called *New Directions for News*. (East was the issue specialist on this project.) She became a board member of the newspaper think tank, also called New Directions for News, located at the University of Missouri. She worked for the National Commission on the Observance of International Women's Year, 1975–1979; participated in the National Women's Conference in Houston, 1977. In 1988, she was awarded the University of Missouri Distinguished Service to Journalism Award.

Marjorie Paxson

Marjorie Paxson was one of two children raised in Houston, Texas; she said she was raised to believe that she and her brother were equals. After sometime at Rice University, she transferred to the University of Missouri to study journalism. She graduated during World War II and thus was able to work at a wire service because so many men were away in the service. She was allowed to cover everything but football games and executions, according to her oral history.

In peacetime she was forced back to the women's pages; she had signed a waiver promising to give her job up when the men returned. She worked in radio and was a women's page editor in Houston after the war. It was in the 1950s that Paxson first began publishing pictures of black brides in the *Houston Chronicle*—something rarely done at metropolitan newspapers in the South. She attributed many of the changes that occurred in her section to changes in the community: "It was more a matter of let's keep up with the times and stay current. It was clear that our coverage would need to change."[62]

Later, Paxson moved to the *Miami Herald* where she worked with Anderson and Jurney. These women developed a journalism community together and pushed the definition of women's news. This period was described by Paxson as the "golden era" for women's pages.[63] She wrote an article for the

Iowa Publisher newsletter in the 1960s about the progress women were making in journalism, although she also recognized that sexism still existed. "The walls of resistance to women in the newsroom are yielding, a complete turnaround from 1945," she wrote.[64] But due to gender-based stereotypes, women were coming into the newsroom at a disadvantage. She wrote, "Most city editors are men, and there is an inborn prejudice against sending a woman on certain kinds of stories."[65] She concluded the article by telling young women they did not have to make a choice between a personal life and a professional life: "A woman needn't worry either about having to make the old choice between marriage or a career. More than half the women who work in this country are married. A smart girl has her cake and eats it, too."[66]

Paxson was elected president of Theta Sigma Phi (now known as the Association for Women in Communications) in 1963, as the organization took on a more professional approach. Paxson's 1966 advice to women's page editors on stories about women who were rising through the ranks: "Let's stop downgrading women executives. How many times have you heard and printed the comments, 'I hate to work for a woman boss'? No specifics, just that. I have worked for some men who weren't so great as bosses, but nobody will sit still for a generalization about male bosses. As women, let's give other women a chance."[67]

Then, just as society was beginning to pay serious heed to the changing role of women, the women's pages were eliminated. Some of the women journalists were able to move into other sections, while others were demoted or lost their jobs. Paxson said one of her lowest career points came when she was meeting with a group of professional women and she described her firing and demotions due to the end of women's pages. Paxson recalled, "One of the participants heard me out and then told me: 'Marj, you have to accept the fact that you're a casualty of the women's movement.'"[68] Paxson said she agreed with that assessment despite the work she had done for women's rights.

Paxson took leave from her newspaper in Philadelphia to become the editor of *Xilonen*, the eight-page daily newspaper published for the NGO for the United Nations World Conference for International Women's Year held in Mexico City in 1975. After the media sensationalized events at the conference and minimized the women's concerns, she wrote a series of articles that was picked up by several newspapers. Along with Jurney and East, she worked on the federal government report *To Form a More Perfect Union*. (After some conflict by those overseeing the report, Glaser wrote the introduction.) She eventually became the fourth female publisher in the Gannett newspaper chain and continued to fight for equality for women, including changing editorial stance to support the ERA in her second publisher position.

Marie Anderson

Marie Anderson was a Florida native and an only child who was the daughter of a wealthy judge. Both of her parents earned law degrees although her mother never practiced nor had a career outside of the home. Anderson earned a degree in English from Duke University and moved to New York City to go to secretarial school. Letters in the 1940s between Anderson and a college friend describe shock that a classmate would be "a housewife with no outside job."[69] Anderson returned to Miami to work at the Servicemen's Pier during World War II. She became the first single woman to head the Junior League in Miami. Her connection to the organization led to a job at the newspaper, the *Miami News*. It was there that she met Jurney. Anderson said her new friend introduced her to both journalism and feminism.

The two women later moved to the *Miami Herald* where Jurney was the women's page editor and Anderson was her assistant throughout the 1950s. In 1960, Jurney left for Detroit and Anderson became women's page editor in Miami. She won so many Penney-Missouri Awards, the top prize for the women's pages, in the 1960s that she was retired from the competition. The women stayed in touch and Jurney often returned to Miami. In a speech to female high school students, Anderson said, "Marriage, of course, is a fine institution and I don't want to knock it but don't get upset if you don't make it."[70] In that same speech, she encouraged the students to develop their own skills—and be independent. "Don't go to college just to find a husband," she said. "Be selfish about it. Learn things for your own good. It's good insurance to be able to do something on your own."[71] Anderson had a community of friends she socialized with regularly. "I don't mind being alone," she said. "I have lots of friends I feel I can communicate with if I want to."[72]

For much of women's page history, society coverage was of the upper-class, but it was beginning to change under the watch of these women's page editors emerging from a post-World War II Florida. In a 1964 *Editor & Publisher* article about Anderson, she said women's sections were covering less society news and more hard news. "We need to operate a little more like the city desk," she said.[73] In a 1967 presentation, Anderson told women's page journalists to "de-emphasize society activities and emphasize events and features of interest to the whole community."[74] She emphasized that the trend in women's pages was to play down society news.[75] In another speech, she urged women's page editors not to forget the subject that was at the heart of the sections. She wrote: "There is still a mighty fertile field for the encouragement of good reporting about the subject 'women.' She is a big subject—and she's not likely to yield her identity or place in the sun, which grows larger with every week and month."[76]

Some critics have expressed concerns about progressive news being located near recipes and fashion pictures, feeling that it diminished women's issues.[77] Anderson, however, was not bothered by this. This is likely because she saw these things as intertwined. The letters that went back and forth between Jurney and Anderson included paragraphs addressing job inequities for women followed by mentions of gardening and what dish had been recently served.[78] In various letters, they wrote about hyacinths,[79] a diet,[80] and the health of friends and family.[81] In another letter, Jurney included a 1970 magazine advertisement for a resort. In the ad, a young couple stands in the water holding hands. His pants are rolled up and hers are not. Jurney wrote to Anderson, "It's bad enough these people have to push sex at the exclusion of everything else but why do they have to have a pix where he has the sense to roll up his pants and she hasn't?"[82]

Anderson syndicated the "Washington Offbeat" column, written by Glaser, in her *Miami Herald* section. East subscribed to the *Herald* from Washington, DC, and then sent copies of the women's pages of the *Miami Herald* to other women's liberation leaders across the country. When the White House initially refused to release the report from the Task Force on Women's Rights and Responsibilities, Anderson ran parts of it in her women's pages. Later, Anderson chaired Florida's Commission on the Status of Women and oversaw a Continuing Education for Women program in Miami. Her obituary noted that she was "an editor who took chances, often publishing stories on subjects that were not popular."[83]

Their Connections

After covering hard news in Washington, DC, during World War II, Jurney became the assistant women's editor of the *Miami News* from 1946 to 1949. While at the *Miami News*, Jurney got to know Anderson, who would become a colleague and lifelong friend. In future years, they traveled the world and spent many holidays together.[84] It was Jurney who taught Anderson to look at women's news as about more than the four Fs (family, fashion, food, and furnishings), as Anderson had no background in journalism[85] and was mentored by her new friend. Jurney quit the newspaper in 1949 because the editor defined women's news as only weddings and club notices.[86] *Miami Herald* Editor Lee Hills soon called Jurney and asked her a question: "Could you take on the women's editorship so that we could get something in the paper that is worth reading?"[87] She took the challenge at the *Miami Herald*, where she stretched the definition of women's news for a decade.[88] She soon hired her friend Anderson as her assistant. When Jurney transferred to the *Detroit Free Press* in 1959, Anderson took on the role of women's page editor at the *Herald* where she would remain for more than a decade.

Although Glaser was already aware of women's issues from both her political and journalism work, she often wrote stories based on material provided by East. (East was nicknamed "Deep Throat" for her undercover relationship with reporters.) Her friendship with East led to her being a member of the President's Task Force on Women's Rights and Responsibilities. Glaser had already written many articles and gave several speeches about women's rights before she got national attention for asking President Nixon a question about women in his cabinet. The question caused East to call Glaser and a longtime partnership was formed. They went on to work together in both formal and informal ways.

East and Glaser seemed destined to be partners in the fight for women's rights. The two women had worked within a system that typically excluded women—the government and the mainstream media. Yet, they found their own ways to make a difference. By the time they met, in relation to Glaser's questioning of President Nixon, they were in a position to take a stand on women's roles—although they still needed to walk a fine line in order to keep their jobs. Among the strategies they used were educating politicians and raising awareness about political appointments, using the media, breaking the rules and working behind the scenes. These women were both powerful in the impact that they made in governmental documents yet subtle enough to be forgotten in some documents and records in women's history. For example, the 506-page book, *Feminists Who Changed America 1963–1975*, did not include profiles for Anderson, Jurney, or Paxson.[89]

Glaser was also friends with Jurney and Anderson. Jurney used Glaser's column in the *Detroit Free-Press*. Anderson ran "Offbeat Washington" in her *Miami Herald* women's pages and hired Glaser for freelance reporting assignments. For example, Anderson and Glaser exchanged letters when the Women's Bureau was celebrating its fiftieth anniversary with a conference in 1970. In an April 23 letter Glaser responds to a request by Anderson to cover the event. Glaser agrees but mentions that in previous meetings, there was little news value. She wrote: "To tell the truth, this meeting over the years has been dullsville. May be different this time because they are getting worked up over rights, etc."[90] After receiving the conference's program, Glaser contacted Anderson again. She planned to cover the speeches given by Koontz and others. Glaser wrote: "I sort of doubt Virginia Allan is going to say anything newsworthy. If the task force report is out by then, it's possible she may have something important to say, but I'm beginning to think it will not be released at all now."[91]

East has said that Jurney was "born too soon" for her forward-thinking perspective.[92] It is not clear when the two women met although they may have gotten to know each other through Anderson who by the 1960s was leading the top women's section in the country. Later, Jurney and East, along with Paxson worked together on the governmental document *To Form a More Perfect Union*. In their retirements, East and Jurney worked together on the New Directions for News project that documented the media's coverage of women's issue.

East was instrumental in the creation of National Organization for Women. She, along with EEOC member Richard Graham, brought up the idea of creating a group similar to the NAACP. Later, she helped gather the women together in Betty Freidan's hotel room, which led to NOW. One history noted: "Catherine East was becoming a one-woman clipping service, reading everything she could find about women, copying it and mailing it to her network. Though not a member of NOW, East remained at the center."[93] In going through papers, there was the regular appearance of "ce" indicating that the letter was from East. One of those women at the center of NOW was Clarenbach. Numerous letters demonstrated the partnership between the women. At one point, the University of Wisconsin cut her funding and impacted her work on the state's commission on the status of women. So, she wrote to East and asked her to make copies of the needed materials.[94]

Additional Women

There are numerous additional women who were helpful in the fight for equality. Esther Peterson was the head of the Women's Bureau from 1961 to 1964 and was East's boss for much of that time—although East had worked for the federal government prior.[95] Peterson was involved with the Kennedy Presidential Commission on the Status of Women and she was the one who recommended that states create their own commissions. She was the keynote speaker for the February 1963 University of Wisconsin conference "Professional Opportunities for Women" for three hundred attendees. The next day, she encouraged establishing state commissions on the status of women. By 1963, the state's governor announced the establishment of a commission that Clarenbach would oversee for many years. Peterson's work for women has largely been overshadowed by her work in the consumer movement. According to her *New York Times* obituary, Peterson was "a dogged consumer advocate whose work had an impact on Americans every time they buy a can of soup or a box of laundry detergent."[96]

Representative Martha Griffiths, a Democrat from Michigan, was another ally of the women. They worked together to make legal arguments and pass legislation helpful for women. Both the civil rights and the beginning of the women's liberation movements crossed paths in 1964 with the passing of the civil rights act. This act outlawed discrimination based on race, color, religion, sex, or national origin. It was originally written in a way that excluded gender, but an amendment was made at the proposal of Representative Howard Smith and has been considered authored by Representative Martha Griffiths. As she said of her strategy: "I used Smith."[97] A review of Griffiths' letters at the Bentley Library at the University of Michigan lead to a better understanding of how female leaders fought for women's rights while adjusting their messages as to not sound too extreme.

Marguerite Rawalt was a groundbreaking lawyer and a club woman leader, active with the Business and Professional Women. She started working as an attorney in the office of chief counsel for the Bureau of Internal Revenue 1933. In 1943, Rawalt was elected as president of the Federal Bar Association, the first woman to hold the position. She also served as president of the National Association of Women Lawyers during that year. Rawalt became involved with President's Commission on the Status of Women. In 1964, Rawalt wrote to members of Business and Professional Women and Zonta International, persuading the groups to lobby for the passage of provision VII of the Civil Rights Act of 1964, which prohibited discrimination by employers on the basis of sex. In 1966, Rawalt became a member of the National Organization for Women, and acted as their first legal counsel. In 1972, Rawalt founded the Marguerite Rawalt Legal Defense Fund, a group focused on funding legal cases involving women's equity, particularly relating to financial equity. She retired from the IRS in 1965, having been employed there for thirty years. The 1986 book, *Be Somebody*, outlined Rawalt's career and explored her relationships with East and Clarenbach.[98]

Elizabeth Duncan Koontz, the first black president of the National Education Association and director of the Women's Bureau in President Nixon's Department of Labor, was raised in the segregated South and trained as a teacher. She spent her career championing equal rights for blacks, women, and the working poor. In 1967 the National Education Association elected her its 110th president. At her inaugural, she spoke out for "teacher power." Gone, she said, was the era when teachers merely did as they were told because the school boards were in the driver's seat. She was described as "soft-spoken, tactful, and tough" and "unflagging in her commitment to what she thought was right."[99] Halfway into her term with the teachers' organization, President-elect Richard M. Nixon asked her to become head of the Women's Bureau. As head of the Women's Bureau, she promoted equal pay for women and allowed East to be engaged with women's rights organizations. Koontz was not reappointed for Nixon's second term, and she returned to North Carolina.

Gene Boyer was one of the twenty-eight women who gathered in Betty Friedan's hotel room on June 28, 1966, and participated in the discussion that inspired NOW. She was also a founding member of the National Organization for Women and served as NOW's national treasurer from 1968 to 1974. She was appointed to the Governor's Commission on the Status of Women by Wisconsin Governor Patrick Lucy in 1971 and, in 1977, served as a delegate to the International Women's Year Conference held in Houston. She specialized in improving the economic status of women. She advocated for allowing women as equal players into the business world. She took part on local chambers of commerce in Wisconsin and in Florida. Boyer was a member of the Veteran Feminists of America and appeared in the 1998 film, *Step by Step: Building a Feminist Movement*.[100]

Virginia Allan was a president of the National Federation of Business and Professional Women's Clubs. She chaired President Nixon's Task Force on Women's Rights and Responsibilities, of which Glaser was a member. Later, she was named deputy assistant secretary of state for public affairs and was a member of the US delegation to the World Conference for the International Women's Year in Mexico City. As head of the Women's Studies Program at Washington State University, she oversaw the New Direction for News project. East and Jurney worked on the project, which examined the media's coverage of women's issues such as the Equal Rights Amendment.

Pauli Murray was a lifelong friend of Eleanor Roosevelt. She worked to end segregation on public transportation that resulted in her arrest for refusing to sit in the back of a Virginia bus in 1940. She was denied entrance to Harvard University Law School because of her gender. She eventually became the only woman in the 1944 graduating class of Howard University Law School—where she was first in her class. She was a member of the President's Commission on the Status of Women and was outspoken about the EEOC allowing newspaper help wanted ads that segregated by gender. She knew both East and Clarenbach.

Roxcy O'Neal Bolton first got involved in community issues and in the Democratic Party during the 1950s. She was influenced by Eleanor Roosevelt's address at the 1956 Democratic National Convention. Shortly after, Bolton began her activism when she spoke to a women's group in Fort Lauderdale to advocate for equal pay for equal work. Bolton was one of the first Florida women to join the National Organization for Women after its founding in 1966, serving as national vice president in 1968. She also founded and was the first president of the Miami-Dade Chapter of NOW in 1968. A 1971 article in the *Orlando Sentinel* about a Women's Political Caucus meeting, Bolton encouraged more women to run for public office in Florida. Marie Anderson's name was put forward as a candidate for lieutenant governor. The female reporter noted: "'Women's lib' was a term never mentioned. These seemed resolute, serious women, deeply convinced of the rightness of their objective but far removed from the bra-burning ladies associated with the women's liberation movement." Bolton pushed to establish August 26 as Women's Equality Day. The 1972 proclamation by President Richard Nixon establishing the day was later presented to Bolton in recognition of her work.

Malvina Stephenson was born in Texas but spent most of her life in Oklahoma while not in Washington, DC. Her father was a pioneer lawyer and in the early 1930s, he served on the Oklahoma Supreme Court Commission. She was an only child and her father pushed her to succeed. She applied for her first newspaper job at the *Tulsa World* in the 1930s. She was nervous because there were so few women in journalism. Her father who brought her to the interview responded: "Now you are going and if they throw you out, I will be down in front to catch you."[101] She earned a master's degree in journalism from the University of Oklahoma in 1936. In 1940, Stephenson moved to Washington, DC, to launch a one-woman news bureau. She quickly became a regular political correspondent for several newspapers. She also contributed stories to King Features Syndicate and the North American Newspaper Alliance news service. In addition, she reported for the West Virginia Network's weekly radio program. From 1951 to 1963, Stephenson worked as press secretary for Senator Robert S. Kerr of Oklahoma. After the senator's death in 1963, Stephenson did freelance journalism work and resumed contributing stories to the *Tulsa World*. In 1969, Stephenson and Vera Glaser formed what was likely the first female political columnist team when they began writing the syndicated column, "Washington Offbeat."

From World War II to International Women's Year, Houston, 1977

This book examines the experiences of the previously described women during the World War II years through the meeting in Houston in 1977, with an afterword about the later lives of the women. By the mid-1970s, the question of women's roles in American society was openly questioned. In some ways, the rest of the country caught up with the kind of roles women held during World War II and that the commissions on the status of women had encouraged in the 1960s. Jurney had said she was frustrated later by women who were not using their educations outside of the home in the 1940s. She said, "I was very disappointed when I found that the women who were in college around the time of World War II were not career-minded. They were marriage and family and children minded. And that struck me as regression for women."[102] In another example, letters in the 1940s between Anderson and a college friend describe shock that a classmate would be "a housewife with no outside job."[103] These women's page journalists rejected a more traditional path for middle-class women during this period for themselves. Yet, they did not judge other women—covering various kinds of women in their newspaper sections and covering the activities of clubwomen (outside of the business and professional women's clubs) who often were not part of the paid workforce.

NOTES

1. Miriam Horn, *Rebels in White Gloves: Coming of Age with Hillary's Class—Wellesley '69* (New York: Random House, 1999), 44.
2. Judy Klemerud, "International Women's Year Torch Arrives," *New York Times*, November 19, 1977.

3. Anne S. Orwin, "Labor Roots and the Women's Movement," *Women's Studies Quarterly*, Fall–Winter 1999, 269.

4. "Anti-ERA leader Schlafly predicts Houston meeting," *Houston Chronicle*, November 3, 1977.

5. Fran Henry, Voices of Feminism Oral History Project, October 22 and 25, 2004, 43, Sophia Smith Collection, Smith College.

6. Laurel Thatcher Ulrich, *Well-Behaved Women Seldom Make History* (New York: Knopf, 2008).

7. Janet M. Martin, *The Presidency and the Women: Promise, Performance & Illusion* (College Station, Texas: Texas A & M University Press, 2003), 50.

8. Articles in major news magazines described Betty Friedan as an "angry battler for her sex." Marcia Cohen, *The Sisterhood: The Inside Story of the Women's Movement and the Leaders Who Made It Happen* (New York: Fawcett Columbine, 1988).

9. Cohen, *The Sisterhood*, 129.

10. Deborah Siegel, *Sisterhood Interrupted: From Radical Women to Grrls Gone Wild* (New York: Palgrave Macmillan, 2007), 71–93.

11. Susan Brownmiller, *In Our Time: Memoir of a Revolution* (New York: Random House, 1999), 59.

12. Carolyn G. Heilbrun, *Writing A Woman's Life* (New York: Ballantine Books, 2002), 16.

13. Kathryn Clarenbach, Oral History, University of Wisconsin, 134.

14. Susan Douglas, *Where the Girls Are: Growing Up Female with the Mass Media* (New York: Random House, 1995), 244.

15. Douglas, *Where the Girls Are*, 223.

16. Gerda Lerner, "Midwestern Leaders of the Modern Women's Movement: An Oral History Project," *Wisconsin Academy Review*, Winter 1994–95, 12.

17. Suzanne Braun Levine and Mary Thom, *Bella Abzug* (New York: Farrar, Strauss and Giroux, 2007).

18. National Organization for Women, "Honoring Our Founders and Pioneers," NOW Website.

19. Cohen, *The Sisterhood*, 134–135.

20. Cohen, *The Sisterhood*, 139.

21. Genevieve McBride, *Women's Wisconsin* (Madison, Wisconsin: University of Wisconsin Press, 2005), 437–8.

22. Ellen Chesler, "Lives Well Lived: Kathryn F. Clarenbach," *New York Times*, January 1, 1995.

23. Patricia Sullivan, "Vera Glaser, veteran Washington reporter, dies at 92," *Washington Post*, January 5, 2009.

24. Catherine East, "Remarks for Veterans of Feminist America Meeting," May 26, 1993, 5, Veteran Feminist of America Papers, Duke University.

25. Vera Glaser, March 17, 1971, *Congressional Record*, E1987.

26. Vera Glaser, "A Few Good Women" Oral History Project, Penn State University, August 19, 1997, 32.

27. "Oveta Culp Hobby," Famous Texans, http://www.famoustexans.com/OvetaCulpHobby.htm

28. Marjorie Paxson, "Women in Journalism," Washington Press Club Foundation, Session 6.

29. Kirstin Downey, *The Woman Behind the New Deal* (New York: Anchor Books, 2009).

30. Lee Ann Banaszak, *The Women's Movement: Inside and Outside the State* (New York: Cambridge University Press, 2010).

31. Stephanie Gilmore, *Groundswell: Grassroots Activism in Postwar America* (New York: Routledge, 2013).

32. Brigid O'Farrell and Joyce L. Kornbluh, *Rocking the Boat: Union Women's Voices, 1915–1975* (New Jersey: Rutgers University Press, 1996).

33. Judith Hole and Ellen Levine, *Rebirth of Feminism* (New York: New York Times Book, 1971).

34. Alice S. Rossi, *Feminists in Politics: A Panel Analysis of the First National Women's Conference* (New York: Harcourt Brace Jovanovich, 1982).
35. Nancy A. Hewitt, ed., "Introduction," *No Permanent Waves: Recasting Histories of U.S. Feminism* (New Brunswick, New Jersey: Rutgers University Press), 5.
36. Kelly C. Sartorius, *Deans of Women and the Feminist Movement* (New York: Palgrave MacMillan, 2014), 3.
37. Vera Glaser letter to "Jim," January 13, 1988. Papers of Vera Glaser, Heritage Center, University of Wyoming.
38. Vera Glaser letter to Marie Anderson, April 29, 1970. Papers of Vera Glaser.
39. Marie Anderson letter to Vera Glaser, May 12, 1970. Papers of Vera Glaser.
40. Vera Glaser, Women's News Service, "Women Discriminated Against?" October 16, 1963.
41. Ken Hoyt and Frances Spatz Leighton, *Drunk Before Noon: The Behind-the-Scenes Story of the Washington Press Corps* (Englewood Cliffs, New Jersey: Prentice-Hall, Inc., 1979), 292.
42. KNOW, Inc. memo, "Reporters You Can Trust," nd. Papers of Catherine East, Carton 16, folder 34, Schlesinger Library, Radcliffe Institute for Advanced Study, Harvard University.
43. "History," National Press Club Website. http://www.press.org/about/history
44. Kimberly Wilmot Voss, "Vera Glaser: A Journalist's Ode to Offbeat Washington Politics," Hall Institute of Public Policy, May 5, 2009.
45. Cally S. Zann, "Catherine East: Gatekeeper of the Women's Movement," Graduate paper, University of Maryland, May 1987, 8. Available in the papers of Catherine East, Schlesinger Library, Radcliffe Institute for Advanced Study, Harvard University.
46. Zann, "Catherine East," 7.
47. Judith Paterson, *Be Somebody: A Biography of Marguerite Rawalt* (Austin, Texas: Eakin Press, 1986).
48. Lee Stout, *A Matter of Simple Justice: The Untold Story of Barbara Hackman Franklin and a Few Good Women* (University Park, Penn: Pennsylvania State University Libraries, 2012).
49. Cynthia Harrison, *On Account of Sex: The Politics of Women's Issues 1945–1968* (Berkeley, Calif.: University of California Press, 1988), 183.
50. David Callender, "Henry Clarenbach Dies From a Long Illness," *Capital Times*, June 20, 1987.
51. Stephanie Gilmore, "Thinking about Feminist Coalitions," in *Feminist Coalitions: Historical Perspectives on Second-Wave Feminism in the United States* (Urbana, Illinois: University of Illinois Press, 2008), 228–229.
52. Ellen Chesler, "Lives Well Lived: Kathryn F. Clarenbach," *New York Times*, January 1, 1995.
53. Russ Feingold, "Kathryn Clarenbach," *Congressional Record*, Vol 140, Number 26, March 10, 1994.
54. Barbaralee Diamondstein, *Open Secrets: 94 Women in Touch With Our Time* (New York: Viking Press, 1972), 227.
55. Kay Murphy, "What Makes Women's Department Tick?" A Green-Eyed Editor Named Dorothy," *Miami Herald*, April 17, 1955.
56. "Select Committee on the Centennial History of the Indiana General Assembly: Indiana Historical Bureau," *A Biographical Directory of the Indiana General Assembly*, Vol. 2. 1980–1984.
57. Dorothy Jurney, Autobiography, 1. Papers of Dorothy Jurney, National Women and Media Collection, State Historical Society of Missouri.
58. Dorothy Jurney, "Women in Journalism," Washington Press Club Foundation, Session 1, 16.
59. Jurney, "Women in Journalism," Session 2, 55.
60. Jurney, "Women in Journalism," Session 2, 55.
61. Jurney, "Women in Journalism," Session 1, 15.
62. Kimberly Wilmot Voss, "Marjorie Paxson: From Women's Page Editor to Publisher," *Media History Monograph*, 2008. http://facstaff.elon.edu/dcopeland/mhm/mhm.htm.

63. Marjorie Paxson quote was mentioned by Anne Kasper in the introduction to Marie Anderson's interview. "Women in Journalism." Washington Press Club Foundation.
64. Marjorie Paxson, "Where the Girls Are Going," *The Iowa Publisher*, October 1967, 13.
65. Ibid.
66. Ibid, 14.
67. Talk by Marjorie Paxson, Penney-Missouri Awards Banquet, March 31, 1966, 2. Papers of Penney-Missouri Awards, National Women and Media Collection, State Historical Society of Missouri.
68. Marjorie Paxson, *New Guardians of the Press: Selected Profiles of America's Women Newspaper Editors*, Judith Clabes, ed. (Indianapolis: R.J. Berg & Co. Publishers, 1983), 126.
69. Kay Pancoast letter to Marie Anderson, August 9, 1946. Papers of Marie Anderson. National Women and Media Collection, State Historical Society of Missouri.
70. Marie Anderson, *Commencement Speech*, 5. Papers of Marie Anderson. National Women and Media Collection, State Historical Society of Missouri.
71. Anderson, *Commencement Speech*. 5.
72. Anderson, *Women in Journalism*. 42.
73. Dick Sherry, "Women's Page Revolt: To the Classifieds!" *Editor & Publisher*, December 26, 1964.
74. "Penney-Missouri Workshop is Another Classic Event," *Southern Advertising and Publishing*, April 1967, 15–16.
75. Pam Hanlon, "Women's Rising Status Will Affect News Coverage," *Columbia Missourian*, March 17, 1967.
76. Marie Anderson, "So What's Ahead? Some Attitudes," *Penney Press*, 1972. Papers of the Penney-Missouri Awards, National Women and Media Collection, State Historical Society of Missouri.
77. Gaye Tuchman, *Making News* (New York: Free Press, 1978), 147; Susan Douglas, *Where the Girls Are: Growing Up Female With the Mass Media* (New York: Random House, 1995), 157.
78. Anderson's files include letters to and from Dorothy Jurney, as well as correspondence with other women's page editors. Papers of Marie Anderson, Box 1. National Women and Media Collection, State Historical Society of Missouri.
79. Dorothy Jurney letter to Marie Anderson, January 27, 1984. Papers of Marie Anderson.
80. Dorothy Jurney letter to Marie Anderson, January 1, 1976. Papers of Marie Anderson.
81. Dorothy Jurney letter to Marie Anderson, July 25, unknown year. Papers of Marie Anderson.
82. Dorothy Jurney letter to Marie Anderson, 1970. Papers of Marie Anderson.
83. Jo Werne, "Marie Anderson," *Miami Herald*, July 2, 1996.
84. Jurney wrote several letters to friends while staying at Anderson's home. Dorothy Jurney letter to Virginia Allan, February 25, 1980. Papers of New Direction for News, National Women and Media Collection, State Historical Society of Missouri. Letter from Dorothy Jurney to Virginia Allan, January 3, 1984. Papers of New Direction for News, National Women and Media Collection, State Historical Society of Missouri.
85. Marie Anderson earned an English degree from Duke University and did not take any journalism classes. Kimberly Wilmot Voss and Lance Speere, "A Women's Page Pioneer: Marie Anderson and Her Influence at the Miami Herald and Beyond," *Florida Historical Quarterly*, Spring 2007, 398–421.
86. Jurney, Autobiography, 1.
87. Marie Anderson, "Women in Journalism," 24.
88. Dorothy Jurney, "Women In Journalism," *The Bulletin*, American Society of Newspaper Editors, January 1, 1956, 5.
89. Barbara J. Love, *Feminists Who Changed America 1963–1975* (Urbana, Illinois: University of Illinois Press).
90. Vera Glaser letter to Marie Anderson, April 29, 1970. Papers of Vera Glaser, University of Wyoming.
91. Vera Glaser letter to Marie Anderson, May 25, 1970. Papers of Vera Glaser, University of Wyoming.

92. Dorothy Jurney Introduction, http://beta.wpcf.org/oralhistory/jurnint.html
93. Paterson, *Be Somebody*, 172.
94. Kathryn F. Clarenbach letter to Catherine East, July 9, 1968. Papers of Kathryn Clarenbach, Box 2, Commission on the Status of Women, 67–69, University of Wisconsin.
95. Esther Peterson, "Working Women, *Daedalus*, 1964, 671–699. Esther Peterson, *Restless: The Memoirs of Labor and Consumer Activist Esther Peterson* (Washington, DC: Caring Publishing, 1997).
96. Irvin Molotsky, "Esther Peterson Dies at 91; Worked to Help Consumers," *New York Times*, December 22, 1997.
97. Emily Gore, *Martha W. Griffiths* (Washington, DC: University Press of America, 1982), 150.
98. Paterson, *Be Somebody*, (Austin, Texas: Eakin Press, 1986).
99. Wolfgang Saxon, "Elizabeth Koontz, 69, Dies; Led Teachers' Union," *New York Times*, January 8, 1989.
100. *Step by Step: Building a Feminist Movement*, 1998.
101. Malvina Stephenson Oral History, Tulsa Library, March 12, 1980.
102. Jurney, "Women in Journalism," Session 2, 55.
103. Kay Pancoast letter to Marie Anderson, August 9, 1946. Papers of Marie Anderson.

Chapter Two

World War II, Women's Pages, and Women's Clubs

The women's liberation movement of the 1960s and 1970s was much more than a book or marches—although too often that is how it is portrayed. Many women's page journalists were well aware of issues that were central to women's liberation. Glaser, for example, was enlightened well before the second wave of the women's movement, and her stories on inequalities predate any of the more visible mediated feminist events such as protests. It was a time when other women were working for rights in more organized ways— one that aimed at avoiding conflict. East said: "I hope that the women who are the militant types can come up with some new form of non-violent resistance that will be effective. It's particularly suitable to women, as a powerless group, to engage in those tactics."[1] According to one of the government women from the President Nixon years:

> Women's groups during that era—the ones that were trying to get something done—were noisy. This was a calmer, cooler kind of modus operandi. And I think the women involved were much respected. Not that other women weren't, but the technique was different.[2]

It is difficult to overestimate how hostile journalists (usually male) were to the messages of feminism in the 1960s. Numerous studies have looked at the intersection of the media and the women's liberation movement—and found mostly negative coverage in the news pages of newspapers and on television.[3] For example, in a study of the print media's framing of the women's movement from 1966 to 1986, researchers Laura Ashley and Beth Olson found that the descriptive coverage of feminists often delegitimized their goals. On the other hand, anti-feminists were listed as well organized and attractive.[4] It reinforced what media scholars, Maurine Beasley and Shelia Gibbons wrote earlier:

> Many people, knowing only what the mass media told them about the movement, lacked sufficient information to judge the movement's significance. What they thought of the movement was generally a reflection of what they had read or heard or were shown about. And indeed, most reporting on the "second wave," as modern-era feminist activism was known, trivialized the issues and mocked the movement's leaders.[5]

One of the national events that came to represent the women's liberation movement was the Women's Strike for Equality on August 26, 1970. The strike was in ways symbolic, as many women could not simply walk away from their jobs. Instead, there were sit-ins, lunch-hour rallies and a march down Fifth Avenue in New York. It was the largest women's protest in US history.[6] Those within the movement considered the event a success, although media coverage was largely condescending.[7] According to historian Ruth Rosen, the media used the march to "sensationalize and discredit the women's movement."[8] Yet, for many women who had not been a part of the movement, this was a significant moment. For example, Ogilvy advertising women Jane Maas and Gloria Guarnotta looked out their Fifth Avenue office window and watched women marching by the hundreds. According to Maas's memoir, they did not say anything but walked to the elevator and went down. They linked arms and walked the eight blocks to Bryant Park. Maas later recalled, "I had never considered myself a feminist and was secretly scornful of the bra burners, but this one time, marching with all those women, I felt exuberant."[9]

Women and World War II

While questions of women's rights in the country go back to its beginnings, the foundation that led to what has been described as the second wave of the women's movement can be traced back to World War II. The war made a significant impact on the lives of American women, and the women of this book were no different. The opportunities that wartime provided these women stayed with them when peace returned. It was the time of the famed Rosie the Riveter and her sisters who joined the paid workforce in unheard of numbers when men went off to war. (It's worth mentioning that government-run daycare centers took care of the real-life Rosie the Riveter's children.)[10] For some of the women, the overt discrimination that followed World War II opportunities shaped the rest of their careers, and for others, it opened up a future career path that went beyond the limits that the women's work options had provided.

For the women at the center of this book, the war provided opportunities that would likely not have happened during peacetime. Clearly, the positions in hard news that Paxson and Jurney held would not have happened if there had been men available to take the jobs. East's government work during the war allowed for unprecedented opportunities, as did Glaser's work. Clarenbach, too, had significant work opportunities that would not have been possible without the war.

After the war, many women lost their jobs and their government-sponsored child care. By 1947, more than three million women had been laid off from their wartime employment.[11] There were picket lines with signs such as "How Come No Work for Women" and "Stop Discrimination Because of Sex."[12] Of course, this does not include the many women who were employed in the working class, often taking care of the children or homes of other employed women. Anderson recalled the war in a 1960 speech to other women's page editors: "The child care problem is desperate. We had child care programs during the war. Why not now? Young girls are being encouraged only to get a husband or teach. Why can't she be a mathematician and have a husband, too?"[13]

While Anderson was doing volunteer work during World War II, she met Kay Pancoast, who oversaw the volunteers.[14] Like many upper-class women, they initially found their calling to be in women's club positions. They both continued to do volunteer work before beginning professional careers—journalism for Anderson and art for Pancoast. Many of these women volunteers continued to do important work after the war was over. As Associated Press women's editor Dorothy Roe noted, "The public began to find out that if a community needs a new school community center, or somebody to tame its teenagers, the local women's clubs could usually get the job done, often succeeding where generations of politicians and aimless 'do-gooders' had failed."[15]

During World War II, Dorothy Jurney had opportunities that never would have been available to her in times of peace. She had years of journalism education and newspaper experience by the time she was in her thirties. During the war, Jurney was hired as a "city-side deskman" at the *Washington Daily News,* a Scripps-Howard newspaper in the nation's capital. She initially walked into the office of Charles Stevenson, the executive editor, and detailed her background. His response was: "Can you start tomorrow?"[16] At the time, many newspapers were in need of staff members because male journalists were serving in World War II. During this time, many women's page journalists were able to move into the news side of the newspaper. For example, the United Press employed one hundred women during wartime, or 20 percent of its staff.[17] A former Northwestern female classmate wrote of Jurney's new position: "That must be a dream, too bold to be expressed even yet, of every dame who ever got mixed up in newspapering."[18] Stevenson later wrote he hired Jurney reluctantly as he had "an antipathy toward women in news shops."[19] Jurney soon was promoted to assistant city editor and eventually she became acting city editor. According to Stevenson, Jurney at that point had become "one of the greatest finds ever to enter our doors. She was an excellent copy reader, a good writer, an editor of rare judgment, an exceptional executive—and one of the hardest workers it ever has been my privilege to know."[20]

Then, the war ended and Jurney—despite her significance—lost her position like most of the women journalists who had taken men's jobs during the war.[21] As men were returning, Jurney received a phone call from a top editor. He said there was a young man who was a cub reporter in the sports department who management wanted to make the city editor. The managing editor instructed her to teach him his job. He said that she was not a candidate for city editor because she was a woman.[22] Years later, Stevenson wrote he knew that Jurney's treatment was unfair but that it was the practice at the time to discriminate against women. He wrote that Jurney was actually city editor but without the official title. "We were unfair to her in this."[23] This would happen again to Jurney later in her career when she would be overlooked for management positions because she was a woman. These experiences led to her being an advocate for women who had also been marginalized.

Paxson graduated from journalism school when the nation was at war. She recalled: "Our involvement started in December. The classes at the University of Missouri were still full of men. And within six weeks, suddenly all the guys were gone. I think the enrollment at J School was cut about in half."[24] The new job opportunities allowed her to cover hard news for a wire service, the United Press in Nebraska—something almost unheard of during peacetime. In fact, the only topics she could not cover were football games and executions. When she took the job, she had to sign a waiver that guaranteed that she would give up her job for a man who returned from the service. She left the position after the war ended and would spend most of the rest of her journalism career in the women's pages until she went into newspaper management.

East's experiences in the federal government allowed her to see women in positions of equality than would otherwise have been unlikely. In 1937, she married Charles East, and by January 1939, she was a reviewer and supervisor in the federal government. She had her children while she remained in the workforce. She said that her pregnancy was treated like any other disability, and she used her sick time after the birth of her children. She said: "You didn't quit until you felt you needed to physically. A number of women worked until a day or two until their babies were born. Things were much better then than they were later."[25] Women were able to work in many federal jobs during World War II although there were agencies that wanted to remove women after the war. She stayed in her position after the war and continued to be promoted. She recalled in the late 1950s that she had wanted to add gender to an employment bill but her male supervisor rejected it. She recalled that he asked her: "Now, you're not going to pull that feminist stuff on me, are you?"[26]

Clarenbach worked in the Office of Policies and Procedures at the War Production Board in Washington, DC, during World War II. Her job was to simplify the paperwork process for materials in war production. She and another young woman were hired as what she described as an experiment to see if women could be more than secretaries. She noted that the "experiment went so well that by the time she left the office, half of the office's staff was female. In fact, it wasn't very long before these men would call up the head of our office and say 'send one of your girls over.' It was never 'women,' of course."[27] She also recalled equality of the office—including creating a schedule so that both female and male employees made coffee, as well as the fact that there no differences in pay based on gender. "There as great congeniality in the office. We weren't on the fighting front, we were sending things." She left the job for graduate school after two years. At that point, she was making $3,600 a year.

Women's Clubs

Women's clubs have a long history in the United States. Women's page columnist "Jennie June" or Jane Cunningham Croly, herself a women's club member, wrote an 1898 history of these organizations. These clubs not only focused on culture as was common in the earliest days—there was also an element of community development: "Reform-minded women turned the concept of women's sphere, with its concern for family well-being, into a justification for moving from the home into the public arena to confront situations that had an adverse impact on their families."[28] For example, in 1933, women's clubs were credited with initiating 75 percent of public libraries in the country. James H. Canfield, a librarian at Columbia University and wife of a club founder, said: "I know of no one power, no one influence, which has accomplished more for education in this country than the organization known as women's clubs."[29] In later years, Miami women's page journalist Helen Muir would take the tragedy of her young daughter's accidental death into a drive for funding and supporting libraries that would eventually result in the development of the Coconut Grove and then Miami-Dade library systems.[30] From modest beginnings these organizations were soon tackling social issues in the community from politics to education. As early as 1922, researchers noted that "the one powerful agency through which a woman has been able to express her individuality is though the woman's club movement."[31]

Dorothy Roe wrote in 1961 that "No group of women in history has provided such a hilarious target for cartoonists, humorists, and professional woman-baiters as the thirty million clubwomen of America."[32] Caricatures of these women noted their flighty ways and inability to remember names—most obviously pictured in *New Yorker* cartoons. The mocking of women club members began almost as soon as women attempted to gather outside the home. A May 15, 1869, cartoon in *Harper's Weekly* gauged the reaction to a meeting to one of the earliest women's clubs, Sorosis. The cartoonist featured nervous and distressed husbands forced to care for their babies.[33] The idea was that women who left the house, even for meetings, would lead to the breakdown of the family.

Yet, these women got things done. They changed their communities and developed their political and business skills along the way. Anne Firor Scott has noted that historians have largely overlooked these women and their voluntary organizations that had been around for decades and significantly changed their communities. She wrote:

> The most obvious way in which voluntary associations had brought about social change was by creating a public role for women who, deprived by custom and law of access to the formal, male-dominated institutions had slowly worked their way to social power by organizing and operating their own groups. Forming societies came as naturally to enterprising nineteenth-century women as creating business firms or organizing railroads did to ambitious men.[34]

Many women's page journalists would have agreed with Scott. As Roe noted in 1961, "Today's typical clubwoman is likely to know a lot about any subject she tackles, and if she doesn't know at the start, she finds out in short order."[35] Indeed, the clubs often featured expert speakers on numerous topics. In South Florida, Roberta Applegate worked to elevate the image of clubwomen in the pages of *Miami Herald* in the 1950s and 1960s. (She had covered hard news in Detroit during World War II and was one of the first women to serve as a press secretary to a governor.)[36] At times, those stories were picked up by wire services, and her stories ran in newspapers throughout Florida. Applegate was also a speaker at club meetings where she validated the work of the clubwomen. In one such speech, Applegate said:

> For many years, women's clubs have been the butt of jokes—their hats, their pink teas, and their gossip. I object to that interpretation of clubwork. Sure, sometimes we wear odd hats, we enjoy teas, and I'm afraid we gossip. But look at men's ties, their get-togethers—and did you ever hear a bunch of men talking? Women have no monopoly on gossip. And women do so much that is fine and outstanding, both in their own right and as a prod to the men.[37]

For Anderson, her social standing and club work led to her eventual journalism career. After growing up in Florida, earning her bachelor's degree in English from Duke University and being a secretary in New York City, she returned to Miami. In April 1941, US Army soldiers transformed Miami Beach into a training camp. The local Junior League, which included Anderson, asked for women to volunteer at the Filter Center, also known as the Air Raid Information Center. By October 1942, the Junior League was a "commanding presence" at the Servicemen's Center, helping the more than 100,000 Air Force officers being trained in Miami.[38] In a speech, Anderson said: "It still didn't occur to me to get a job because I thought you worked only if you needed the money. So I became the Available Woman. I was available to every cause that came along."[39] She was an example of a woman who, while not part of the paid workforce, was making a difference in her community.

There are numerous examples of how the women's page journalists provided a non-judgmental place for news about women's issues that originated from clubwomen. For example, most newspapers sponsored an annual meeting for women's clubs—often accompanied by a contest for best club projects in the community. Part of the reason for the success of women's club campaigns was the publicity that women's page journalists gave them. At times, it was for the fundraising activities and other times it was a matter of writing about issues that gave credence to the cause. During Progressive Reform, Dallas women's page writer Pauline Periwinkle followed that model. She said, "Printer's ink judicially applied to the club idea is a great lubricator and will make it run further and smoother than anything I know."[40]

After losing her position at the Washington newspaper to a man, Jurney and her husband moved to Miami, Florida, in 1945. She then became the assistant women's editor of the *Miami News* in 1946. While at the *Miami News*, Jurney got to know Anderson, who got a job at the newspaper due to a friend from the Serviceman's Pier. The two women would become colleagues and lifelong friends. In future years, it was Jurney who taught Anderson to look at women's news as beyond traditional content; Anderson had no background as a reporter.[41] Their partnership would change the content of women's page journalism across the nation, as they presented their approach at conferences.

Women's Page Journalists and Clubwomen

Whether part of the paid workforce or not, many American women were members of one or more women's clubs. The clubwomen often interacted with the women's page editor of their local newspaper. According to a 1946 *Time* magazine article about the clubwomen:

> They had been invited to hear an expert tell them how bad their stuff was. Six hundred showed up. They were all women and all amateur correspondents—presidents and press chairmen of Los Angeles clubs. Like clubwomen everywhere, they habitually send their local papers the kind of disheveled copy that prematurely ages the editors of women's pages. Last week, for the sixth time in six years, *Los Angeles Times* Club Editor Bess Wilson crisply told them to mend their ways.[42]

Her suggestions focused on adhering to news values and spelling names correctly. The women's club members were ready for the advice. In a December 1950 article in the General Federation of Women's Clubs newsletter, club members were advised to hone their public relations skills. According to the author, one of the club's assets was the club's support of suffrage.[43]

Before she came to Miami, Jurney worked hard to help women in her community become news makers in their own right in Indiana. She learned the lesson from her father who likely recognized the value of women's organizations from his suffragette wife. Jurney based her Miami workshop on what she had done at her father's newspaper while women's page editor there. The goals were two-fold: to increase community readership and to improve the content of the sections by adding more news. For example, rather than reporting there was a meeting—the focus was on who would be speaking at the meeting and what that person was going to speak about. By doing this, women who were active in the community were highlighted and served as role models for other women.

Anderson and Jurney often helped to raise the status and activities of women's clubs. They did this by educating the women about how to create events and projects that would be worthy of newspaper coverage. A 1953 invitation to women's club leaders from the *Miami Herald* to women's section workshops encouraged women to tackle significant issues.[44] The annual Miami workshops began small and grew large enough to draw more than 750 clubwomen at a hotel ballroom. The featured guest speakers were columnists whose work appeared in women's pages: Ann Landers and Dorothy Ricker. The goal of the workshops was to retain the goodwill and cooperation of the clubwomen and to explain the publicity chairman's role in producing the type of club news the newspaper could use. To demonstrate the kind of news the journalists were looking to run, the *Miami Herald* held contests to reward clubs with the most significant community projects. These competitions encouraged women's clubs to work on significant issues and projects in the community. For example, in 1954, Applegate wrote a two-part series about a home for the disabled. She visited the home and described the setting and the people. Her first story begins:

> The power of women working as a unified group is being recognized more and more. Their material contribution to their communities is recognized in their

various projects—school equipment, nurseries, building beautification, etc. More intangible is the influence they exert in civic matters, which sometimes manifests itself in tangible ways. The expanded program at the Florida Farm Colony is one of these. The Florida Federation of Women's Clubs supported the appropriations bill passed by the 1953 legislature.[45]

In 1953 the Florida legislature appropriated much more than was originally requested after being lobbied by the women's organization. The superintendent of the home thanked the women for their help and asked for continued support, saying "because a word from you can mean a great deal."[46] In the second article, Applegate again pointed out the significant work that the clubwomen did. She wrote about the work of the Junior League women to raise money to buy occupational therapy equipment and other women's groups who were putting together a survey to learn the needs of children in the state.[47]

Women's page journalists were often in a conflicted position as society questioned women's roles—especially middle-class women. Former women's page editor Marie Saulsbury wrote in a 1975 Associated Press Managing Editors report that not all of the women in her community of San Bernardino, California, were supporters of the women's liberation movement and enjoyed a traditional role in the household: "We hated to admit that clubwomen did have their place in the world and that society stories were not always bad. And that many women not only couldn't care less about the women's lib movement, they were openly hostile to it."[48] Of course, part of the women's view about feminism clearly came from the media's representation of women's liberation. A study of suburban Chicago club women leaders in the late 1970s found an interesting dynamic between the roles of women and self-identifying as a "feminist." According to a survey, only 29.2 percent of the responders would describe themselves as a feminist. Yet, 97.7 percent of responders noted that no person should be denied opportunities due to gender.[49] This concept of rejecting the term but embracing the real meaning behind if would continue. Douglas describes this as the "I'm not a feminist, but ..." concept. She wrote:

> The speaker has been cowed by stereotypes of the feminist as a hateful, obnoxious, repellent shrew. But the speaker also knows that these women have something to say to her, that some of the feminists she has seen and heard she even likes, and she suspects they might not be as hideous as they're made out to be.[50]

Women and the Federal Government

Research has found that the federal government's Women's Bureau, along with the State Commissions on the Status of Women in the 1960s, "were integrally involved with the reformist branch of the resurgence."[51] In fact the government had long been helpful in women seeking paid employment. The American Governmental Woman in Industry Service published the federal report "Standards for the Employment of Women in Industry" in 1918. The report was later republished several times, into the 1960s. The labor standards from the report were later incorporated into labor laws at the state and federal levels. The United States' entry into World War I created a strain on the country's labor force. The War Labor Administration wanted to resolve the problems by replacing male workers with female workers. To address women's labor issues, the Department of Labor created the Women in Industry Service in 1918. W.I.S. conducted field investigations to find what was happening to women in the readjustment period after World War I. In addition, it started several investigations of women's employment conditions in different states. The first investigation was done in Indiana at the request of Governor James Goodrich. Later, the bureau conducted the same type of survey in thirty-one other states. The findings were collected and used as the basis for legislation. Several state laws were passed because of the bureau's reports.[52]

The United States' Women's Bureau was established in the Department of Labor by Public Law No. 259 on June 5, 1920. The bureau was assigned to "formulate standards and policies which shall promote the welfare of wage-earning women, improve their working conditions, increase their efficiency, and advance their opportunities for profitable employment." The governmental bureau also had the authority to investigate and report to the US Department of Labor on matters regarding employed women. Among the bureau's initial studies examined working conditions of "Negro" women workers in 1922. The first director of the Women's Bureau was Mary Anderson and was the longest-serving director, serving until 1944. She wrote in her autobiography:

> I think our most important job was issuing the standards for the employment of women. It was the first time the federal government had taken a practical stand on conditions of employment for women, and although the standards were only recommendations and had no legal force, they were a very important statement of policy and were widely used in all parts of the country.[53]

Presidential Commission on the Status of Women

The federal government, and a few states, advocated for women well before the women's liberation movement pointed out inequities in society. Educated, middle-class women have long worked in fields outside of teaching and nursing. They may have been in limited numbers and not necessarily in powerful positions, but they were part of the workforce. After all, the organization Business and Professional Women has been around since 1919. As historical studies have shown, the foundation for what would later be the women's liberation movement was laid years earlier: "The rebirth of the women's movement paralleled this transformation in the Washington community, forcing presidents to respond to this new contingency while at the same time influencing the direction of the movement."[54] Change was on its way even if the more visible media images of marches and protest were still a few years off. The challenge at this point was to include women in the workforce, as well as stay-at-home mothers. Further, the commission wanted to explore the next stage of a woman's life after her children were at school or out of the house.

Likely the most visible governmental body regarding women in the post-World War II era was the Presidential Commission on the Status of Women, created by President John F. Kennedy in 1961. According to a history of women and the presidency:

> A commission is designed to act independently of any existing government structure, adding fresh insight, it is shaped by the administration responsible for its establishment. The president sets forth the mission and the goals of the commission, and, in fact, shapes its final recommendations by selection of the commission's members.[55]

In 1961, President Kennedy put forth a reorganization plan in the Department of Labor that created a new assistant secretary position that went to Esther Peterson. While Peterson had not been a formal staff member in the Kennedy campaign, he did call her for advice due to her work in the labor union movement. In her new position, Peterson was in charge of the Bureau of Labor Statistics and the Women's Bureau. At the time, not much was known about the lives of women working outside of the home. Peterson wrote in 1964: "Very little light is shed on the great majority of America's twenty-five million working women."[56] Some demographic information was available, including that one-third of the nation's married women worked and they contributed 35 to 45 percent of the household income, if they worked fulltime. The greatest increase in women's employment during the previous two decades had been in clerical work although women's employment in all job categories had increased, other than farm work.[57]

East was a part of every commission from President Kennedy until her retirement in 1977. She had initially learned about the organization by reading about it in the women's pages of newspapers.[58] Before long, she was an executive secretary for two groups within the commission. Her early experiences as a federal government employee were mostly free of gender discrimination. She later recalled: "It was an eye-opening experience for me."[59] It was the beginning of East's long career of collecting information about inequities for women, which made her valuable to the commissions and those writing the reports.

Six years before Glaser and East would connect after President Nixon's press conference, Glaser wrote about the commission's potential findings. At this point she had spent more than a decade working in government or covering it as a journalist. She offered her opinion: "Whether the commission's report, which is the fruit of its two-year existence, will serve to change deep-seated attitudes is doubtful. However, many see it as an initial step."[60] She went on to quote Peterson, who had hoped that the same presidential tactics used to help the lives of African Americans would be used to help women. She said: "Personally, I think it would be an effective way. Discrimination against women is part of the same principle and problem. At the moment, of course, we do not know whether the presidents will do it or whether some of us will be allowed to do it."[61]

States Commissions on the Status of Women

The creation of the States' Commissions on the Status of Women was largely a reaction to President Kennedy's Presidential Commission on the Status of Women established in 1961. The national commission report, *American Women*, published in 1963, recommended that each state form a similar commission on the status of women. The Business and Professional Women's Foundation helped set up state commissions, as did other women's organizations. At the national level, the Women's Bureau also worked with these organizations toward establishing the commissions. The various states' research regarding women's status in society demonstrated that discrimination against women was a wide-ranging and serious problem.

The state commissions were created in different ways. For example, Michigan Governor John Swainson created the Governor's Commission on the Status of Women by executive order in 1962. It was likely the first state commission in the country. In 1968, the Michigan Legislature, under the guidance and leadership of Senator Lorraine N. Beebe, enacted Public Act No. 1, which created the Michigan Women's Commission by statute. All fifty states had commissions in operation by 1967 that were addressing women's issues. Most of the state commissions lacked budgets, clerical staff, and office space. This lack of support prevented some commissions from making significant changes.

The National Conference of Governor's Commissions on the Status of Women took place in 1964, and the Women's Bureau sponsored the Annual National Conference of Commissions. In 1970 at the fiftieth anniversary conference of the Women's Bureau, the commissions created their own organization, the Interstate Association of Commissions on the Status of Women. Clarenbach was the first president. In the early 1970s, local commissions gained momentum, starting with local commissions in Wisconsin and Iowa. The IACSW continued annual meetings from 1969 through 1975, when a constitutional convention in Chicago was held. The bylaws were changed and the IACSW became the National Association of Commissions for Women.

Wisconsin Commission on the Status of Women

The Clarenbach family moved back to Madison, Wisconsin, in 1960. The following year, Kay Clarenbach began teaching at Edgewood College, an independent liberal arts school. She also began teaching an evening class at the University of Wisconsin's extension program. She soon started overseeing the University of Wisconsin–Extension, and she began by interviewing women about what potential employable skills the homemakers had. Neighbors often babysat her children when she was at work. In addition, her husband had become a Realtor so that he could be home when school got out. As she developed the continuing education program, she did run into some resistance. She said she "often encountered husbands who did not appreciate her efforts to find jobs for their wives. Some of the wives were looked on as freaks."[62]

It was around this time that Clarenbach went to a national conference where she heard Labor Department Women's Bureau Director Esther Peterson speak about women's roles. It was at this point that Clarenbach realized that to truly help women, she needed to do more than just run the university's continuing education program. In fact, she worried that her program was offering false hope to women in terms of their employment opportunities.

It was a time when many women were largely unaware of just how many overall inequities they faced. Clarenbach recalled one woman who came into her office after the commission was established in Wisconsin. The woman's professor husband was away studying the jungles in Brazil. Their son had just turned sixteen and she had not been allowed to sign him up to get his driver's license—only the father had the legal right to do it, according to state law. During the same week, her washer broke. The repairman would only allow her husband to sign the credit bill. Even Clarenbach was amazed by the limited control women had in their on households under the law. She described it as "an absolute shock for me. I didn't know about either of those things. We had a nose out for that 'what elses' from then on."[63] In 1965, she asked the governor to change a law that prevented mothers from signing the form that allowed their minor children to get a driver's license. The request was overruled by the head of the motor vehicles department who responded that only fathers were the heads of a household.[64]

Third National Conference of Commissions

The theme of the Third National Conference of Commissions was "Targets for Action," although it was a lack of action at the meeting that led to the establishment of NOW. The State Commissions on the Status of Women were scheduled to meet a few days after Griffiths' speech about the lack of attention that the Equal Employment Opportunity Commission gave to issues of gender discrimination; Griffith was scheduled to speak at the closing luncheon of the commission's meeting. Unofficially, East invited Friedan to attend the meeting, as a member of the press.[65] Friedan was best known for her book, *The Feminine Mystique*, which largely appealed to educated, middle-class homemakers. Research has found that the book had an impact on women, even if they did not read it or skim it. The justification of the problem that "had no name" was beneficial for many women who understood that feeling.[66]

While Friedan was well-known, East played a pivotal role for women's rights behind the scenes. She helped organize commission meetings, and the gathering of the women in Friedan's hotel room was a strong example. Friedan noted East was a "prime mover" in the 1966 birth of National Organization for Women. Friedan said of East, "She and others kept saying how what we needed is an NAACP (National Association for the Advancement of Colored People) for women. I thought of myself as a writer, not an organizer, but Catherine kept emphasizing that what was needed was outside pressure on the government."[67] It was at a conference of these commissions in June 1966 that a group of women came to Friedan's hotel room to urge the formation of the group that, four months later, became NOW.[68] Although East was not present in the hotel room (some histories have incorrectly put her in the room), she had invited many of the women who were there to lobby Friedan to create the organization.[69] East's influence often went unnoted, so much so that friends called her "Deep Throat"[70] after the shadowy Watergate figure Mark Felt.

East, Murray, and Eastwood had quietly held a meeting with Friedan in the hopes of creating a women's organization. In their words: "If we're going to budge, we've got to have pressure from the outside."[71] They often met at night with Friedan in her hotel room or a restaurant where no one from the Women's Bureau would see them. According to a history of the time: "Women with government jobs had to be careful, they told her; but Betty was independent, she could speak out."[72] A meeting in Friedan's hotel room was arranged for the night before the final day of the commission meeting. Clarenbach and several of the members of the Wisconsin group attended and were taken aback by the discussion that challenged the federal government. Clarenbach hadn't been privy to any of their previous conversations in which they had talked about the importance of what Betty Friedan was to the

NAACP for women.[73] While she shared the women's concerns, Clarenbach still believed they could work through Peterson and others within the Women's Bureau based on her previous experiences.[74]

While Clarenbach had wanted to work through official channels, the tide was about to change. A storm of discontent was brewing among the women. They were frustrated by the lack of action by the EEOC regarding women's employment, especially the continued practice of employment ads in newspapers with separate columns for men and women. Further, the group was concerned that Richard Graham would not be re-appointed to the EEOC. Graham and Aileen Hernandez had fought hard to support cases of sex discrimination, only to lose on 3–2 votes. Both people would go on to be leaders in NOW.

Peterson said the commission meeting was to be information only—although a resolution would not have any real power. The resolutions were not brought to the floor—blocked by Peterson, Margaret Hickey, and Mary Keyserling. Clarenbach said in her oral history: "Each one said this would sound critical of the federal government, and you are here at the invitation of the federal government and therefore it's inappropriate to have any resolutions. I was absolutely appalled."[75] With that message Clarenbach was ready to create the organization that had been discussed in Friedan's hotel room. Rawalt's biographer wrote of the moment: "Marguerite watched two round tables in the middle of the room fill up with the most militant women at the conference. They were not to be placated. Clarenbach joined the leaders and now the other women were ready to follow."[76] The word "militant" in its most common usage in the women's liberation movement is hard to apply to Clarenbach and her colleagues. They had come to the conference in the hopes of passing resolutions—non-binding but forward-looking statements that would have indicated the next step for women. They were only forced to become "militant" and create an organization (one that would include men as members, too) when their simple request for resolutions regarding the EEOC were rebuffed.

Initially, Clarenbach was inclined to follow the official governmental path because of her success in Wisconsin. She was used to getting things done and had clout in her home state. She ran the commission out of the University of Wisconsin's Continuing Education Office and headed the Wisconsin Commission from 1964 to 1969 and again from 1971 to 1979. The newspapers in the state respected Clarenbach and offered sympathetic coverage of her causes. There was a national Handbook for Commissions on the Status of Women that was produced by Clarenbach and published by the University of Wisconsin–Extension in cooperation with the Women's Bureau in the Department of Labor. The first came out in 1968. A third edition was published in 1979. In that decade, the commissions had grown and had significant influence. According to the handbook:

The part Commissions are taking in eliminating sex-based discrimination continues to increase in range and effectiveness. The initial efforts of most state and local Commissions to research and publish reports on women's status are a far cry from the sophisticated and knowledgeable efforts now being exerted by the majority of Commissions to bring about change in the economic and social fabric of the nation.[77]

Creation of National Organization for Women

With Clarenbach's new understanding about the conference's political process, she was ready to consider establishing a women's organization. She told Friedan: "You were absolutely right! It's a no go with these resolutions." At the conference's closing event, Clarenbach sat at a table with Friedan, Catherine Conroy, and BPW member Inka O'Hanrahan—who went on to be NOW's treasurer. Clarenbach remembered:

> As we sat there, dreaming up a name and an acronym, and a Statement of Purpose for this 'to be' organization, Inka would see somebody she knew on the other side of this huge ballroom, and she would run over to tell somebody what we were up to, and run back again.[78]

Catherine Conroy, who had come out of the labor movement, said: "Let's put our money where our mouths are," and put five dollars on the table. It quickly grew to forty dollars. Clarenbach said: "That looked like a sizable chunk. Here I was, from the Wisconsin Commission, which didn't have a penny of budget for its first ten years."[79] Clarenbach ended up as the temporary chair because she had a desk and a secretary. They also put together a temporary steering committee. It was not yet clear exactly what the organization would look like. At one of the early board meetings, Pauli Murray asked: "Are we a leadership organization or are we thinking about a mass membership organization?" Clarenbach responded: "That was something that (we) hadn't been talked or thought about."[80]

On November 22, 1966, the *New York Times* covered a NOW meeting that served as a press conference. The tone of the article was condescending: "Although no one in the dim ruby and sapphire Victorian parlor actually got up and cried: 'Women of the world, unite! You have nothing to lose but your chains,' that was the prevailing sentiment yesterday morning at the crowded press conference held by the newly formed National Organization for Women." The new group was clearly trying to find its footing as it debated being exclusive or seeking a large membership. The reporter wrote: "Mrs. Friedan said last week in her apartment that NOW had 'just begun to think about methods' to implement its goals of enabling women to 'enjoy the equality of opportunity and freedom of choice, which is their right.'"[81] She claimed five hundred members at that time, according to the article, although it would have been difficult to judge as different chapters were being created across the country. The organization continued to grow, and Clarenbach would eventually leave the leadership while still working for women's causes.

NOTES

1. Lee Ann Banaszak, *The Women's Movement Inside and Outside the State* (New York: Cambridge University Press, 2010).
2. Stout, *A Matter of Simple Justice*, 31.
3. See Patricia Bradley, *Mass Media and the Shaping of American Feminism, 1963–1975* (University Press of Mississippi: 2003). Susan Brownmiller, *In Our Time: Memoir of a Revolution* (New York: Random House, 1999). 136–166. Laura Ashley and Beth Olson, "Constructing Reality: Print Media's Framing of the Women's Movement, 1966–1986," *Journalism and Mass Communications Quarterly*, Summer 1998, 263–277.
4. Ashley & Olson, *Constructing Reality*, 263–277.
5. Maurine Beasley and Sheila Gibbons, eds., *Taking Their Place: A Documentary History of Women and Journalism.* (Washington, D.C.: The American University Press, 1993), 150.
6. Carol Mueller, "Conflict Networks and the Origins of Women's Liberation," *New Social Movements*, eds. Enrique Larana, Hank Johnston and Joseph Gusfied (Philadelphia: Temple University Press, 1994), 253.
7. Susan Douglas, *Where the Girls Are* (New York: Three Rivers Press, 1995), 171.
8. Ruth Rosen, *The World Split Open: How the Modern Women's Movement Changed America* (New York: Viking Penguin, 2000), 296.
9. Jane Maas, *Mad Women: The Other Side of Life on Madison Avenue in the '60s and Beyond* (New York: St. Martin's Press, 2012), 131.
10. Rhaina Cohen, "Who Took Care of Rosie the Riveter's Kids?" *The Atlantic*, November 18, 2015.
11. Coontz, *A Strange Stirring*, 50.
12. Ibid.
13. Rodger Streitmatter, "Transforming the Women's Pages," *Journalism History*, 24 (2), 1998, 72–81.
14. Kay Pancoast, a graduate of Cornell University, was very active in the Miami community. Several letters from Pancoast to Anderson are included in the Papers of Marie Anderson.
15. Dorothy Roe, *The Problem With Women in Men* (New York: Prentice-Hall, 1961), 124.
16. Dorothy Jurney, "I Was Replaced As a City Editor By An Ex-Copy Boy," *ASNE Bulletin*, November 1992, 27.
17. David Davies, *The Postwar Decline of American Newspapers, 1945–1965* (Westport, Conn.: Praeger Publishers, 2006), 4.
18. Mary Welsh Hemingway letter to Jurney, September 11, 1958. Papers of Dorothy Jurney.
19. Charles Stevenson letter of recommendation, February 28, 1949. Papers of Dorothy Jurney.
20. Ibid.
21. Paxson described this in her introduction to the National Women and Media Collection, State Historical Society of Missouri.
22. Jurney, "Women in Journalism," Session 4, 126.
23. Stevenson letter, Papers of Dorothy Jurney.
24. Marjorie Paxson, "Women in Journalism," Session 6, 144.
25. Catherine East, Oral History, Schlesinger Library.
26. Ibid.
27. Clarenbach, Oral History, 52.
28. McElhaney, *Pauline Periwinkle*, 15.
29. Karen J. Blair, *The Clubwoman as Feminist: True Womanhood Redefined, 1868–1914* (New York: Holmes & Meier Publishers, 1980), 101.

30. "Library System Announces the Passing of Library Advisory Board Chair Emeritus Helen Muir," February 17, 2006. Miami-Dade Public Library System.
31. Nellie Roberson, "The Work of Women's Organizations," *The Journal of Social Forces*, November 1922, 50.
32. Roe, *The Problem With Women*, 123.
33. Blair, *The Clubwoman*, 25.
34. Anne Firor Scott, *Making the Invisible Woman Visible* (Urbana: University of Illinois Press, 1984), 283.
35. Roe, *The Problem with Women*, 125.
36. Kimberly Wilmot Voss, "Roberta Applegate: Breaking Barriers in Michigan," *Michigan History Magazine*, March/April 2008.
37. Roberta Applegate, "Association News and the Club Editor," undated speech, Coral Gables. Papers of Roberta Applegate.
38. Carmen Morrina, *The League Goes to War*. The Junior League of Miami. http://www.jlmiami.org/the-league-goes-to-war
39. Marie Anderson, *Commencement Speech*. Papers of Marie Anderson.
40. Pauline Periwinkle, *Dallas Morning News*, June 4, 1900. Cited in Jacquelyn Masur McElhaney, *Pauline Periwinkle and Progressive Reform in Dallas* (College Station, Texas: Texas A & M Press, 1998), xvi.
41. Kimberly Wilmot Voss and Lance Speere, "A Women's Page Pioneer: Marie Anderson and Her Influence at the *Miami Herald* and Beyond," *Florida Historical Quarterly*, Spring 2007, 398–421.
42. "Class for Clubwomen," *Time*, September 30, 1946.
43. Pauline Mandigo, "Good Public Relations," *General Federation of Women's Clubs Newsletter*, December 1950, 12.
44. "Herald Extends Club Invitation," *Miami Herald*, September 13, 1953. Papers of Marie Anderson.
45. Roberta Applegate, "'Children at Florida Farm Colony Range from 6 to 60," *Miami Herald*, October 14, 1954.
46. Ibid.
47. Roberta Applegate, "Emphasis at Florida Farm Colony Placed on Rehabilitation, Training," *Miami Herald*, October 15, 1954.
48. Saulsbury, 23.
49. Trudy Haffron Bers and Susan Gluck Mezey, "Support for Feminist Goals among Leaders of Women's Community Groups," *Signs*, Summer 1981, 741.
50. Susan Douglas, *Where the Girls Are*, 270.
51. Georgia Duerst-Lahti, "The Government's Role In Building the Women's Movement," *Political Science Quarterly*, Summer 1989, 251.
52. "Women's Bureau Anniversary 90 Years: Still Working," Women's Bureau, http://www.dol.gov/wb/90years.htm.
53. Anderson autobiography, undated. Marie Anderson Papers.
54. Janet M. Martin, *The Presidency and the Women: Promise, Performance & Illusion* (College Station, Texas: Texas A & M University Press, 2003), 51.
55. Martin, *The Presidency*, 57.
56. Esther Peterson, "Working Women," *Daedalus*, 93:2, 1964, 617.
57. Peterson, "Working Women," 683.
58. East, Oral history, 93.
59. East, Oral history, 93.
60. Vera Glaser, "Women Discriminated Against?" *Amarillo, Texas Globe-Times*, October 16, 1963.
61. Ibid.
62. Clarenbach, Oral History Project, 16.
63. Clarenbach, Oral History, 177.
64. Genevieve G. McBride, ed., *Women's Wisconsin: From Native Matriarchies to the New Millennium* (Madison: Wisconsin Historical Society, 2005), 437.
65. Paterson, *Be Somebody*, 164.

66. Coontz, *A Strange Stirring*.
67. Anthony Ramirez, "Catherine East, 80, Inspiration For National Women's Group," *New York Times*, August 20, 1996.
68. Harrison, *On Account of Sex*, 192–199.
69. Most stories of the initial creation of NOW indicate that East was not in Friedan's hotel room and her later note to Clarenbach seems to support that theory. However, one researcher wrote that East was included in Friedan's hotel room: Duerst-Lahti, "The Government's Role," 265.
70. Ramirez, "Catherine East."
71. Clarenbach, Oral history, 127.
72. Paterson, *Be Somebody*.
73. Clarenbach, Oral history, 127.
74. Paterson, *Be Somebody*, 165.
75. Clarenbach, Oral history, 128.
76. Paterson, *Be Somebody*, 166.
77. National Association of Commissions for Women, *Handbook for Commissions on the Status of Women* (Madison, Wisconsin: Regents of the University of Wisconsin System, 1979), 3.
78. Clarenbach, Oral history, 128.
79. Ibid.
80. Clarenbach, Oral history, 129.
81. Lisa Hammel, "They Meet in Victorian Parlor to Demand 'True Equality'—NOW," *New York Times*, November 22, 1966.

Chapter Three

Women's Journalism Organizations, Women's Political Writing, and Offbeat Washington

The women's pages were a part of metropolitan newspapers for decades. The sections included club news and photos of brides. Much of the coverage has been described as the four Fs: family, fashion, food, and furnishings. Yet, amid the more traditional stories in women's pages were stories that addressed serious issues and challenged the notion that a woman should remain at home. This was especially true in the post-World War II years and into the 1960s. It was the assumption that the sections were non-threatening that gave them a platform to address progressive content for women. According to journalist Zena Beth Guenin in 1973:

> First-rate women's sections do exist and some were doing a top reporting job long before the theme of women's liberation was heard. And there have been women who strived for excellence despite the indifference from management.[1]

Yet, for many years, women's pages were dismissed as "fluff sections" and a "ghetto" for women. The reality was much more complex. By devaluing the work of women journalists—who fought for change, important voices are marginalized. Many women's page editors worked within the system to make a difference. One study of Anderson and Jurney's work by media historian Rodger Streitmatter examined the ways they strove to change the traditional content found in their sections. For example, when Jurney was at the *Detroit Free Press* in 1959, she heard the United Presbyterian Church was having a conference and birth control would be discussed. She volunteered to cover the event as a favor to the news editor. She said: "If a man had covered that conference, he wouldn't have mentioned the words birth control." Streitmatter concluded: "The pioneering editors did not reject the news values and conventions that male editors had developed, but they assiduously—and sometimes with a high degree of manipulative skill—used the long established system to their advantage."[2]

The visible women's liberation movement that caught media attention beginning in the late 1960s was a complex one. Leila J. Rupp and Verta Taylor wrote that many have given Friedan significant credit and ignored the "old ladies who sat in that vine-covered building and made repeated phone calls to congressional leaders,"[3] in a quote from National Woman's Party member Caruthers Berger. Additional projects have sprung up in recent years that have demonstrated other pockets of support for women's rights. In *The Sisterhood*, Marcia Cohen argues that in addition to the well-known movement leaders, there were "brushfires burning, a grassroots movement."[4]

The women's pages of newspapers had long addressed women's social and political issues. For example, in 1959, the *Miami Herald's* women's page addressed the needs of widows in a six-part series written by women's club editor Applegate. According to census figures at the time, 12 percent of adult women were widowed, and the Florida retirement communities would have meant it was a good part of the readership. Applegate interviewed many widows and spoke with guidance counselors, legal and sociology experts; her intent was to empower her female readers who may not have been as independent in their marriages. It was titled, "What would you do if your husband died?" and was syndicated through United Features. It ran in the women's pages of newspapers across the country.[5]

There were several stories about women in the workforce—not as a "first," but simply as women who held jobs outside of the home. One example can be found in a 1960s *Miami Herald* series on women who worked at Cape Canaveral in central Florida. With the space race running on the front page of newspapers across the country, more attention was paid to Patrick Air Force Base. For the women's pages, this would have been a natural female angle. The five-part series featured the stories of four women who, Applegate wrote, "are working to unlock the secrets of space."[6] Eleanor Livingston was the deputy chief of the community relations branch. Prior to this position, Livingston was a medical and science writer in New York.[7] The next article told the story of Dorothy Laidlaw, who had been a contract expert at the base for a decade. She was one of three women in this position. Applegate noted that Laidlaw was married and that her housework load was easier because they lived in a trailer.[8] The third woman was June Luther, who was a missile mathematician who worked in computer language.[9] Last featured was Ollie Porto, who was secretary to the base manager. He said: "Ollie is the catalyst that holds us together here. I don't know what we'd do without her."[10] All of these women were recognized for their professional work—without focusing on the fact they were female.

A 1958 women's page article, written by Applegate and edited by Jurney, profiled Marion Martin, who was the nation's only woman commissioner of a state department of labor. She had been in that position in Maine for more than a decade. She was in Miami to address the Florida Industrial Commission's Workmen's Compensation Conference. In the story, Applegate included a quote from Martin that may have spurred some women into action:

> Labor-management relations after all are just human relations and the woman in the household is the one who resolved conflicts. The same techniques a woman uses to solve family quarrels are used in labor and management conflicts.[11]

In another example, the *Miami Herald* featured a women's page story about the views of a Republican committee woman, Claire B. Williams, and her opinions about woman in politics. Williams, of St. Petersburg, Florida, said she was insulted by statements made by male politicians about the woman's vote: "As if we weren't human beings, too." She addressed a stereotype of the female voter: "It's insulting to women to say a candidate must have dimples and wavy hair to appeal to the women. We look for the same thing men do and so often we're better informed." She also said that a woman was not ready to be president. Not for a stereotypical reason, but that the path to the presidency needs to be in place. She said women would not be ready until there were more women in Congress and more women governors.[12] Other women's page journalists addressed the stereotype of women voting for candidates based on their handsome appearances. For example, women's page columnist Beverley Morales urged her female readers to use their political power. In her column, she wrote:

> Women now hold the balance of voting power in Florida and in the nation. They outnumber men, 107,000 to 97,000 on Broward County's voter books, for example. ... They could change the face of the nation if they cared to.[13]

A 1964 *Miami Herald* story, edited by Anderson and Paxson, profiled five women who would play major roles at the upcoming Republican Convention. Although this story by the Associated Press addressed the hard work of the women, the writer also described the women as "good-looking," illustrating the mixed messages that the sections conveyed. While the story did not challenge the status quo, there was a recognition of gender inequality. For example, "Since little girls rarely dream of growing up to be president—they know it's a waste of imagination, at least right now—they are taking on more important political jobs every year instead, to show they are here to stay."[14]

Another story in that same issue, a UPI wire story, profiled Katie Louchheim, a top-ranking woman in the State Department. She was known for taking new approaches to traditional governmental programs. A colleague said: "Sometimes the State Department gets used to doing things a certain way. Then someone like Mrs. Louchheim walks in, does things a little differently and injects new life into the job."[15] The story focused on her professional life rather than her personal life or familial roles.

Journalism Organization Theta Sigma Phi

Throughout the early part of the century, male and female journalists were often members of separate professional organizations—as they were prevented because of their gender from joining several journalism organizations. For example, the Society of Professional Journalists did not allow female members until 1973. Instead, women journalists often belonged to the sorority Theta Sigma Phi, which had state-wide chapters. (The organization is now known as the Association for Women in Communications.) Many of the Florida women's page editors were leaders in the state chapter, but it was Paxson, then of the *Miami Herald*, who made a national name for herself. Anderson wrote of Paxson, "She certainly has done an excellent job of putting Theta Sig on a more professional and businesslike basis."[16]

Paxson was the national president of the Theta Sigma Phi during its transformation from a sorority to a professional organization. Paxson was elected the national president of the 4,500-member professional journalism organization. She held that office from 1963 to 1967. When she took office, the organization—which was founded in 1908 as a sorority for journalism students—was more of a social group. According to Paxson, "I turned the organization from a narrow, journalistic social sorority concept to a professional approach. I motivated volunteers who paid dues for the privilege of working in the organization . . . to change direction."[17] Paxson's campaign for more professionalism was not always well received. The race for the presidency was bitter. Many members resisted Paxson's emphasis on professional training. She was at a local Theta Sigma Phi meeting when she learned she had won. She got a telegram from Anderson with a sarcastic message: "Congratulations, I guess."[18]

According to Chicago journalist Mary Jane Snyder, it was an important time for the women's organization. She said:

> Those were decisive years when a philosophy of change was at stake. We needed a woman with strong leadership qualities, a real professional. Marj was the right person at the right time. She hits the ground running. She's a woman with high expectations who has the talent to mesh divergent people together, yet do it in a non-threatening manner so everybody feels comfortable.[19]

Paxson's goals included establishing a national headquarters. At that time the organization's files were housed in a member's garage. She also wanted to put more professional information in the organization's magazine, the *Matrix*. She spent much of her free time traveling and speaking to local chapters. While she served as president, she visited around forty chapters and traveled more than 75,000 miles. She also corresponded with different groups within the organization—writing more than 4,000 letters for an average of twenty-five a week. In her farewell address as president, Paxson called for the organization to change its name from the Greek letters denoting a sorority to a more professional title, Women in Communications, Inc., although it took several more years for this to occur. She said, "I always had a high regard for the organization. It did spread across the country and there were a lot of prominent women in it. I felt like it could be a force to help women as things changed in the sixties."[20]

In Fort Lauderdale in 1966, some women journalists took a stand when the city advertised for a public relations position and specified it must be a male. According to Paxson, the reason was a woman could not accompany the male city commissioners on civic trips. She said, "I don't know who they were more worried about—a woman or the city commissioners."[21] The local Theta Sigma Phi chapter went to speak to the city officials and the policy was changed. None of the women wanted the position—it was simply the principle of being excluded by gender. Paxson wanted the women's pages to cover more stories like that one. She told women's page journalists:

> As women's editors, we have a lot of very precious white space at our disposal every day. It's time we started putting some hard news into that valuable space. It's time we accepted the responsibility of making our readers aware.[22]

In the years following Paxson's presidency, the women whom she had recruited stayed involved and pushed for continued professionalism. Decades later, the organization continues to be a professional association that provides a female voice for communications professionals. In 2003, Paxson was inducted into the organization's national hall of fame. The organization noted: "Her career is truly a documentary of women in journalism. She has lived the evolution of change from society section to lifestyle section . . . society editor to managing editor and publisher."[23] Further, her establishing of the National Women and Media Collection allows for the stories of more women journalists to be told.

Journalist Turned Spokeswoman

While many women who went into journalism in the 1950s were relegated to women's beats in newspapers and in radio, some women took another path.

They created their own jobs as correspondents, bureau chiefs and political representatives. Glaser had decided to be a journalist while in high school. She began her career in magazines before turning to governmental public relations work in the 1950s, including being the publicity director for the women's division of the Republican National Committee. Glaser had served as press officer for Michigan Republican Senator Charles E. Potter from 1956 to 1959. During that time, she also directed publicity for the Michigan "Minute Men for Eisenhower."[24] She noted her gender was unique while her boss was running for re-election. She said: "This is a man's game, but I think a woman can be effective in it." She also noted that the Democratic rival had four men assigned to the job while she had no publicity colleagues.[25]

In her new national role, she was giving speeches about getting media attention. She advised making friends with local journalists and inviting them into their homes for interviews. In a 1959 speech to a Republican Women's Conference, Glaser explained:

> Always remember that the opportunity carries with it a responsibility. Your answers to reporters' questions and your publicity releases must be accurate and truthful. You must always stand or fail on the facts—even if this means giving replies that are not entirely pleasant.[26]

Later that year, she wrote a memo for her boss, Clare B. Williams, about women's roles in state-wide elections. They were still expected to keep a home and raise a family but they should also fill their roles as active citizens. Glaser noted, "America's women have accepted this double challenge and they are chalking up a magnificent record of service to the nation. I predict that the upward trend of their advances will continue."[27]

By 1962, Glaser was a press secretary to Senator Kenneth B. Keating, a Republican from New York. That year she spoke to the League of Women Voters in Washington, DC and explained the significance the GOP gave to women voters. She showed this through President Eisenhower's role from 1952 to 1960. She said that the president "broke all records in the number of women appointed to top-level government posts."[28] She cited as examples Oveta Culp Hobby, first secretary of the US Department of Health, Education, and Welfare, first director of the Women's Army Corps, and Clare Boothe Luce, who had been named an ambassador to Italy. Attendees were given the booklet, "Win with Womanpower." Glaser pointed out that the majority of the Republican votes in the last three elections were women. In return, women had equal representation in the Republican National Committee. According to the structure of their party, there was one male and one female representation from each state. Further, she cited the number of women who were involved in the 1960 national convention in Chicago. At the event, eleven women were in top positions. According to Glaser, women held "positions of real eminence in organizing the convention, writing the party platform, and making major addresses to the delegates."[29]

In October 1966, Glaser spoke at a meeting of the Massachusetts State Federation of Women's Clubs, which was celebrating its seventy-fourth year. The audience included more than seven hundred club members. She advocated for the women to take on political issues: "If there were a natural vocation for women, it is politics. Women are political naturals because politics call for an abiding interest in people. It calls for the ability to persuade."[30] She concluded her talk with the lack of women in national political positions. She mentioned that only two women had been named to a president's cabinet and that only seven women had served as ambassadors.[31] She also said that no woman had ever been named to the Supreme Court—a foreshadowing of the campaign that she and East would later wage during the Nixon administration.

Glaser left her post as a spokesperson and returned to journalism as a reporter for the North American Newspaper Alliance in the 1960s. Then she became the Washington bureau chief for the Alliance in the 1960s. Her articles typically ran in the women's pages of newspapers. By September 12, 1963, her employer North American Newspaper Alliance wrote a letter to White House Press Secretary Pierre Salinger verifying her employment and noted that she officially worked for the Alliance's subsidiary Women's News Service.[32]

Women in Politics

While women were largely excluded from politics, there were typically a few women able to hold positions of power who women journalists covered. One example was Republican Elly Peterson. She was known of the "Mother of the Moderates" in the GOP.[33] In fact, she was often called "mother" by the young workers she attracted to the Republican Party. In 1963, she became the assistant chairwoman of the Republican National Committee. She retired from the committee in 1970 after a second term. *Washington Post* columnist David Broder wrote that she would have been named to lead the GOP "were it not for the unwritten sex barriers both parties have created around the job."[34] She was a strong supporter of Michigan Governor George W. Romney. He said of Peterson: "She thinks like a man, looks like a woman and works like a dog." She said she appreciated the thought but not the wording.[35]

Frequently, her speeches and activities were covered by women's page reporters. In August 1968, Peterson was featured along with a story about the GOP keynote address in the *Miami Herald*, which would have been edited by Anderson. She was described as "Mrs. William Peterson." It was written by women's page reporter Janet Chusmir, who would go on to be one of the first female newspaper executives at a newspaper that was not family owned.[36] Chusmir wrote about Peterson's experiences: "At first, the men would say 'pardon me,' after they had said 'damn.' Now, they've dropped the 'pardon me.' That's a sign of acceptance of a woman in a man's world."[37] Peterson also said "Men admit women do a lot of work, but to be a delegate is a competitive thing. It's very difficult to beat a man."[38] In March of 1970, Glaser wrote about Peterson, also for the *Miami Herald*. She had taken a stand against the nomination of potential Supreme Court Justice G. Harrold Carswell of Florida. She also spoke out about those in her party who were not moving forward with school desegregation. She said: "I happen to be a strong promoter of civil rights and I do not look forward to neglect of any kind."[39] By October of that year, Peterson was ready to leave her post and was again interviewed by Glaser. Peterson explained: "I've always felt that the strength of any political party lies in new ideas and new people. I have been on the scene quite a while. I never intended to hang on by my teeth forever. If I move on, it makes for more diversity and action."[40]

Women and Washington, DC, Journalism

For decades, political coverage was dominated by male journalists. There were, however, a few women who broke the barriers—especially if they approached their beat from a women's perspective or with a society angle. One example was journalist Betty Beale, who covered Washington, DC, parties and social life from 1945 to 1990. She described her colorful career in her book *Power at Play: A Memoir of Parties, Politicians, and the Presidents in My Bedroom*.[41] It is estimated that she attended about 15,000 parties ranging from the Truman to the Reagan administrations. At the height of her career in the 1960s, approximately ninety newspapers published her column.[42] After one party, she angered the Eisenhower administration by reporting that the White House was serving hard liquor at an afternoon reception. It led to a protest by non-drinkers, and the practice was discontinued when reporters were present.[43] In her book, she wrote:

> The essence of Washington was not to be found in presidential pronouncements or congressional commitments. Instead, it was alive and thriving on the nightly social scene where the activities of the day and the predictions of the morrow were reported, sorted, aborted, or distorted and promptly exported to the next pair of ears at the next party. Indeed, in the Capital the laws of physics were reversed. Sound traveled faster than light.[44]

Beale was not the only woman covering Washington politics at those parties. The city's social gatherings made women journalists welcome. According to historian Maurine Beasley's research about Washington, DC, female journalists, there was a discriminatory environment, yet some prevailed.

Washington women journalists have viewed news differently and more broadly than their masculine competitors. Due to their own roles, engendered by societal expectations, they had to move beyond the limitations of a journalism that focused on reporting and commenting about conflicts and controversies.[45]

Longtime political newspaper columnist Mary McGrory said she had deeply resented the practice as she described "some fat lobbyist lighting his cigar and having his second cup of coffee."[46] (In another story, *New York Times* Bureau Chief Scotty Reston had wanted to hire McGrory but told her that she would also have to learn to operate the switchboard. She rejected the offer.)[47] In 1975, two equally important events happened to McGrory; she won the Pulitzer Prize for commentary for her coverage of Watergate, and it was revealed that she was on President Nixon's enemies list. There was no love lost between the two. "If he were a horse, I would not buy him," McGrory wrote of Nixon. *Time* described McGrory as "Queen of the Corps" and the United Press's Washington bureau chief said her writing was the best he had ever seen. President Johnson called her "… the best writer in Washington, and she keeps getting better at my expense."[48]

Sometimes the marginalization of female journalists was due to being overshadowed by male editors. *Washington Post* editor Ben Bradlee has been recognized for his creation of the Style section in 1969 and its groundbreaking role in lifestyle journalism—away from the traditional women's pages. Yet, when looked at through the lens of current journalism history, this accomplishment becomes an overstatement. The women's page editors made the most of their situations and often innovated pioneering moves under the radar of their male editors. The women's page editors had already begun implementing changes to their sections well before Bradlee created the Style section and eliminated the women's section.

What happens when Bradlee is recognized for his work is that the women who were true groundbreakers get forgotten. Marie Sauer, who headed the *Washington Post's* women's section prior to the Style section's debut, was an impressive journalist. Her women's section was a progressive mix of hard and soft news in a city where political decisions were often crafted at social events. It was she who wanted to change the name of the section in the 1950s to "For and About People" but was denied. A Columbia University School of Journalism graduate, Sauer came to the *Post* in 1935 as assistant Sunday editor. She became Sunday editor a year later and held that position until 1942, when she joined the US Navy. She was the first woman staff member of the *Post* to join the armed forces in World War II.

After her return in 1946, she became woman's editor where she remained until her retirement in 1969 (and the launch of the Style section). Some people considered the role of women's editor as a demotion for her; Sauer did not. She saw this as an opportunity to provide news about "prominent women, average women, white women, black women—their fashions, their foods, their lifestyles, their fight for equal rights and civil rights, their involvement in community actions" that would "inform, amuse, challenge, and intrigue." She was also a dogged journalist. Sauer would often instruct her staff on what to ask and whom to talk to, such as requesting a reporter to "See what the secretary of defense thinks about this." In turn, her obituary noted, this approach "won recognition as required reading for anyone hoping to understand how Washington worked."[49] She produced eight stand-alone sections each week and sent her reporter to the White House, State Department and embassy parties. Judith Martin worked for Sauer in the 1960s and recalled her power. As a young reporter, Martin had been assigned to ask a difficult question to President Kennedy. While she was nervous to ask the question, she recalled thinking who she was more scared of—the president or her editor. She wrote: "I asked him the question."[50]

Sauer long believed in the value of hard news in her section, and in truth believed newsroom policies often restricted the scope of her section and what it could or could not cover. Bradlee may get the credit for turning the *Post's* Style section into more, but Sauer clearly wanted to improve the section in the decade before he made his move. Had Bradlee done nothing, chances are the transformation of the women's pages to lifestyle sections was predestined by both the messages from the women's liberation movement to better integrate women's news throughout newspapers, and the growth of the "Sectional Revolution" experienced at newspapers in the early 1970s.[51]

Offbeat Washington

Longtime Washington reporters Glaser and Malvina Stephenson officially became journalism partners on the presidential election night in 1968. They were at Richard Nixon's headquarters at the Waldorf-Astoria in New York City. Reporters were stuck in the press room being supplied with briefings and alcohol. The two women found California Lieutenant Governor Bob Finch and "rode his coattails," according to Stephenson. "How heady to forge past the barricades of police and security guards, escorted as 'ladies' in the company of VIP Finch." She recalled that the pair took mental notes and subtlety scribbled details as they interacted with Nixon's inner circle. They lingered as Glaser claimed a headache and waited for pills to be delivered. Stephenson said: "Before being kicked out, we obtained a batch of exclusive interviews, which were the price of the entire excursion."[52] They got information from John Mitchell, future attorney general, and other Nixon insiders. She recalled:

> Even as we retired from that battlefield we managed another triumph. Since we were both sober, we were able to concentrate on a bunch of what seemed

like routine releases, only to discover that one was a secret memo prepared by campaign director Bob Ellsworth, coaching his aides on the handling of election returns. Using it as a source, we were able to write a hilarious report comparing the confidential analysis with what the campaign spokesmen were feeding out to the public as the returns came in.[53]

By the time they were spotted by Nixon's director of public relations, they had found a copy of the campaign director's confidential guide to election returns. Then they broke the story. This was a formula that they perfected during their tenure together. Their partnership was based on the love of a good story and their variety of contacts—Glaser had been the press secretary for a Republican and Stephenson had been a spokesperson for a Democrat. Glaser had reached out to Stephenson and suggested the arrangement. Several male reporters had teamed up for columns, and they would be the first women. They worked on several projects before they signed on with the Knight newspaper chain a year later. Stephenson said: "Some of our friends made dire predictions about the 'shackling together' of two strong-willed, independent women. I think they gave us but a short time to last. We fooled them."[54]

One of their big stories included writing about First Lady Jackie Kennedy's view of the White House—scooping her own secretary's tattletale book. From an unnamed source, Glaser and Stephenson were leaked memos from the First Lady's Office. They wrote that Mrs. Kennedy worried about the drunken behavior of guests and damage to the Red Room rug. They documented her battles with her social secretary. They wrote about the First Lady's view of women reporters at White House social events:

> Their notebooks bother me, but perhaps they should be allowed to keep them, at least, then you know they are the press. But I think they should be made to wear big badges and be whisked out of there once we sit down to dinner.[55]

One of their biggest scoops was learning that former First Lady Kennedy had renounced her widow's pension. The request had been hidden and when it was finally revealed, the date was blackened out. They wrote: "The hush-hush attitude of the Treasury appears strangely protective."[56] They further noted that many people had been surprised that she had applied for the pension after she received ten million dollars from her late husband's estate. They went on to analyze Kennedy's new wealth now that she had married billionaire Aristotle Onassis. Glaser and Stephenson concluded: "The Kennedys could now be called Jackie's poor kinfolk, but they hold political clout, and with Teddy's drive now under way, may one day be back in the White House." (The Chappaquiddick tragedy on July 18, 1969, would largely end the youngest Kennedy's White House aspiration.) Their wire service sent out a press release to newspaper editors about the scoop, noting:

> You may have noted that the scoop by Vera Glaser and Malvina Stephenson—that Jackie Onassis has renounced her widow's pension—was picked up and confirmed by the Associated Press. Vera and Mal's story, of course, was far more developed and detailed than the belated AP version.[57]

A 1970 story by the pair received a great deal of press. It involved a story about a case against Green Beret officers in Vietnam. They wrote that the officers' wives were heading to Vietnam to fight the charges. The Army dropped the charges the day after the column appeared.[58]

Glaser and Stephenson rarely named their sources, but were known for having many friends in Congress who leaked them information. They wrote about a rumor that members of the House Foreign Affairs Committee were not pleased that President Nixon's Administration was using expensively trained astronauts for non-space-related positions. Their column noted, "Astronaut Michael Collins soared to the moon and back in eight days, but seems unable to get into orbit at the State Department after four months as assistant secretary of public affairs."[59] They were the first to report that Shirley Temple Black, US delegate to the United Nations General Assembly, was charging a five-hundred-dollar fee for every speech she gave at a major Republican function—including a five-hundred-dollar fee for appearing at her own birthday party. In a column that began "Who is spying on whom . . .," they noted that the director of the Central Intelligence Agency and a Russian correspondent for *Pravda* lived in the same Washington, DC, apartment building.

At times, it was their following a rumor that led them to report that the gossip of other journalists was not completely correct. One example was an exclusive interview that Glaser earned with Passport Director Frances Knight. It was at a time when some in the State Department were trying to get Knight fired, and she was not speaking to anyone in the media. Knight, who oversaw the office for twenty-two years, was often criticized for denying passports to those who were thought to be Communists during the Cold War.[60] Glaser kept calling Knight's secretary and explained that Knight's voice should be heard. The resulting story clarified the attacks that Knight had been under. Glaser said of the interview: "I had heard that Miss Knight was mean, an absolute impossible woman, and she turned out to be delightful. The rumors about that poor woman are just incredible, and she is as nice as can be."[61]

The women wrote what they described as the appointment of a "Republican segregationist" to a twenty-thousand-dollar-a-year job in Nixon's State Department. The two columnists produced a picture of the woman at a Wallace rally carrying a sign that read: "They say intergration (sic). They mean miscegenation." The appointee was dismissed from the position as soon as the story ran in the newspapers. She had been on the job for forty-eight hours.⁶² This is just one of the examples of the transparency of government that the columnists provided to readers.

In another column, the women wrote about a rumored proposed appointment to the Equal Employment Opportunity Commission. This was at a time when the federal agency was under fire for not taking accusations of discrimination against women seriously. The columnists wrote that the potential appointee was a well-connected socialite who had served on arts and gambling boards.⁶³ She had no legal experience for the position. The column led to a letter from Aileen Hernandez, the president of the National Organization for Women and former member of the Equal Employment Opportunity Commission, to President Nixon. She cited the column and the "journalistic credibility" of the women writers. She wrote, "I do feel it is unlikely that Mrs. (Irene) Walczak has much experience, which could be related to the Herculean tasks she will be called upon to perform as a commissioner to the EEOC."⁶⁴ Ultimately, Walczak was not named to the commission.

One of the more common sources for "Offbeat Washington" was Martha Mitchell, wife of Attorney General John Mitchell. The Nixon administration had invited wives to cabinet meetings, as a way of reaching out to women. One wife complained to Glaser, and said she had called Martha Mitchell to say she did not want to be part in a particular program, "but Martha is someone you don't say 'no' to. Martha didn't realize until later that her zeal for what she termed 'helping both the country and the administration' wasn't shared by everyone. She forged ahead, looking for meaningful things for the wives to do."⁶⁵ Apparently, Nixon later became concerned. Glaser noted that an unnamed cabinet wife that the president had turned to her husband and "completely out of the blue, in the middle of another conversation, asked, 'What are going to do with Martha Mitchell'?"⁶⁶

According to Stephenson: "Martha was comparatively anonymous until our first column in October 1969, which proved her a talking doll. She would call us very early in the morning."⁶⁷ Glaser recalled that the pair were threatened by John Mitchell, "who told us if we quoted him he'd see that we never got inside the White House or Justice Department again. That was because we tracked down Martha Mitchell's first husband, Clyde Jennings, Jr., regarding a twenty-five-thousand-dollar lawsuit pending against him."⁶⁸ It was the result of back child support for their then-grown son. The phone calls led to a story co-authored by Glaser and Stephenson. Jennings would contact the attorney general in hopes of settling the matter. He would say: "'That's between you and Martha.' So we knew that there were many problems in the attorney general's home life," Stephenson said.⁶⁹

In another offbeat Washington column, they wrote about China-born yet American citizen Anna Chan Chennault, the widow of a wartime hero. There were questions about the woman's role in American politics—a potential violation of the Logan Act. The legislation forbids a private citizen from engaging in negotiations with a foreign government. The women reported that President Johnson had "exploded" the previous fall when he heard about her messages that the government had taped. According to the story, "the Nixon administration appears to be giving her a longer leash" and she was no longer being taped. They also cited Attorney General Mitchell. They wrote: "He pretended to be unaware of the flap she caused in the campaign, although other Nixon aides have admitted she gave them the scare of their lives and could have cost them the election."[70]

The joint column ended a few years later when both women were overwhelmed with their own projects. Glaser continued to get exclusives, including an interview with Midge Costanza—the token woman in the Carter Administration. She also wrote the first story about what she described as "Tongsun Park's skullduggery on rice deals" in March 1975. She noted that the *Washington Post* began an exposé a few months after her initial story. Glaser again wrote about the Tongsun Park wrongdoing in 1977 with karate schools.[71]

Covering Politics in the Women's Pages

To broaden the coverage in her women's section, Jurney offered to cover issues or events that the news desk did not have time or staff for. She said that while she was in Detroit: "We always did stories on women in politics because it didn't seem to me that a woman who was campaigning for state representative or for the city commission got a fair shake from the news side. So we just said, we will also do a story on her."[72] Jurney wanted to include news of the African-American community that was not being covered in the news sections. She said, "They were ignored. Just like women's things were ignored."[73] She persuaded the managing editor to hire one of the first African-American journalists at the *Detroit Free Press*, a woman whom Jurney wanted to cover the African-American community for the women's section. Jurney also helped to name a Detroit home for teenage mothers for Lulubelle Stuart, an influential doctor in the African-American community. As women's editor, Jurney oversaw stories on race relation issues and women in labor unions that were ignored by the news section.[74] Jurney was so progressive about covering issues in her section that one city reporter went through the *Free Press's* library and found that all the stories he was interested in writing had already run in the women's section.[75]

Jurney assigned a series of stories about women and working conditions that she later said she was most proud of producing.[76] The series was filled with charts that documented pay inequities and the lack of women in management positions. One of the stories addressed a program at General Motors that encouraged women to enter male-dominated fields like engineering.[77] Several other stories pointed out that not all businesses welcomed policies that forced the hiring of women. One executive said: "We're being forced to play the number game with women."[78] Yet, the tone of the series was that the changes would occur so society needed to prepare for them. Reporter Helen Fogel wrote, "It is a fact that the women's movement and women's demands for equality, both of which seemed laughable to many a few short years ago, are laughable no longer."[79] A concluding story in the series addressed how businesses would react to more women in the workforce. Fogel wrote:

> It may take all of America's celebrated business and industrial know-how to implement a regulation that looks far into the future where traditional sex roles are erased, at least in the work world, and to implement it with today's women who grew up in a society that taught her success beyond her home is unfeminine.[80]

NOTES

1. Zena Beth Guenin, "Women's Pages in the 1970s," *Montana Journalism Review*, 27.
2. Streitmatter, "Transforming the Women's Pages," 72–81.
3. Leila J. Rupp and Verta Taylor, *Surviving the Doldrums: The American Women's Movement, 1945 to the 1960s* (Columbus, Ohio: Ohio State University Press, 1990), 3.
4. Marcia Cohen, *The Sisterhood: The Inside Story of the Women's Movement and the Leaders Who Made It Happen* (New York: Fawcett Columbine, 1988), 25.
5. United Features Syndicate letter to editors, nd, Papers of Roberta Applegate, National Women and Media Collection, State Historical Society of Missouri.
6. Roberta Applegate, "Cape Canaveral: A New World," *Miami Herald*, July 3, 1960.
7. Roberta Applegate, "Ellie Knows Her Space Facts—From Monkeys to Catnip," *Miami Herald*, July 4, 1960.
8. Roberta Applegate, "Her Missile Base Work's a Huge 'Clean-Up' Chore," *Miami Herald*, July 5, 1960.
9. Roberta Applegate, "June Tells Missiles Where To Go," *Miami Herald*, July 6, 1960.
10. Roberta Applegate, "Ollie's a Housekeeper—for Cape Canaveral," *Miami Herald*, July 7, 1960.
11. Roberta Applegate, "Women Keep Peace at Home; They Can Do It in Industry," *Miami Herald*, October 31, 1958.
12. Roberta Applegate, "Dimples Don't Sway a Woman's Vote," *Miami Herald*, August 29, 1959.
13. Beverley Morales, "Candidate Use of Sex Appeal Woos Women," *Sun-Sentinel*, October 7, 1966.
14. Associated Press, "GOP? It Means Gals' Own Party," *Miami Herald*, June 18, 1964.
15. "What Katie Did—Use Imagination," *Miami Herald*, June 18, 1964.
16. Marie Anderson letter to Paul L. Myhre, September 4, 1967. Penney-Missouri Awards Papers, National Women and Media Collection, State Historical Society of Missouri.
17. Paxson, *New Guardians of the Press*, 124.
18. Paxson, "Women and Journalism," Session 3, 66.
19. Diane K. Gentry, "Women in Journalism," Introduction, 1, 1991.
20. Paxson, "Women and Journalism," Session 3, 71.
21. Talk by Marjorie Paxson, Penney-Missouri Awards Banquet, March 31, 1966, 4. Papers of the Penney-Missouri Awards, National Women and Media Collection, State Historical Society of Missouri.
22. Ibid.
23. The Association for Women in Communications website, Hall of Fame page.
24. Republican National Committee, News Release, January 6, 1959. Papers of Vera Glaser.

25. Marie Smith, "Blows Bugle for Senator But Can't Vote for Her Boss," *Washington Post*, October 24, 1958.
26. Vera Glaser, "A Nose for News," speech to the Seventh Annual Republican National Committee, April 12, 1959, 5. Papers of Vera Glaser.
27. Clare B. Williams, Memo, Republican National Committee, September 20, 1959. Papers of Vera Glaser.
28. Vera R. Glaser, "A Woman in Politics," Speech to the League of Women Voters, Washington, DC, September 20, 1962, 1. Papers of Vera Glaser.
29. Vera R. Glaser, "A Woman in Politics," 1962, 2. Papers of Vera Glaser.
30. Vera Glaser, "Women's Role in Politics," Speech to Massachusetts State Federation of Women's Clubs," October 31, 1966, 2. Papers of Vera Glaser.
31. Vera Glaser, "Women's Role in Politics," 1966, 5. Papers of Vera Glaser.
32. Sid Goldberg letter to Pierre Salinger, September 12, 1963. Papers of Vera Glaser.
33. Sara Fitzgerald, *Elly Peterson: Mother of the Moderate* (Ann Arbor, Michigan: University of Michigan Press, 2012).
34. William Grimes, "Elly Peterson, 94, a Leader of Moderate Republicans, Is Dead," *New York Times*, June 30, 2008.
35. Ibid.
36. Kimberly Wilmot Voss, "'You Can't Hug a Newspaper': Janet Chusmir, the *Miami Herald* and Newspaper Management," *FCH Annals: Journal of the Florida Conference of Historians*, May 2012.
37. Janet Chusmir, "First Female Party Chief" 'Effort, Time and Energy,'" *Miami Herald*, August 5, 1968.
38. Ibid.
39. Vera Glaser, "Elly Peterson Raps GOP Senator, Aide," *Miami Herald*, March 20, 1979.
40. Vera Glaser, "Elly Peterson Is Bowing Out," *Detroit Free Press*, October 17, 1970.
41. Betty Beale, *Power at Play: A Memoir of Parties, Politicians, and the Presidents in My Bedroom* (Washington, DC: Regnery Gateway Books, 1993).
42. Maurine H. Beasley, *Women of the Washington Press: Politics, Prejudice, and Perspective* (Evanston, Illinois: Northwestern University Press, 2012), 134.
43. Beale, *Power at Play*, 135.
44. Beale, *Power at Play*, 9.
45. Beasley, *Women of the Washington Press*, xv.
46. John Norris, *Mary McGrory: The First Queen of Journalism* (New York: Viking Press, 2015), 34.
47. Ken Hoyt and Frances Spatz Leighton, *Drunk Before Noon: The Behind-the-Scenes Story of the Washington Press Corps* (New Jersey: Prentice Hill, 1979), 133.
48. Norris, *Mary McGrory*, 34.
49. Martin Weil, "Pioneering Post Journalist Marie Sauer," *Washington Post*, October 9, 2001.
50. Judith Martin, "In Defense of 'Women's Pages,'" *Washington Post*, December 12, 2014.
51. Kimberly Wilmot Voss, "Remembering the Real Pioneers of Lifestyle Journalism," *Ms Magazine* blog, November 4, 2014.
52. Hoyt and Leighton, *Drunk before Noon*, 195.
53. Hoyt and Leighton, *Drunk before Noon*, 195–196.
54. Hoyt and Leighton, *Drunk before Noon*, 194.
55. Vera Glaser and Malvina Stephenson, "Inside the White House In the Kennedy Years," Knight Newspaper Syndicate, July 6, 1969. Papers of Vera Glaser.
56. Vera Glaser and Malvina Stephenson, "Jackie's Renounced Pension is Surrounded by Secrecy," *Boston Globe*, January 9, 1969.
57. Women's News Service Report, January 10, 1969. Papers of Vera Glaser.
58. Knight Newspapers, Inc. press release, February 2, 1970. Papers of Vera Glaser.
59. Winzola McLendon and Scottie Smith, *Don't Quote Me: Washington Newswomen & the Power Society* (New York: E.P. Dutton & Company, 1970), 41.
60. William Honan, "Frances Knight, 94, Director Of Passport Office for Decades," *New York Times*, September 18, 1999.

61. McLendon and Smith, *Don't Quote Me*, 41.
62. Ibid.
63. Melinda Robinson, "Irene Walczak on Betting and Arts," *Palm Beach Daily News*, January 5, 1971.
64. Aileen Hernandez letter to President Richard Nixon, June 28, 1970. Papers of Catherine East, Carton 16, folder 27.
65. Winzola McLendon, *Martha: The Life of Martha Mitchell* (New York: Ballantine's, 1979), 158.
66. McLendon, *Martha*, 161.
67. Hoyt and Leighton, *Drunk before Noon*, 193.
68. Ibid.
69. Hoyt and Leighton, *Drunk before Noon*, 194.
70. Vera Glaser and Malvina Stephenson, "Far East Visitor—No Official Status," *Evening Star*, July 20, 1969.
71. Vera Glaser, "Karate School Linked to Korean Power Play," *Evening Independent (FL)*, November 19, 1976.
72. Jurney, "Women in Journalism," Session 2, 77.
73. Jurney, "Women in Journalism," Session 4, 123.
74. Dorothy Jurney letter to Laura Fraser, June 1, 1981. Papers of Dorothy Jurney.
75. Jurney, "Women in Journalism," Session 1, 20.
76. Dorothy Jurney note, October 9, 1988, about *Detroit Free Press* Order 4 stories. Papers of Dorothy Jurney.
77. Helen Fogel, "GM and Women Today," *Detroit Free Press*, April 1972.
78. Helen Fogel, "GM Executive Looks at the Impact of Women Workers," *Detroit Free Press*, April 1972.
79. Helen Fogel, "Putting New Rules into Effect," *Detroit Free Press*, April 1972.
80. Helen Fogel, "U.S. Industry, Women Head For New Era," *Detroit Free Press*, April 1972.

Chapter Four

Washington Press Club, Fundraising Cookbooks, and Glaser's Years as Head of Washington Press Club

Female journalists were often in a difficult place concerning women's rights in the 1960s. They clearly saw the discrimination around them. Yet, they struggled between being objective or being seen as advocates. A poignant example can be found in the marketing of popular syndicated humor writer Erma Bombeck whose column, "At Wit's End," largely ran in the women's pages of newspapers across the country. The column became syndicated in 1965, running three times a week in hundreds of newspapers across the country. In it, a writer noted that the message was "housework, if it is done right, can kill you. It was that the women who kept house in the happy hunting ground called suburbia were so lonely that they held meaningful conversations with their tropical fish."[1] Bombeck's humorous ability to satirize housework helped her connect with readers who recognized the limited value of homemaking. Her funny jabs at the monotony of cooking, cleaning, and child-raising allowed homemakers to recognize some of the difficulties they faced without disparaging them.

The mid-1960s marketing material for Bombeck's column show photos of the writer taking care of her three children and contains information about her role as a mother. (Ironically, the children were well dressed and well behaved in a clean house—the image that she routinely mocked.) Then, the copy reads: "Typical suburban housewife, except—Well, she claims she hasn't lost her identity. Putting on the kids' muddy boots is okay with her, she says." Yet, she was pro-birth control and fought for passage of the Equal Rights Amendment. Maybe more importantly, she pointed out the silliness of homemaker and mother perfection. She allowed women to admit they could find humor rather than hopelessness in a dirty house and messy children. She also pointed out the potential loneliness of a woman restricted to her home and husbands who did not communicate. According to columnist Art Buchwald, "She became the Betty Friedan of the Women's Humor Movement."[2]

Time magazine's initial review of her work noted her positioning in connection to the women's liberation movement. When asked if she had burned her bra, she answered that she had taken a halfway measure: "I scorched mine on the ironing board." The reporter went on to write: "Erma has been called a champion of the Great Silent Majority. That upsets her. For one thing, she is a staunch Democrat. Worse, 'It sounds like I'm totally uninvolved—like being a ski instructor in Berlin during World War II.'"[3]

Public feelings about women's roles were not always openly shared—and sometimes women who believed in feminism did not feel included by the movement. Bombeck's view about Friedan did not mean that she was not an active feminist—especially in later years. In 1978, she began a two-year national tour in favor of the Equal Rights Amendment. She recalled a lieutenant governor of a Southern state patting her on the head and said she should be home having babies. Her response was "My babies were old enough to vote against him."[4] She said she took the defeat of the Constitutional amendment hard, and she had little respect for younger women who opposed the ERA.[5] She was able to have an impact by allowing her voice to be one of a mother and homemaker. As fellow columnist Ann Landers said of Bombeck: "She is savvy and sophisticated enough not to come across as too savvy and sophisticated."[6]

Her approach to women's roles in society appealed to many suburban women. She had put herself through school and had a career before she had children. She believed that feminism and being a homemaker could co-exist. Bombeck recalled going to hear Friedan speak at an Ohio event and that she scolded the audience for finding housework funny rather than demeaning. Bombeck's view was "first we had to laugh; the crying had to come later."[7] It was a slight that she did not forget in later years. Bombeck said of Friedan and some other feminists: "These women threw a war for themselves and didn't invite any of us. That was very wrong of them."[8]

The label "feminist" could be a loaded one. Many women were most familiar with the concept by media representations that were rather extreme. It took time for even forward-thinking people to understand women's liberation. Journalist Bill Moyers began a speech on November 3, 1971, by announcing he was a newly recruited member of the movement. He told of his conversion after a conversation with his nine-year-old daughter. She said she wanted to be a nurse when she grew up. When asked why she did not aspire to be a doctor, she replied: "Oh, Daddy, don't be silly. I'm a girl." It led Moyers to ponder: "I know there are thousands of women who are doctors. But what invisible inheritance in our society has been working upon the consciousness of a nine-year-old girl to cause her to see her potential as limited by the accident of being a female child."[9]

Many women were in a difficult position during the women's movement—especially those who were in positions of power. For example, Gloria Biggs was hired in 1966 to oversee the women's section of a new Florida Gannett newspaper in 1966. The following year, she gave a speech to male Gannett editors about how to attract female readers that was also published in the Gannett newsletter. It was rather stereotypical advice. She recommended content for women should be centered on appearance, people, and emotion. She concluded her talk by saying: "I'd like to emphasize that I'm not a feminist. I'm happy to have men run the show." Many years later, she wrote a note on that speech: "I weep when I read the lines about not being a feminist but then realize that in 1968 that's the way it was and the way I thought I was supposed to say I was!"[10] She was not in a position to share her real feelings while at the newspaper.

Press Clubs

The marginalization of women in journalism was evident for decades. On a broader level, in the 1960s women journalists were still denied access to national and local professional press associations. This was shown in Wisconsin at the Milwaukee Press Club, the oldest continuously operating press club in the United States. On September 19, 1966, the city's women's journalists began their five-year fight to be members of the club with a demonstration in front of the club's building. Their picket signs read "Our Sex Edited Out," "Way Past Deadline," and "Oldest and Most Archaic." In a press release, the women journalists expressed their concerns: "When the spittoons were thrown out of news offices long ago, you forgot to get rid of another archaic practice. Our picketing today is to remind you that you are not addressing yourself to this problem and that it is time to act." [11] Clarenbach was aware of the discrimination and spoke to the Milwaukee chapter of Theta Sigma Phi in 1967. She addressed the issue of gender segregation in the news media. She said: "'People's news' is almost always by, for and of men." [12] In the summer of 1971, after the American Civil Liberties Union threatened a lawsuit, women were allowed to become members of the press club. [13]

Press clubs often held fundraisers to sponsor speakers or events. As women's changing roles in society were being discussed in the late 1960s and early 1970s, traditional expectations were often under fire. Concepts like cooking and home economics were considered ways of keeping women in the home—an enemy of feminism. Yet, in more recent examinations of cookbooks, some scholars have found that the act of producing the publications was more an act of feminism than a reinforcement of traditional roles for women. For example, a study of the Iowa Lutheran Church Women found distinct feminist actions in gathering information, producing and marketing a cookbook. The researcher wrote of the women's work:

> They entered the economic sphere both to produce and to sell their cookbooks, and they negotiated and developed a corporate process that gave them an important voice in the community. Of course, they did so in the service of a domestic ideology that feminism opposed, but their methods were closer to those of contemporary feminists than either side was then likely to admit: a politics of celebrating women getting together, creating collectively, valuing women and women's work.[14]

These kinds of organizations and their fundraising actions can be found in communities across the country. One of the most successful of the well-behaved women fundraising projects occurred in Tampa, Florida. Members of that city's Junior League produced the acclaimed *The Gasparilla Cookbook*. The fiftieth anniversary edition of the cookbook was published in 2011—the book's twenty-third reprint. That edition of the book included a "History of The Gasparilla Cookbook," photos from its early publications and sample menus compiled of readers' favorite recipes. The anniversary edition of the cookbook included 712 of the original recipes, featuring dishes with Spanish, Italian, Greek, Cuban, and Southern influences. Net proceeds from all cookbook sales directly support league programs and projects. The name comes from the legend of José Gaspar, or "Gasparilla," who was a mythical Spanish pirate captain who supposedly operated in Southwest Florida. A week-long celebration of the pirate is held each year in Tampa.

The idea for a fundraising cookbook began in 1960 when the Junior League of Tampa wanted to raise funds to establish a headquarters. At that time there were 217 members, many of whom were wives of local civic leaders. They formed a six-member committee with Deedee Gray as chairman. They organized the recipe collection, tested, wrote, typed, proofed, and designed the layout. They initially published 712 recipes in a hardbound book, selling for $3.75 a copy. The printing of the first edition of 7,800 books sold out in about three months. Another ten thousand cookbooks sold within the following two years. Club members could be seen selling stacks of the books on card tables along the downtown Franklin Street Mall. Copies were available in hotels and sold to other junior league clubs across the country.

Tampa Tribune food editor Ann McDuffie wrote of the book: "Magazine and newspaper food editors across the nation are just as impressed as I am."[15] In the early 1970s, the *Tribune* would publish astrological menus in the paper, helping readers to cook entire Gasparilla-inspired dinners according to their birth signs. According to one headline: "Good-Natured Scorpios Enjoy Good Meals." The cookbook came into the national spotlight in April 1964, when former First Lady Jacqueline Kennedy was photographed holding the book while leaving the Florida pavilion of the New York World's Fair with young daughter Caroline. A special edition was issued for the World's Fair.

The funds from the cookbook continue to make an impact. One cookbook can buy four bags of food for people who do not have enough food to eat on the weekends. Four cookbooks can buy twenty-three books for an underprivileged kindergarten student for his or her home library. Four cookbooks can buy two backpacks filled with items for two children taken into protective custody.[16] Over the years, numerous social causes were aided by sales of the book.

Several press clubs have produced cookbooks as fundraisers. Two Washington, DC cookbooks in particular exemplify the culture of power and prestige in the city. The first was the 1955 cookbook *Who Says We Can't Cook* by the Women's National Press Club. The members stressed the book was not a defense of their culinary talents but rather a fundraising venture so they could rent space for a clubhouse. A story by the journalists accompanied each set of recipes. One contributor was Henrietta Poynter, the editor of *Congressional Quarterly* and mentor to many of the reporters in the women's page section of the *St. Petersburg Times*. (Her husband, Nelson Poynter, was the more well-known of the couple—as publisher of the newspaper. They had shared a bylined column in the newspaper that her husband owned, and she influenced content in the women's pages.) She offered recipes for Heavenly Hamburger and Cheese Wafers and described her kitchen experiences as a young girl:

> I learned to cook at about fourteen when my mother went on a three-month speaking tour for suffrage and left me to keep house. Whatever I saved out of the budget was mine, so I specialized in recipes for making cheap cuts of meat delicious and managed, without starving the family, to indulge in new clothes, theatre tickets, and other things not covered by my allowance.[17]

The initial cookbook had a press run of five thousand copies, and the books were sold out in the first week. For the next three years, the cookbook was regularly reprinted with requests coming as far away as Australia.[18] The book included recipes, some culinary history and short narratives about food. It also included insights into women who both worked as reporters and as home cooks. *Washington Post* food journalist Elinor Lee, who contributed a recipe for oatmeal refrigerator rolls, noted that she collected recipes the way others collect stamps or coins. "It's my hobby as well as my job," she wrote.[19]

The cookbook of the Washington press women proved so popular that a second edition, called *Second Helping*, was released in 1962. This time, Lee shared her recipe for "Whipped Butter," which included brandy and finely chopped blanched almonds. "The recipe, I was told, is a specialty of the Kansas City Club," she explained. Esther Peterson added a recipe for Danish pastry. It was noted that she was of Danish descent and had lived in Europe from 1948 to 1957 when her husband was stationed in Sweden.[20] A representative from the General Federation of Women's Clubs contributed a recipe for "The Best Gingerbread in the World." She noted: "I stake the claim to the title for this recipe because I have used it with success for nigh on to forty years and have heard no dissenting voice."[21] In addition, Mildred White Wells, another member of the group, contributed a recipe for rum punch: "The recipe first came to my attention when I was faced with the problem of giving a cocktail party for an undetermined number of guests in attendance at a medical convention."[22] Glaser's writing partner Malvina Stephenson offered the recipe "Dixieland Butterscotch Pie." She wrote of her culinary background: "The daughter of a Confederate veteran, my mother first learned to cook with limited supplies in postwar Tennessee. Her originality thrived on necessity and, in our kitchen, if we forgot to replenish an item, she eagerly improvised."[23]

Washington Press Club Foundation

The women's press organization that produced those two fundraising cookbooks had a long history. It began in 1919, when six women gathered in correspondent Cora Rigby's office at the *Christian Science Monitor* and created the Women's National Press Club. Their goal was for women to come together to promote the journalistic profession and to enhance the role of women in the newspaper industry. They noted that they faced discrimination in their newsrooms and were banned from membership in the all-male journalism organizations, such as the National Press Club and Gridiron Club. Within months, the women's club grew to twenty-eight charter members.

In the early New Deal days of the 1930s, Eleanor Roosevelt joined the Women's National Press Club; she had a regular column that ran in magazines and newspapers. She soon began holding women-only press conferences that caused many previously all-male news bureaus to hire women. Her role as both the president's wife and a journalist helped women in the profession overall. For example, the First Lady invited women's press club members to perform their annual political lampoon in the White House. After her death, the club established an Eleanor Roosevelt Golden Candlestick Award given for service to humanity.

The Women's National Press Club featured numerous significant speakers, including President Franklin Roosevelt as well as kings, queens, prime ministers, and world leaders. Senator Margaret Chase Smith announced her historic run for the presidency at the women's club meeting. Presidential candidate Barry Goldwater held a question-and-answer session before the club as he launched his 1964 campaign. President Lyndon Johnson announced the appointment of ten women to his new administration at the club's 1964 Congressional dinner. The club celebrated its half-century anniversary with more than seven hundred members. In 1970, the club voted to admit qualified male journalists to membership and changed its name to fit the occasion, becoming the Washington Press Club. The National Press Club voted soon afterward to admit women journalists for the first time since it was founded in 1908.

The first day that it was open to women, Glaser and a few other women had lunch at the club. Journalist Chalmers Roberts came over and glared at the women. He angrily said: "Well, are you satisfied now?" Glaser later said: "Well, of course, these are words one can never forget."[24]

Women and History of the National Press Club

Women journalists were excluded from membership in the Washington, DC, based National Press Club until 1971. This was a significant exclusion as important politicians and celebrities delivered speeches at the press club. Prior to 1955, women were not even allowed in the club building to cover the speeches that made news. As a compromise, the male members came up with a plan that allowed women journalists to cover speakers from the balcony of the ballroom; but they had to stand—because the balcony was too narrow for chairs—while their seated male colleagues ate, drank, and asked questions from below. According to Bonnie Angelo, chief of the *Newsday* bureau in Washington,

> Here were the people in the balcony, distinguished journalists treated like second-class citizens. I *had* to cover the stories there. Some people equated the balcony with the back of the bus, but at least the bus got everybody to the same destination just as well. We could not ask questions of the speakers. All this standing—it was like a cattle car. And all the time you were really boiling inside. You entered and left through a back door, and you'd be glowered at as you went through the club quarters. It was discrimination at its rawest.[25]

The concept that the National Press Club was a male environment was obvious—an oil painting of a nude Phryne the Courtesan, was displayed in its lounge. As one history of the club noted:

> For newswomen operating out of the same (Washington) bureau, the club remained forbidden territory. They could not walk ten feet inside it to read the teletype, contract co-workers in the bar, or take a meal there, regardless of how late they worked in the bureaus downstairs or the weather outside.[26]

Wives of the male journalists made some inroads in 1946 when a room used to store broken furniture was converted into the Ladies Dining Room. "So long as a woman reporter was married to a member, or was invited as a member's guest, she could use the small dining room in the evening, provided she did not venture into the rest of the club."[27] During the 1950s, the press wives extended their privileges to enter the main dining room of the club. Yet, they apparently went too far when they requested access to the bar. According to columnist Frederick Othman: "I can tell you that anguish prevailed in the board room." He noted that some club members threatened to resign "if a female ever stuck her powdered nose past the swinging door."[28]

The male journalists struck a compromise by opening a Ladies' Cocktail Lounge and posted a plate on the door of the members' bar: Accompanied Male Guests Only.[29] Otherwise, women had to remain in the balcony where they could not question the speakers, and had to enter and leave via the back door. They were expected to vacate the premises as soon as the programs ended. *New York Times* women's page journalist Nan Robertson said: "It couldn't have been meaner."[30] The newswomen did take a stand:

> Dissatisfied with their perch, the newswomen petitioned scheduled speakers not to address the Press Club unless women could sit in the dining room as guests. One of the few to comply was Soviet premier Nikita Khrushchev, who in 1959 gladly seized the opportunity to publicize an American injustice.[31]

Candidates for the 1960s presidential race spoke at the National Press Club. Vice President Richard Nixon compensated by bringing his wife, Pat, to a club luncheon, while then Massachusetts Senator John F. Kennedy looked up at the women reporters in the balcony and said, "'My mother is in Chicago and wasn't able to be with us today so I invited May Craig to come along.' Craig took a bow from the balcony."[32] According to a history of Washington, DC journalism, on the day that women journalists were admitted to the Press Club, UPI reporter Roy McGhee approached previously mentioned women's page journalist Judith Martin (later known as Miss Manners) and said "Come with me, we're going to integrate the men's bar. The bartender served her a beer and expressed his hope that she would choke on it."[33] Esther Van Wagoner Tufty was one of the first females to be admitted to the club. In 1952, she was shown on a national television audience as she climbed up on a table to get an interview.[34] She described the long journey to become a member of the press club as "positively insulting." She said the worst reaction that she heard came from Bill Lawrence of the *New York Times* when someone asked him what he thought of having women admitted: "I don't mind sleeping with a newspaper woman, but I'll be damned if I want to have lunch with her in my club."[35] Several members of NOW were friendly with female journalists. The board sent a letter to the Press Club:

> The general public has assumed that the "gentleman of the press" are mature professionals and not some journalistic offshoot of the aficionados of the Play-

boy Club. Women journalists have contributed much to the profession as serious, dedicated, competent chroniclers of the present, and yet cannot become full members of the National Press Club.[36]

Further, if the club's membership did not begin to accept women as members, NOW planned to urge all public officials and political leaders to refuse to speak at or use the National Press Club facilities and would encourage members to resign from an organization "backward enough to perpetuate discrimination against a significant segment of their profession."[37]

The vote to allow women as official members of the National Press Club was 227 ayes and 56 nays. According to an account of the vote: "One man at that moment left the club with a vow never to return—and he didn't."[38] When at the last the walls were breached, some two dozen of the press, of assorted ages and sizes, were inducted into full card-carrying membership while the orchestra played, 'Thank Heaven for Little Girls.'"[39]

Glaser's Reign as Press Club President

Glaser initially joined the Women's Press Club in 1959. (The Women's Press Club was established in 1919. It was renamed the Washington Press Club in December 1970.) According to the writer of a recommendation letter for her application into the club: "Mrs. Glaser is a first-rate newspaper woman."[40] Glaser also included a letter from radio station WGMS where she had worked in 1948 and again in 1954 as a writer, producer, and commentator for women's programs. Her former employer noted in a letter: "Each time she left us it was completely voluntary on her part and amicable, if regretful, on ours."[41]

Glaser became the president of the Washington Press Club in 1971—the first year that men were allowed to become members. The *Washington Star* included a smiling photo of her taking the oath of office on a stack of newspapers.[42] President Nixon wrote Glaser a letter of congratulations: "It is a special pleasure to be able to salute a new President who is also First Lady—and I know that as one who has been in the kitchen, you will be able to stand the heat."[43] Nixon's special assistant Charles Clapp wrote to Glaser a sarcastic note:

> Why did you and your associates discriminate against men? I note that no men were elected to office. This may call for strong steps. Seriously, I was pleased to read of this recognition of at least some of your many talents. I wish you well.[44]

The two national press organizations merged in 1985. To bring the two groups together, a task force was created that included three women. The mezzanine floor of the National Press Club included paintings of the previous club presidents. During the merger, past presidents of the women's club were added to the wall. Glaser recalled going up to look at her image, along with legendary journalists and past presidents Helen Thomas and Fran Lewine. As she rode the elevator down, she overheard a conversation between two older male members. One said to the other: "If I had known this was going to happen, I never would have joined this damn club."[45]

In an oral history, Glaser remarked about the lack of open mindedness of male journalists. She recalled being invited to speak at the 1971 Minnesota Newspaper Association convention soon after the task force issued its report. She spoke about the lack of progress that the Nixon administration had made based on the report. She also spoke about the lack of support for the women's movement by many men. "The response by the average male ranges from amusement to intense hostility. Rarely does it include the open-mindedness with which men discuss other issues."[46] She further explained that the women she knew in the women's movement were reasonable and not radical. She said: "The women I have mentioned are not kooks. They are potent establishment groups. They are not strident. Their weapon is the law of the land."[47] The journalists did not like what they heard: "At the reception later, I was treated like a leper. The experience kind of showed how far along the news profession had not come at that point."[48] A member of Congress, Joseph Garth, was in the audience and later read it into the *Congressional Record*. Glaser said of the experience: "It just showed how deep this movement went. It took a while to communicate itself to members of the press who were supposed to be open minded."[49]

The lack of open-mindedness toward women in the journalism field was quite common. *Milwaukee Journal* women's page editor Aileen Ryan addressed the lack of opportunities for women in the Milwaukee Press Club's annual publication, *Once a Year*, in 1961. Ryan had spent decades at the newspaper when she wrote: "There is no line of promotion for women on newspapers. Women, regardless of their attainments, are not in line for executive positions."[50] She had been fighting for equality for decades. In the 1930s, she asked why the women on staff were paid five dollars less than men in comparable jobs. (The answer was "Miss Ryan, there is no justice in the world."[51]) Later, she went back again and asked for equality in journalists' paychecks regardless of gender and got the raises in question.[52] In the 1960s, Ryan wrote that the inequities that female reporters faced often came as a shock to young women journalists beginning at newspapers that they viewed as tools of correction for social injustice. She paraphrased the views naïve, new female employees might ask, "Aren't newspapermen the foes of prejudice, champions of tolerance, fighters on the side of justice, searchers after truth, exposers of inequalities, fair-minded exponents of human rights?" Ryan said her response would be: "We can only point out that newspaperwomen are not even permitted to become members of the Press Club."[53]

NOTES

1. John Skow, "Erma in Bomburbia," *Time*, July 2, 1984, 2.
2. Susan Edwards, *Erma Bombeck: A Life in Humor* (New York: Avon Books, 1997), 119.
3. Skow, "Erma in Bomburbia," 8.
4. Ibid
5. Ibid.
6. Skow, "Erma in Bomburbia," 10.
7. Ibid.
8. Ibid.
9. Bill Moyers, 1971 Penney-Missouri Magazine Awards Luncheon, November 3, 1971, New York, New York. Papers of J.C. Penney, Southern Methodist University, Dallas, Texas.
10. Gloria Biggs, "To Catch a Woman," *Editorially Speaking*, Gannet Group of Newspapers, Vol. 25, 1967, 21. Papers of Gloria Biggs, National Women and Media Collection, State Historical Society of Missouri.
11. Kimberly Wilmot Voss and Lance Speere, "Way Past Deadline," *Wisconsin Magazine of History*, Autumn 2008, 40.
12. Kathryn Clarenbach, "Where We Have Been—Where We Are Going," Theta Sigma Phi, Milwaukee, Wisconsin, 1967, 1. Papers of Kathryn Clarenbach.
13. Voss and Speere, "Way Past Deadline," 40.
14. Kennan Ferguson, "Intensifying Taste, Intensifying Identity: Collectively through Community Cookbooks," *Signs* 37, no. 3 (Spring 2012): 696.
15. Jeff Houck, "50 Years Later, 'Gasparilla Cookbook' A Tasty Classic," *Tampa Tribune*, September 13, 2011.
16. "The Gasparilla Cookbook's 50th Edition Media Kit." www.jltampa.org/documents/17931/85667/The_Gasparilla_Cookbook_Media_Kit.pdf
17. Women's National Press Club, *Who Says We Can't Cook!* (Washington, DC: McIver, 1955), 38.
18. Women's National Press Club, *Second Helping* (Washington, DC: 1962), 5.
19. Women's National Press Club, *Who Says*, 18.
20. Women's National Press Club, *Second Helping*, 60.
21. Women's National Press Club, *Second Helping*, 82.
22. Women's National Press Club, *Second Helping*, 109.
23. Women's National Press Club, *Second Helping*, 127.
24. Vera Glaser Oral History, Penn State, August 19, 1997, 27.
25. Nan Robertson, *The Girls in the Balcony: Women, Men, and the New York Times* (New York: Random House, 1992), 101.
26. Donald A. Ritchie, *Reporting from Washington: The History of the Washington Press Corps* (New York: Oxford University Press, 2005), 173.
27. Ritchie, *Reporting from Washington*, 173.
28. Ibid.
29. Ibid.
30. Ritchie, *Reporting from Washington*, 175.
31. Ibid.
32. Ibid.
33. Ibid.
34. Times Wire Service, "Esther Van Wagoner Tufty, Newswoman, Dies at 89," *Los Angeles Times*, May 6, 1986.
35. Hoyt & Leighton, *Drunk Before Noon*, 141.
36. Aileen C. Hernandez, National President, NOW, n.d, Martha Griffiths Papers, Bentley Library, University of Michigan.
37. Ibid.
38. Hoyt & Leighton, *Drunk Before Noon*, 143–144.
39. Ibid.
40. Robert J. Donovan letter to Membership Chairman, Women's National Press Club, September 1, 1959. Vera Glaser Papers.

41. Robert Rogers letter to membership chairman Women's National Press Club, July 31, 1959. Vera Glaser Papers.
42. Donnie Radcliffe, "New Order at Press Club," *Washington Evening Star,* September 17, 1971.
43. Richard Nixon letter to Vera Glaser, September 16, 1971. Papers of Vera Glaser.
44. Charles Clapp letter to Vera Glaser, June 30, 1971. Papers of Vera Glaser.
45. Vera Glaser, "A Few Good Women," Penn State, August 19, 1997, 26.
46. Vera Glaser, *Congressional Record,* March 17, 1971.
47. Ibid.
48. Glaser, "A Few Good Women," 33–34.
49. Ibid.
50. Aileen Ryan, "Women's World: 'Not so,'" *Once a Year,* 1961, 57. Box 10, folder 21. Milwaukee Press Club. UWM Manuscript Collection 146. University Manuscript Collection. Archives. University of Wisconsin–Milwaukee.
51. Robert Wells, *The Milwaukee Journal: An Informal Chronicle of Its First 100 Years* (Milwaukee: The Milwaukee Journal, 1981), 257.
52. Barbara Salsini, "Fashion Pioneer," *Milwaukee Journal,* April 7, 1983.
53. Ryan, "Women's World."

Chapter Five

Questions of Feminism, the 1969 Press Conference, and the President's Task Force on Women's Rights and Responsibilities

Near the end of the decade of the 1960s, many of the well-behaved women found themselves in a time when they agreed with the concepts of women's liberation leaders but not necessarily the methods used—such as protests and rallies. ERA supporter and Florida State Senator Lori Wilson remarked that some in the feminist movement were not in favor of public demonstrations, yet "during a long history of struggle, there may be controversial methods inspired by impatience."[1] Letters to Michigan lawmaker Martha Griffiths demonstrated the sometimes difficult place that women—who had long fought for other women—were put in when it came to the Women's Liberation Movement. Griffiths received numerous letters from constituents: "I regret so much that the 'Women's Lib' movement has been the great hindrance that it has. I hope we can overcome the effect of their extreme demands and manner of attempting to further the aims and objectives of our legitimate groups."[2] Another person wrote to Griffiths: "I sincerely hope that you will be successful in accomplishing rights for women across the board. We have women's lib stirring up a ruckus, which I think in the end will alienate men more than help us."[3] Another letter writer mentioned: "I will readily confess that I am not, nor do I support the 'Women's Lib.' They have done a great injustice by causing the whole effort to be ridiculed."[4]

The term "feminism" has a complicated history. A 1914 announcement for a women's meeting included the headline: "What is Feminism? Come and find out."[5] Historian Nancy Cott has noted that in its early American use, the word "feminism" had a shock value. In the early years, those who considered themselves feminists were looking for more than just the right to vote—they wanted equality in numerous areas. For example, a speaker at the time stated, "All feminists were suffragists, but not all suffragettes are feminists."[6] By 1920, women had the right to vote. The fight for more rights for women would ebb and flow in the ensuing decades. By 1960, the word "feminism" was being used again.

In 1972, the *New York Times* featured a story about some of the limitations of the women's liberation movement. Reporter Judy Klemesrud visited Hope, Indiana and spoke with women who did not identify with feminism. The headline clearly described the theme of the article: "In Small Town U.S.A., Women's Liberation Is Either a Joke or a Bore."[7] Klemesrud quoted numerous women about their lack of interest in the movement or the concern over radical feminists. (The one exception was a divorced, single mother who liked the potential of the term "Ms.") She concluded:

> It has been called a major weakness of the women's movement, this failure to reach the boondocks. It is not that the people haven't heard of women's lib. They hear about it and read about it. It's just that they don't care enough about it.[8]

Clarenbach recalled that feminist was a term not used in the initial public fight for women's rights in her community. She said: "We didn't use the word feminist to begin with. I don't even know to what extent people identified themselves in that language. In fact, the current expression was 'women's liberation/women's lib' so that was almost a pejorative, especially when it was used in the press."[9] While she had studied the issues regarding discrimination, there was not necessarily language to describe it. Clarenbach said: "I know that the first time I used the word 'sexist,' I even thought I invented it because I'd never read it anywhere, in 1969. 'Racism' I knew but I had never heard or read the words 'sexist' or 'sexism.' They might have been around but I had never encountered it."[10] Yet, the media did assign the terms to women in the movement. By 1971, a *Milwaukee Journal* story described Clarenbach as a feminist in a headline: "Feminist Sees Improving Climate."[11]

As mentioned in an earlier chapter, one of the national events that came to represent the women's liberation movement was the Women's Strike for Equality on March 26, 1970. Those within the movement considered the event a success, although media coverage was largely condescending.[12] According to historian Ruth Rosen, the media used the march to "sensationalize and discredit the women's movement."[13] For example, ABC began its coverage by quoting Spiro Agnew: "Three things have been difficult to tame. The ocean, fools, and women. We may soon be able to tame the ocean, but fools and women will take a little longer."[14] On CBS, anchor Eric Sevareid said, "The plain truth is, most American men are startled by the idea that American women generally are oppressed, and they read with relief the Gallup poll that two-thirds of women don't think they're oppressed either."[15]

In her memoir of the women's movement, Susan Brownmiller doesn't mention the negative press but rather how the media responded to issues for the first time. She wrote of the Women's Strike for Equality Day: "For the first time since the passage of the Nineteenth Amendment, newspapers and magazines seemed to expect women to stand up for their rights."[16] Historian Carol Mueller also theorized that the media's coverage of the strike was a unifying force in the development of the movement.[17] Journalist David Broder agreed that the impact of the strike was significant. He wrote, "The tactic worked. The agenda of causes was spelled out in full, and for the first time, debated."[18]

President Nixon's 1969 Press Conference

It was early in 1969 when Vera Glaser received a phone call from Catherine East. She asked if Glaser would be interested in some statistics about inequities women faced throughout American society. Glazer replied: "Indeed."[19] The interaction between Glaser and East was the beginning of a political and media partnership that helped promote rights for women at a pivotal time in the country. While they were recognized by the time of their deaths for their contributions to feminism, their work was largely done behind the scenes and their methods have only recently been uncovered in their papers and the papers of other government women. Together, East and Glaser worked inside and outside both the government and the media to raise awareness for women's position and issues.

The phone call from East was in relation to Glaser's question to President Nixon during a 1969 televised press conference. It was the President's second press conference and Glaser felt the journalists were asking easy questions. Glaser, representing the North American Newspaper Alliance, was lucky enough to be in the third row—reporters further back were unlikely to be called upon. One of the only women in the room, Glaser wanted to ask a tougher question than her colleagues. When it was Glaser's turn, this was her question: "Mr. President, since you've been inaugurated, you have made approximately two hundred presidential appointments, and only three of them have gone to women. Can we expect some more equitable recognition of women's abilities, or are we going to remain the lost sex?"[20]

The question led to audible chuckles from the many male reporters in the room, and the president also initially responded as if it was a joke before seeming to realize he was on television. This was at a time when nearly every question from a female reporter at a presidential press conference led to laughter. Nixon recovered his composure and then said he would look into the issue. The question also led to numerous phone calls and then follow-up stories across the country, crediting Glaser for raising the topic of women's limited roles in the leadership of the federal government.

Nixon's Administration and Complicated Gender Roles

Some recent scholarship, grounded in the oral history project "A Few Good Women," has given broad credit to Nixon for encouraging a change in women's roles. Later, the book *A Matter of Simple Justice* chronicled the positive story of Barbara Hackman Franklin. She was a special assistant to Nixon and was charged with recruiting women for positions of leadership in the federal government. Her appointment followed Glaser's question and the need to appeal for more female voters for Republican candidates. She said:

> The closer I got to the election of 1972, the more clout I had in terms of getting anything done, be it appointments or be it interjecting into the campaign, saying, "You don't have any women on the platform or chairing anything, and you need a woman keynoter". . . Some of my clout began to recede after the election.[21]

While Nixon clearly helped some women gain momentum in governmental roles, there was not universal support for women. One of the debated points during his administration was the nomination of a woman to the Supreme Court, as mentioned previously. Glaser and East put together a list of potential female candidates for the Supreme Court. Glaser sent a letter including the list to First Lady Pat Nixon and also sent a copy to East.[22] Naming a woman to the Supreme Court was one of the few political issues that the First Lady was outspoken about. She told Glaser: "I don't think one person can speak for another. The candidate should speak for himself."[23] The hopes of nominating a woman to the Supreme Court had been ongoing in the media. A July 1969 *Chicago Tribune* story noted a White House meeting that Rep. Catherine May and other lawmakers had with Nixon about the appointment of women. "We're trying to put sex into civil rights." This included the possibility of a woman being named to the high court. Rep. Charlotte Reid explained: "He told us he was not excluding the thought of sometime finding a competent woman for the Supreme Court bench." He further said that Attorney General John Mitchell was seeking names for women to nominate for the federal bench.[24]

The First Lady told East and Glaser that she would speak with her husband and appeared to support the judicial nomination of a female candidate. East responded with a handwritten note to Glaser, thanking her for taking the initiative. East wrote, "Thanks so much for letting me see this. Hope this leads to the first woman Supreme Court judge—and it very well may; and if it does, she'll probably never know how it happened."[25] The president told his wife: "Don't you worry. I'm talking it up. If we can't get a woman on the Supreme Court this time, there'll be next time."[26]

When given the opportunity to nominate two potential Supreme Court justices, Nixon named William Rehnquist and Lewis F. Powell, a Virginia lawyer described as moderate. Many people were unhappy about the lack of a woman being appointed. According to papers from the time, the First Lady felt betrayed and "really hit him on his failure to appoint a woman." The president said: "Boy is she mad."[27] According to daughter Julie Nixon Eisenhower: "During dinner, Mother strongly stated that one of the nominees should have been a woman and gave her reasons. My father, with exaggerated weariness, finally cutoff the conversation: 'We tried the best we could, Pat.'"[28] Further, according to Nixon Eisenhower:

> Mother was keenly disappointed that a woman was not chosen. She had spoken out because she felt so strongly that women in 1971 needed the recognition that a female member of the Supreme Court would bring them. She was also annoyed that her advice, offered publicly, had gone unheeded.[29]

While some women were entering governmental roles in the Nixon administration, there certainly was a sexist environment. From most reports, President Nixon was surrounded by men who embraced a rather sexist agenda. Chief of Staff H.R. Haldeman refused to hire women in the re-election campaign; later, Chief of Staff Alexander Haig, Jr., barred women from the White House gym because the "place isn't suited for ladies." He then relented, allowing women to use the gym if they used the "buddy system" to ensure their safety. Press secretary Ronald Ziegler said the first lady's thirty-two-year-old press secretary suffered from a "menopause problem." The author of a book about the thirty-seventh president noted: "Sexist comments were far more common than racist slurs in Nixon's administration."[30]

President's Task Force on Women's Rights and Responsibilities

In September of 1969, Glaser was the guest speaker at the *Miami Herald's* sixteenth annual Club of the Year Award conference. Her speech was called "Tomorrow's Woman" and focused on women's rights as another form of civil rights. She said: "Ironically, this movement comes at a time when women are making progress in the world outside the home but this also happens to be a time of widespread and pervasive discrimination against women in the United States."[31] She encouraged the clubwomen to understand what women's rights were and not shun the topic because of the radical images often presented in the media. She said the movement was "not an attempt by women to dominate our society, but more accurately a movement to achieve a fair share of the nation's economic rewards and political leadership. The reporter mentioned the question Glaser had asked President Nixon about the lack of women among his political appointments. Glaser questioned if Nixon's administration would truly make a change. She asked: "Is this administration willing to use its financial clout—as it does on racial discrimination—to get universities to remove their unwritten quotas on the number of women entering law and medical schools?"[32]

After the speech, while still in Miami, Glaser received a phone call from the White House. On the line was Charles Clapp, a top aide to Burns who had investigated the women's claims and found them correct. He invited Glaser to be a member of the Presidential Task Force on Women's Rights and Responsibilities. East ended up becoming the staff director of the task force. It was chaired by Virginia Allan, although she gave much of the credit for the success of the group to East's contributions.

Allan had a strong background in organizational work, including being president of the National Federation of Business and Professional Women's Clubs. She said that she was aware of discrimination against women and wanted to do something about it. In an oral history, Clapp noted the need to find the right person to head the group. He advocated for Allan while other Nixon administrators pushed for different women. He said he told the others: "The worst thing you could do is pick one of these right wing people to head it. We've got to get a reasonable person."[33]

Allan was ultimately approved to head the committee. In an oral history, she explained that East was the key to the work the committee did. Allan had known East before her appointment to the task force. She said of her friend: "Catherine guided me all the way. I hardly would make a move without consulting her because she was so knowledgeable and so very willing to help. She was the centerpiece of what we did."[34] In February 1970 Glaser delivered the speech "Tomorrow's Woman" to a meeting of the Citizens' Advisory Council on the status of women—Allan and East were in the audience. Glaser said a year had passed since her question to the president and that relatively small progress on appointments had been made, describing it as "a little tokenism to make the ladies happy."[35] About two years after Nixon's response to Glaser's press conference question, Glaser published a story where she gave the administration a ".333 batting average with feminists." Two-thirds of the task force recommendations had not been implemented, but there had been signs of progress.[36]

The official date on the print Presidential Task Force on Women's Rights and Responsibilities report was April of 1970. Yet, the report was not released by the White House at the time. After several weeks of questioning, the report was leaked to the *Miami Herald*. The source has not been clearly identified. Several books give Glaser credit for the leak as she was working for the Knight newspaper chain at the time, which owned the *Miami Herald*.[37] One book author wrote that the White House assumed that Glaser was the source.[38] In East's oral history, East said that the source was not Glaser. Glaser never verified that she leaked the information. The report was given to Anderson who printed a story about the report's findings in an April 22, 1970 article. It included suggestions such as an amendment to the tax laws to permit deductions for child care costs. The report was then serialized throughout the following week.[39]

Anderson fought for advance front-page mention of the report but was rejected by management.[40] The Knight newspapers' publication did not stop the demands for the official release from the White House. In a *Miami Herald* article, Geri Joseph, vice chairman of the Democratic National Committee, was quoted as saying, "I think women are really invisible to Mr. Nixon."[41] After Anderson published the Task Force's results, her editor called her a "pinko."[42]

Political and Media Partnership

Prior to the committee formation, East and Glaser worked together to educate politicians about gender inequity. Before they met, Glaser along with a group of journalists, under the leadership of veteran journalist Sarah McClendon, collected information from top Nixon officials on numerous topics. During his interview, top advisor Arthur Burns denied the lack of progress for women in the administration and in public policy. When she read that, Glaser thought, "We really shouldn't let Arthur Burns away with saying that because the policies have not been fair."[43] This realization led Glaser to write a letter to Burns outlining his inaccuracies about women's roles. A few days later, Burns called Glaser directly and said: "You've leveled some very serious charges against us. I just don't think they are accurate."[44] He invited her to meet with him, and she agreed but asked to bring East along. The two women met to strategize. East had recalled that Burns had been the chief economic advisor to President Eisenhower and that he wanted summaries on one piece of paper.

When not enough had happened by April of 1969, Glaser wrote a story about the lack of progress. She wrote that when she asked Burns what had been done for women, he responded: "I have had other things to do."[45] Glaser cited a letter about discrimination against women sent to Nixon from Rep. Florence Dwyer on February 26. The letter, which asked for action by the President, was printed in newspapers across the country.[46] Glaser wrote of Dwyer's letter: "The letter has been gathering dust on Dr. Burns's desk for two months."[47] She concluded with the low number of women who had been given significant posts in Nixon's administration and noted that the president was expected to soon name a task force to address women's issues.

Among Glaser and East's examples were the low quotas in law and medical schools that excluded women students. Burns, a former chancellor of

Columbia University, described their allegations as "nonsense." They responded by asking him to check the records. After they left, Glaser told East that the meeting was a failure. East disagreed noting that Burns was an economist and as soon as he saw the numbers, he would understand.[48]

Despite their lack of success in securing a female Supreme Court appointment, East and Glaser did fight for more women in political appointments. In one case, Glaser wrote to East about how they could build their campaign for more qualified women in high-level positions and "alert them to the resentment caused by wives-in-cabinet-meetings ploy."[49] The wives were invited to attend the meetings although they were not allowed to speak. Mrs. Romney said that Nixon told the wives that they were there as "listeners." It was described in news' stories as the "first husband-and-wife cabinet session that anyone could recall." The wives learned about pollution, pre-school education, and government budgets.[50]

One of the strategies used by East and Glaser was to spread information about gender inequity that was not included in most media coverage. For example, East, who lived in the Washington, DC, area, subscribed to the *Miami Herald* solely because she considered Anderson's section to be the most substantive women's news being published anywhere in the country. Anderson assigned her reporters stories about abortion, equal pay and domestic violence among traditional stories on homemaking and brides. East created an informal news service to make sure Anderson's work had broad impact. She clipped and duplicated the best of the *Herald's* articles—many written by Glaser, and mailed the packets to a network of other feminists around the country who were using the media in their own ways to spread news about women.

Interestingly, in 1970, Anderson addressed gender discrimination in her *Miami Herald* weekly column, "Monday Musings," in the case of jockey Barbara Jo Rubin. The young woman had been banned from her position in South Florida due to her gender—the male jockeys had threatened to strike. She later went on to win her first race in Charles Town, West Virginia. Anderson wrote: "If Jockey Barbara Jo had been a Latin, Jew, or black, it is doubtful that she would have been deprived of her right to work. But she was just a woman."[51] It turned out that the jockey was Jewish and a reader chastised Anderson for not double-checking this fact and accused her of spreading hate.[52] Anderson responded:

> I am highly in favor of eliminating all bigotry and discrimination—against Latins, Jews, blacks, Catholics, Poles, and anybody else, including women. My point was that most of the others mentioned have been fighting this discrimination for years and through organization have managed to eliminate much of it, not all. Women, however, until just recently have not been organized to fight this discrimination, hence Barbara Jo had no one to help her fight her battle.[53]

The work of Anderson and Glaser was not typical of most coverage about women's issues that were found in other parts of the newspaper—if the topics were covered at all. Due to the invisibility of women's news in the mainstream media, issues central to the women's liberation movement were often ignored or mocked—what sociologist Gaye Tuchman deemed symbolic annihilation.[54] The one place that news about women was treated fairly was the women's pages of newspapers. According to Tuchman's work, there was "a conscious realization by women editors of the section that if these women were not covered on the women's page, they would not be covered at all."[55]

Female Revolt Series

The most visible of Glaser's journalism about feminism was the five-part "Female Revolt" series that ran in more than fifty newspapers across the country. It addressed "the inequities that women must face in a male-dominated society."[56] The series was suggested by a male editor after the response to Glaser's question at President Nixon's televised press conference. In the promotional material, several strategies were used. One approach questioned "Who's Being Protected?" The tease about protective legislation noted: "Actually, the laws work to protect the men from female job seekers."[57] The series also took on women who were tired of being second-class citizens—titled "Militants." The pitch was "One of these days a woman is going to fling her frying pan right smack into The Male Establishment—and the henhouse rebellion will be on."[58] Different newspapers presented the series with a variety of methods.

The *Miami Herald* featured the series in its women's pages in March 1969—although without the "Female Revolt" title until the fourth story. Glaser's first story addressed women's new roles in society. The lead was: "A mink coat, and those shiny electronic appliances are no longer enough, it appears, for the American woman. She wants something bigger, shinier, and far more explosive called 'an even break.'"[59] Glaser also noted:

> The female eying a "male" career area can expect ridicule and roughing up, as Barbara Jo Rubin learned when a man jockey threatened to "ride her into the rail." Or she may be turned down flat for no apparent reason, as were qualified lady scientists who applied for astronaut training.[60]

The third article in the series was titled "For the Female Sex, There Is No Justice."[61] Rep. Martha Griffiths' fight for equality for women was cited at the beginning of the story. The lack of work by the EEOC was also included. A sidebar to the story explained that an equal pay bill had passed the state house. Next to the lead story was an article about the significant work of flight attendants.

The fourth article featured a drawing of a woman in bell-bottom pants carrying a sign reading: "Ballots or Bullets," with the subhead of: "The Women's Revolution Could Go Either Way." Glaser mentioned NOW and Cathryn (sic) Clarenbach, as well as "more radical groups."[62] The article ran next to a story about three different paths of training to become a nurse. The expectation was that women in the traditional career path of nursing could have a diverse career path in the future.

The final article in the series listed what needed to be done to eliminate inequities. The five requests were equal protection under the law, day care centers, legalized abortion, and "a poverty program that does not discriminate against women."[63] In Florida, for example, the series was included in the women's sections of newspapers of various circulation sizes including the *Miami Herald, Orlando Sun-Sentinel*, and the *Pensacola Journal*.[64] East wrote in 1970: "Some top Federal officials now expect women's rights to be a major issue of the seventies. It is fair to say Mrs. Glaser's series was a giant step in that direction."[65]

After its run, Glaser's series led to a variety of responses from readers, according to her personal papers. One reader wrote she was hoping to get more information about women's organizations: "I'm very much interested in conditions affecting women as I have encountered some very cruel and senseless situations."[66] Glaser responded with information about the National Organization for Women and contact information for East.[67] Glaser also received a letter from a Chicago woman who described herself as the "voice of the women's liberation movement." It began "Dear Sister." The author wrote to clarify a point in the series stating the women in the movement "are mostly white and young, we are not students." She provided contact information about her women's organization.[68] Glaser responded with a letter beginning "Dear Sister" and wished the group luck.[69] Not all letters were supportive. One reader wrote, "Just a short time ago results of a survey showed most women abhorred working under a woman, so I don't think women should blame men because they are not top leaders." The letter ended with the damning statement, "Without Christianity, every day is Halloween."[70]

Glaser's ultimate goal of the series was to have the Nixon administration read the stories and take action. She wrote to East, "I'm trying to bring it to the attention of President Nixon. That is in the lap of the Gods."[71] East nominated Glaser and her series, "The Female Revolt," for the prestigious Catherine O'Brien Award for reporting on women's issues. The series was also read into the *Congressional Record* for the historical record—this was a common method for the well-behaved women rather than a protest.

Letters, press releases, and newspaper clippings regularly went back and forth between Glaser and East as their partnership progressed. At times, East provided documentation or anecdotes that Glaser could use in her stories. In other examples, Glaser would provide material that East could either use to prod governmental officials to action or that she could pass on to feminist leaders. In one case, Glaser passed along to East a flier regarding a March for Life event. "I thought you'd be interested in seeing the material this group is distributing to the press."[72]

By February of 1967, NOW addressed the sexist employee policies of the airlines at a time when women were known as stewardesses. The strategizing to address gender inequity can be found in Clarenbach's papers. East sent Clarenbach a press clipping from the *Washington Post* on the topic.[73] One memo explains that only Clarenbach and Friedan could publically be the leaders for the fight—against all US airlines. (For example, being married was rationale for firing for women and the mandatory retirement age was either thirty-two or thirty-five.) East felt the topic was too public for her to be involved in, based on her government job. Instead, Clarenbach, who had more career protection, was requested to appear on a Chicago television station for an interview about the topic.[74]

In 1965, a Northwest Airlines stewardess who was terminated when she married filed a complaint at the EEOC. The organization found "reasonable cause" that the airline had discriminated against women by having a marriage ban for women that did not apply to men. Stewardesses were among the very first employed women to file charges of sex discrimination with the commission, specifically targeting airline age ceilings and marriage bans. In 1968, the Commission ruled that sex could not be a bona fide occupational qualification of being a flight attendant. With this official ruling from the government agency, the stewardess filed a lawsuit. It led to a change in policies that benefited women workers and eventually opened the field to men. In lawsuit after lawsuit, women were making inroads into industry and making strides for gender equality in employment.

NOTES

1. Frances Spatz Leighton, "Has Women's Lib Gone Too Far—Or Not Far Enough?" *Family Weekly*, June 9, 1976, 4.
2. Arizona State Senate, Letter to Honorable Martha W. Griffiths, Papers of Martha Griffiths, Bentley Library, University of Michigan Library.
3. Clara E. Weisenborn letter to Martha Griffiths, August 4, 1971, Papers of Martha Griffiths.
4. Betty Ann Dittemore letter to Martha Griffiths, June 30, 1971, Papers of Martha Griffiths.
5. Nancy Cott, *The Grounding of Modern Feminism* (New Haven, Connecticut: Yale University Press, 1987), 12.
6. Cott, *The Grounding of Modern Feminism*, 15.
7. Judy Klemesrud, "In Small Town U.S.A., Women's Liberation Is Either a Joke or a Bore," *New York Times*, March 22, 1972.
8. Ibid.
9. Clarenbach, Oral history, 132.
10. Ibid.

11. "Feminist Sees Improving Climate," *Milwaukee Journal*, May 23, 1971.
12. Douglas, *Where the Girls Are*, 177.
13. Rosen, *The World Split Open*, 296.
14. Rosen, *The World Split Open*, 296.
15. Rosen, *The World Split Open*, 297; also quoted in Douglas, 163–164.
16. Brownmiller, *In Our Time* 147.
17. Mueller, *Conflict Networks*, 255.
18. David Broder, *Behind the Front Page* (New York: Simon & Schuster, 1987), 127.
19. Glaser, "A Few Good Women," 6.
20. Ibid.
21. Stout, *A Matter of Simple Justice*, 82.
22. Vera Glaser letter to Catherine East, May 9, 1969. Papers of Catherine East.
23. Julie Nixon Eisenhower, *Pat Nixon: The Untold Story* (New York: Simon and Schuster: 1986), 243.
24. Louise Hutchinsin, "Nixon Pledges to Seek Jobs for Women," *Chicago Tribune*, July 9, 1969.
25. Catherine East letter to Vera Glaser, May 13, 1969. Papers of Catherine East.
26. Eisenhower, *Pat Nixon*, 321.
27. Dean J. Kotlowski, *Nixon's Civil Rights: Politics, Principle, and Policy* (Cambridge, Massachusetts: Harvard, 2001), 238
28. Eisenhower, *Pat Nixon*, 321.
29. Ibid.
30. Kotlowski, *Nixon's Civil Rights*, 226.
31. Jo Anne Werne, "Women Demand Fair Share," *Miami Herald*, September 19, 1969, E-1.
32. Ibid.
33. Virginia Allan, "A Few Good Women," 2.
34. Ibid.
35. Stout, *A Matter of Simple Justice*, 41.
36. Stout, *A Matter of Simple Justice*, 54.
37. Kotlowski, *Nixon's Civil Rights*, 231.
38. Stout, *A Matter of Simple Justice*, 44.
39. "Nixon's Task Force Urges U.S. Department of Women," *Miami Herald*, April 22, 1970.
40. Marie Anderson letter to Vera Glaser, May 12, 1970. Papers of Vera Glaser.
41. Molly Sinclair, "Demands Get Louder for Release Of Task Force Report on Women," *Miami Herald*, May 8, 1970.
42. Streitmatter, "Transforming the Women's Pages," 72–81.
43. Glaser, "A Few Good Women."
44. Ibid.
45. Vera Glaser, "Females Are Still 'Forgotten' in D.C." *Miami Herald*, April 30, 1969.
46. Florence Dwyer, "Appeals to President Nixon for Equality," *Sarasota Herald-Tribune*, March 15, 1969.
47. Glaser, "A Few Good Women."
48. Glaser, "A Few Good Women."
49. Vera Glaser letter to Catherine East, May 28, 1969. Papers of Catherine East.
50. Myra MacPherson, "Wives, Silent Partners at Combined Cabinet Session," *Toledo (Ohio) Blade*, April 20, 1969.
51. Marie Anderson, "Too Bad Jo's Just a Girl," *Miami Herald*, July 1970.
52. Mrs. L.V. Olson letter to Marie Anderson, July 15, 1970. Papers of Marie Anderson.
53. Marie Anderson letter to Mrs. L.V. Olson, July 27, 1970. Papers of Marie Anderson.
54. George Gerbner and Larry Gross, "Living with Television: The Violence Profile," *Journal of Communication*, 1976, 172–199.
55. Gaye Tuchman, *Making News*. New York: Free Press, 1978.
56. "Women's News Service Report," North American Newspaper Alliance," March 1969. Papers of Vera Glaser.

57. Ibid.
58. Ibid.
59. Vera Glaser, "Women Demand New Role," *Miami Herald*, March 18, 1969
60. Ibid.
61. Vera Glaser, "For the Female Sex, There Is No Justice," *Miami Herald*, March 20, 1969.
62. Vera Glaser, "Ballots or Bullets," *Miami Herald*, March 21, 1969.
63. Vera Glaser, Women's News Service, "The Female Revolt: Women Don't Want a New Society But They Do Want a Fair Change," March 8, 1969. Papers of Vera Glaser.
64. Partial list of daily newspapers which carried the series "The Female Revolt." Papers of Vera Glaser.
65. Catherine East letter for Vera Glaser's nomination for the Catherine O'Brien Award, January 26, 1970. Papers of Vera Glaser.
66. Marilyn Hamlin letter to Vera Glaser, May 7, 1969. Papers of Vera Glaser.
67. Vera Glaser letter to Marilyn Hamlin, May 12, 1969. Papers of Vera Glaser.
68. Joreen (no last name) letter to Vera Glaser, March 25, 1969. Papers of Vera Glaser.
69. Vera Glaser letter to Joreen, May 1, 1969. Papers of Vera Glaser.
70. Dorothy Foufas letter to Vera Glaser, March 18, 1969. Papers of Vera Glaser.
71. Vera Glaser letter to Catherine East, March 26, 1969. Papers of Catherine East.
72. Vera Glaser letter to Catherine East, January 17, 1976. Papers of Catherine East.
73. "Court Blocks Ruling on Age Limit, Marriage Ban for Airline Stewardesses," *Washington Post*, November 22, 1966.
74. Muriel Fox Aronson letter to Kay Clarenbach, February 13, 1967. Papers of Kathryn Clarenbach.

Chapter Six

Kathryn Clarenbach, Continuing Education Programs, and Helping Traditional Women

Kay Clarenbach's experiences in Wisconsin appear to have been different than those of women's activists in most other parts of the country—especially when dealing with the media. It may have been because of the clout she held. Clarenbach held a doctoral degree and a job at the University of Wisconsin that gave her some secretarial support and an office. She had a respected position on the state's Commission on the Status of Women—which she held during both Democratic and Republican gubernatorial administrations. She was powerful enough to become the head of NOW in the initial years. When she was named to the position, coverage was positive. Newspapers in Appleton, Madison, and Milwaukee were supportive of Clarenbach and her advocacy.

The newspapers—both on the news side and the women's pages—in Southeastern Wisconsin were particularly friendly to Clarenbach and the issues she raised. Jean Otto was a women's page journalist at the *Milwaukee Journal* who often covered women's issues. (The *Milwaukee Journal* and the *Milwaukee Sentinel* were competing newspapers until 1995 when the papers merged.) In a 1970 story, Jean Otto interviewed women about equal rights and explained the mission of NOW and the members' fight for equality. Otto quoted Clarenbach: "This represents enormous effort on the part of a great many people who have worked their heads off."[1] Otto was the kind of woman who understood Clarenbach's appeal to help working mothers. Otto divorced at age thirty-four and went to work in the women's pages of her local newspaper to support her children. She started at the *Milwaukee Journal* in 1968. Four years later, she became the first woman to serve as an editorial writer with the *Journal*—and one of the few women in that position in the country. She was later named editor of the newspaper's expanding Op-Ed page. In 1979, she became the first female president of the Society for Professional Journalists. It was an organization that had only allowed women to be members a decade before.

In another example of a supportive journalist, Harva Hachten was the women's editor of the *Wisconsin State Journal* (in Madison, Wisconsin) from 1961 to 1968. She had an impressive background with an undergraduate degree from Stanford in 1942 and a master's degree in journalism from Columbia University. She worked for numerous newspapers before joining the journalism faculty from 1950 to 1956 at UCLA—where she met her future husband who would become a journalism professor. She had two children while in her thirties and missed the stimulation of the workplace. She was hired by the *Wisconsin State Journal* and wrote for the women's section. This was at a time when Madison children came home from school for lunch each day. "That was very difficult," she recalled. Later, she helped edit her husband's academic articles and books. "Partly because of the women's movement I now insist that I get some title page credit rather than an acknowledgement," she said. Hachten interviewed Friedan one year after *The Feminine Mystique* came out.[2] Hachten said of the experience: "It was great for me. It totally quashed any lingering doubts I had."[3]

Marian McBride covered Clarenbach's work as a women's page reporter for the *Milwaukee Sentinel* from 1963 to 1970. In her reporting she often wrote about the activities and research about the Wisconsin Commission on the Status of Women. In 1968, she wrote a series called "Wisconsin Women, Know Your Rights," which was largely based on the commission's work, as well as input from two local lawyers. It was later republished in a booklet and won the National Bar Association Award of Merit.[4] The booklet begins: "Sex discrimination still exists in many alleys of American life. But often only ignorance of the law leads women to deprivation or loss. Knowing her rights is just as important as having them."[5] It was done in a question-and-answer format, which addressed state law regarding women. For example, women could serve on juries in Wisconsin. This right differed state by state. As late as 1961, the Supreme Court, in a unanimous decision, upheld a Florida law automatically exempting women from jury service in the ruling in *Hoyt vs. Florida*. It also noted that a husband must provide for his family, and if he does not, a wife could charge items of support to his accounts. Women with questions were directed to legal aid or the district attorney's office. The booklet also noted that a wife did not need her husband's consent to work outside of the home, yet if she works in the family business, her husband did not need to pay her.[6]

Milwaukee Sentinel reporter Dorothy Witte Austin was also a common confidant for Clarenbach. Austin had graduated from Marquette University with a degree in journalism in 1940. During World War II, she volunteered with the Red Cross. She eventually wrote for the women's pages and gave positive coverage to women's issues. According to Mary Eastwood: "Her newspaper articles on women's issues were very important in educating women and the public in general, and incidentally contributed to NOW recruitment."[7] In 1983, Austin was named Milwaukee's NOW Woman of the Year. Her biography is included in the book, *Feminists Who Changed America, 1963–1975*.

At times, Clarenbach even trusted Austin to take her place. When there was a NOW meeting in Washington, DC, that Clarenbach did not want to attend, she suggested Austin go to the meeting instead. The reporter "could keep her eyes and ears open and report back to me."[8] She went and Clarenbach got several phone calls, including one from Friedan: "Who is this Dorothy Austin? This meeting is closed to journalists. We're not allowing any journalist to be here, even women journalists." Clarenbach explained: "I wasn't suspicious of Dorothy Austin because she has been an ally, and a very important ally to us here in the state, but apparently others there had had negative experiences with journalists making fun of it in their stories."[9] In May 1971, Austin wrote about a Wisconsin NOW meeting where Clarenbach was the speaker. "We haven't begun to use our political clout in this or any other state and this is one of the tasks to which NOW must address itself."[10] Southeastern Wisconsin journalists were open to the work done by the state commission and were quick to call Clarenbach as a source. Her victories—such as the NOW officer position—were typically treated like victories for the state.

Educating "Displaced Homemakers"

One of the key findings of the commissions—both federal and states—was the need to get more women into the workforce. It was a time when many questioned the value of a woman earning a college degree. For some people—especially in upper-middle class families—college was not necessarily training for a career. A 1962 *New York Times* article noted: "College girl often sees no future but marriage."[11] A 1963 headline in the *National Observer* read: "College for Girls? An Old Argument Takes a New Turn." The caption under a photo of a female student read "The girl in the laboratory—are her hours with the books wasted?"[12] Numerous media stories questioned the need for women to be educated beyond high school—an ongoing debate.

Yet, upper-middle-class women were increasingly going to college in the 1950s. A special 1956 double issue of the popular magazine *Life* provides some perspective. It was titled "The American Woman: Her Achievements and Troubles." It featured a white woman smiling at a young child under the caption "Working Mother." It is a sign that the potential social change for women predated the more visible marches and protests of the late 1960s. The magazine featured an article about women's college Bryn Mawr's campus and curriculum under the headline: "Tough Training Ground for Women's Minds." The reporter noted: "Today, a third of all American college students are women, and college has become almost as much a part of a woman's life as of a man's."[13] It was noted that students took courses in the classics, like Greek and Latin, rather than vocational or domestic science classes, such as home economics. The writer also explored the complicated role that women navigated between intellectual and familial roles. While the college president had said that "only our failures marry," eighty percent of the alumnae had married.[14]

Newspaper advice columns—which often ran in the women's pages—were a common place to debate women's changing roles in society and the point of higher education. As one communication scholar wrote: "Newspaper advice columns, particularly since their modern incarnation in the mid-1950s, have served as one of the few consistent, mainstream, and widely available public forums for the discussion of topics severely limited elsewhere."[15] There were national columnists such as Ann Landers (pen name for Eppie Lederer) and Dear Abby (Pauline Phillips writing under the pen name of Abigail Van Buren). Most newspapers also had community columnists. For example, Eleanor Hart (a pen name for Eleanor Rattelle) was the local advice columnist at the *Miami Herald* in the 1950s and 1960s. On January 19, 1962, letter writer "A Mother" noted that she had an eighteen-year-old daughter who was ready to graduate from high school and she also had a son a year behind in school. She wrote: "I would love to send my daughter to college, but in view of the fact that it's so much more important for a boy to be educated than a girl, I can't see sacrificing as we would have to do to send them both."[16] The letter continued: "My husband agrees. He says a college education is wasted on women and you don't need a diploma to be a mother." Hart, who had earned a college degree in journalism, responded: "Is college wasted on women? Certainly not—not on all women at any rate!" Then, she wrote: "If your daughter qualifies, wants to go to college and you can afford to send her, I believe you are doing her an injustice by not doing so simply because of her sex."[17] If and how a woman would use her college education was openly debated and made the later continuing education programs needed.

At one point in the 1960s, the House Judiciary Committee held a hearing about how the Equal Rights Amendment would impact higher education opportunities for women; some schools had limits on how many female students could be accepted into certain majors. Glaser covered the governmental hearings and later recalled the testimony of numerous women. One young woman had earned a law degree from Harvard University and graduated high in her class. Yet, she was unable to get a job while her male classmates were employed. One of the Congressmen on the panel, Kentucky Republican Judge Marlow Cooke, asked the question: "Are you telling me that my four daughters, that the money, the thousands that I'm putting out on their education, isn't going to buy them the same break in the job market as it buys for a man?" The young law graduate replied: "Yes, I'm telling you that." Glaser recalled: "That caused a hullabaloo. But his question was marvelous because it drew some chuckles, and at the same time was very, very pointed and valid."[18]

That 1950s and 1960s question of what a college-educated woman should do still resonates decades later. This is particularly true when it comes to combining intellect and motherhood. In the midst of her husband's presidential campaign in 1992, future senator, secretary of state and 2016 presidential candidate Hillary Clinton delivered the commencement address to Wellesley College's graduating class. (She graduated from Wellesley College in 1969 and then headed off to Yale Law School.) It was a time when the students had objected to her as the graduation speaker because her main role was that of a spouse—despite her significant legal career. In her speech, she addressed several political issues and then the thorny gender-based issues that women faced. She said:

> As women today, you do face tough choices. You know the rules are basically as follows: if you don't get married, you're abnormal. If you get married, but don't have children, you're a selfish yuppie. If you get married and have children, but then go outside the home to work, you're a bad mother. If you get married and have children, but stay home, you've wasted your education. And if you don't get married, but have children and work outside the home as a fictional newscaster, you get in trouble with the vice president.[19]

The final reference was to then-Vice President Dan Quayle, who had attacked the character Candice Bergen played, Murphy Brown, on the television show of the same name. On the program, the television news anchor decided as a single woman to have a child. It was just another sign that women's choices about motherhood all carry consequences in the eyes of society. So much so, that in the summer of 2013, the *Huffington Post* ran segments from Clinton's 1992 commencement speech. It was because, the writer noted: "It has been two decades, but the issues remain fresh."[20]

Colleges and the Commissions on the Status of Women

The question of whether females should go to college took on a new direction when the several state CSW addressed education for middle-aged women. For example, Clarenbach worked to help "displaced homemakers"—a cause taking place across the country in the 1960s. A 1962 article in the *New York Times* noted that women were likely to eventually enter the paid workforce. The reporter cited a study that predicted that seven million women would enter the workforce and a majority would be in their forties. One expert said: "So many returners are not ready to return."[21] For example, at Washington University in St. Louis in 1963, a program was started to help women go back to school. Its goal was help women bypass the red tape of admission and recommend a flexible schedule. One administrator said: "Often a woman has to take courses whenever she can get a babysitter. And she may be able to take only one or two classes as a time." At the time, about twelve thousand packets about the program were about to be sent out.[22] Other schools adjusted requirements for women returning to college. In 1964, the University of Oregon changed its physical education requirement so that older female students could take golf rather than more strenuous exercise.[23]

Friedan's book, *The Feminine Mystique*, questioned what a college-educated woman who became a homemaker would do with her degree. Friedan had returned to her alma mater Smith College to speak to a group of female college students. Many of the students were not open to Friedan's message. One young woman planned to marry and raise children while doing some volunteer work. She said to Friedan: "We can make a contribution to society without competing with men outside the home." Another said: "Some of us don't want careers. That doesn't mean our education is wasted."[24] A 1962 article noted that one-third of graduates from Barnard College were married within six months of graduation. Experts said that despite research showing that most women will be working by age thirty-five, most college students only thought of marriage and children in their futures. Even if they did consider paid employment, it was short term. One advisor said: "Most girls are thinking in terms of jobs rather than careers."[25]

There were many women who had married quite young and still needed to finish a GED or complete a college degree or obtain certification for a new profession, such as a Realtor license. In other cases, women had college degrees but little workforce experience to gain employment. Continuing education programs at universities and community colleges were used to help women complete degrees or update their skills. Some programs were aimed at employment, while others encouraged volunteering or civic work for women.

Continuing Education for Women

Beginning in the 1960s, various colleges and universities began programs addressing women. They were a mix of training aimed at education, volunteering and paid employment. Miami held a recruiting program for the Council for the Continuing Education for Women beginning in 1970 with Marie Anderson serving as vice-chairman of the program. The two-day event was called "My Fair Lady." It was advertised as appealing to all women of South Florida with an expected attendance of fifty thousand people.[26] The sessions focused on overall self-improvement, preparing for the paid workforce and taking part in volunteer work. The overall message was that women could be and should be more in their communities.

Some of the Continuing Education programs had a complicated relationship with Women's Liberation. An article from the August–September 1970 newsletter of the Miami CCEW showed the relationship. The article began with a question from a Miami-Dade Junior College student: "Is CCEW part of the women's liberation movement?" The initial answer was "Well, no, not really," as the speaker went on to explain that CCEW was about training women for paid employment or volunteer service as well as empowering women. The student responded with: "But, isn't that what women's liberation is all about?" The newsletter editor noted that the CCEW pondered the question of women's liberation. In the article, she noted: "Of course it is, if women's liberation means personal growth, equal opportunity in employment, equal work for work done—and an acceptance of the fact that more and more women are looking for fulfillment outside the traditional role of wife and mother."[27]

Yet the editor was also quick to explain that there were other elements of women's liberation that CCEW was not associated with, such as radical groups like WITCH, SCUM or the Redstockings. She went on to explain: "The bra burners, White House picketers, objectors to men's bars and social clubs have made the headlines but they have gained little sympathy with either men or a majority of women."[28]

One of the key programs was at the extension program of the University of Wisconsin in Madison and headed by Clarenbach. The university's first continuing education conference took place in February 1962. The following year, Esther Paterson, director of the Women's Bureau, spoke at the "Professional Opportunities for Women" conference. About three hundred people attended the event. At the conference, Peterson presented the idea of establishing state commissions on the status of women. States, including Wisconsin, soon established their own commission. Clarenbach was the long-serving chair of the commission—she later said it was her most significant work of her career.

Fighting for Women's Rights

As mentioned previously, the need for NOW drew from many areas. One of the most important was the lack of action by the Equal Employment Opportunity Commission, which was created in 1965. Soon after NOW was created, the otherwise well-behaved women took a stand. According to a biography of Rauwalt: "On November 22, Marguerite, Friedan, and Clarenbach marched into the EEOC office and told the commissioners they wanted the two vacancies on the commission filled by women. Furthermore, they wanted a decision on the employment of female-only airline stewardesses and new guidelines for classified ads, guidelines on retirement, pensions, and maternity rights."[29] As others had found in the 1960s, labor laws could be key to equality for women. According to one study: "The women's movement in the mid-to-late 1960s was both the recipient and creator of political opportunities in the context of employment law."[30]

For many years, newspapers included columns for employment advertising—separated by gender—"Help Wanted-Male" and "Help Wanted-Female." The jobs followed gender stereotypes—clerical employment for women and management positions for men, for example. According to Clarenbach: "For years, the EEOC refused to say that that was discrimination to segregate jobs for men and jobs for women. It took a long time. That was our first but not only meeting with the EEOC, but the first thing we did as Board members."[31] According to a legal history study: "Given the centrality of race—and the ambiguities of sex—in debates over equal employment policy, the EEOC initially understood race and sex discrimination as substantively different issues warranting different administrative and legal responses."[32]

Gender discrimination was being litigated in various industries across the country. "Enlightenment alone did not unlock newsroom doors," historian Kay Mills wrote. "Legal action helped."[33] There were numerous gender-discrimination lawsuits in the 1970s, including cases against the *New York Times*, *Newsday*, and the Associated Press. The lawsuits helped to make male managers more aware of discriminatory promotional practices. As a result, even publications that were not sued began to make changes.[34] For example, Colleen "Koky" Dishon, who started her career in the women's pages, became the first woman to have her name on the *Chicago Tribune* masthead.[35] According to a colleague, the promotion was in part to prevent a lawsuit by women at the newspaper.[36] The story behind the first media lawsuit, filed against *Newsweek* in 1970, is the subject of journalist Lynn Povich's book (and later television show) *The Good Girls Revolt*. Povich, who was a plaintiff in the lawsuit, explained the need for awareness, and other difficulties women faced in their fight for equality. One of their lawyers noted, "It encouraged other women to come forward, it had an effect on journalism, and it had a wide-ranging effect on women."[37] The most famous of the lawsuits was the women's class-action lawsuit *Boylan v. New York Times*; it was chronicled in Nan Robertson's book *The Girls in the Balcony*.[38] (It should be noted that in 1962, more than two hundred delegates to the American Newspaper Guild convention passed a resolution for newspapers to end employment discrimination against "women and minority groups." According to a story about the meeting: "The delegates pledged to press for legislation in Congress prohibiting discrimination in employment throughout the country."[39]) A young Ruth Bader Ginsburg was then working on equality for women through the courts through the ACLU's Women's Rights Project. She won several cases in front of the Supreme Court before she became a member.[40]

NOW & Newspaper Help Wanted Ads

While NOW was not successful in keeping Richard Graham as a member of the EEOC, the members continued to fight against the policy of allowing separate newspaper employment columns for women and for men. On August 30, 1967, NOW organized a protest of the *New York Times* because of the practice. The eight women and three men held picket signs reading: "Women Can Think as Well as Type" and "I Didn't Get a Job Through the *New York Times*." They also handed out leaflets about the practice that they saw as discriminatory.[41] According to a study of the help-wanted ad debate, women were divided into two camps: the progressive women's alliance, which included organized labor and the Women's Bureau. On the other side was the "radical ERA movement" organized within the National Women's Movement.[42] The scholar found: "If 'white' jobs and 'black' jobs were quickly passed into history, 'male' jobs and 'female' jobs remained within accepted sensibilities among the public at large and women's advocates themselves."[43]

In 1965, the EEOC ruled that Title VII of the 1964 Civil Rights Act allowed employers to place employment ads in sex-segregated columns. A few years later, the EEOC reversed its initial ruling and called for the end to the gender-segregated columns. "The debate over help-wanted ads was not only a crucial moment in the initial battle to legally define sex discrimination; it also helped escalate the women's movement and played a central role in the creation of the National Organization for Women," according to an academic study.[44]

Clarenbach and other NOW officers sent a letter to the president requesting that a woman be named to the EEOC. "Surely there are many qualified women—in lower-echelon jobs at the EEOC and elsewhere—who would serve their country with distinction as EEOC officials."[45] The letter went on to address the ongoing problem with sex-segregated help wanted ads in newspapers:

> If cases of job discrimination against Negroes were reviewed only by white persons at the EEOC, there would be a justifiable furor among Negro workers throughout the nation. Surely the current 'men only' review of sex discrimination cases at high levels of the EEOC is equally distressing to women workers and women's organizations.[46]

On October 25, 1967, NOW officers sent a letter to the EEOC and requested a revision of the policy about sex-segregated classified columns: "As long as the EEOC continues to sanction 'Help Wanted-Male' and 'Help Wanted-Female' columns in the newspapers, this reinforces a public impression that the EEOC does not regard its Title VII mandate to combat sex discrimination as seriously as it regards its mandate on other forms of discrimination. In other words, employers and unions are doubly encouraged to discriminate against women—encouraged by the sex-segregated classified columns themselves and encouraged by the protracted inaction of the EEOC." Friedan concluded with: "Warm regards to you (Clifford L. Alexander, Jr.) and Mrs. Alexander."[47] The letter was found in Clarenbach's papers.

Two days later, Clarenbach and other officers sent a letter to the president: "We are pleased to commend you on your new executive order extending to women the protection according to previous executive orders to other victims of discrimination. The twenty-five million working women of this country will be encouraged and inspired by your action."[48] The organization requested that a woman be named to the EEOC.(Aileen Hernandez had been a member of EEOC from 1965 to 1966; she went on to become a board member of NOW.)

Part of the confusion was that neither Congress nor Title VII language defined a "bona fide occupational qualification" or what is known as BFOQ, which would allow for gender distinction. For example, a narrow interpretation of the BFOQ would apply to gender-specific qualifications, such a wet nurse for a women or a sperm donor for a man. A broader interpretation would allow for restrictions based on cultural norms—even if a man or woman could each perform the job. In this case, secretarial jobs would go to women and truck drivers would continue to be men.

During this time, the White House held a meeting to address what was meant by BFOQ. The EEOC was asked, for example, if it would be legal for a hamburger restaurant to only hire "pretty girls . . . to increase sales."[49] The response was that this was an issue that the commission would have to decide. Later, a commissioner told the *Wall Street Journal* that the EEOC would take action on "the most flagrant discrimination based on sex . . . we're not going out on our charter to overturn patterns."[50]

Regional meetings by the EEOC were held around the country to address the segregated help-wanted ads. A meeting was held in Madison, Wisconsin, in September 1968. The meeting was covered by the *Milwaukee Journal* and the story featured the headline: "Panel Backs Separate Job Listing."[51] The short article implied public support for the policy. Yet, one woman went to the meeting and wrote that she was the only citizen at the meeting. Otherwise, the audience included the press, two commissioners (Fagan and Gabriel), and two of their employees—an attorney and a secretary. She reported back to Clarenbach. The woman wrote that one of the commissioners "argued that it would be a big burden for persons to wade through all of those ads. At this point the secretary could not contain herself and stated she would be happy to page through more ads for more opportunities."[52] Further, one commissioner said that men preferred a "pretty young female airline stewardess to fluff his pillow." The woman concluded: "All in all the hearing was pretty much a one-act comedy. I sincerely hope that future events prove me wrong but I saw no reason for optimism."[53]

The woman also told Clarenbach that the commissioners said no one had ever raised an objection regarding the practice of placing ads by gender. Specifically, Fagan said: "To date, we have not received one formal complaint from a Wisconsin resident."[54] Clarenbach responded to the letter: "I've requested both Madison and Milwaukee NOW to get individual letters off and am today sending a memo urging each member of the commission to write. I am not sure what Mr. Fagan meant by 'no formal complaint,' but he obviously needs some reaction."[55] Clarenbach followed through and sent letters to NOW members: "Despite the department's word to us at our November 20th meeting that they 'lean in this direction,'" Mr. Fagan said he had received no complaints from Wisconsin. "Individual letters in addition to the commission resolution seem called for."[56]

East wrote a note to Clarenbach attached to the December 6, 1968 article "Unsexing the Classifieds" from *Life* magazine. The magazine writer described the NOW members as "militant ladies are agitating to forbid US newspapers from running separate male and female want ads." And "Though more than one third of the total US labor force is female, women are still barred from many jobs because of outmoded 'protective' legislation passed in the sweatshop era."[57] East wrote: "We need letters to the editor from as many as possible."[58] Rawalt wrote a memo to Clarenbach on January 10, 1969: "Have had two reports this morning on hearing in DC Court yesterday on the newspapers request for a stay of the lower court's opinion, pending appeal. Phineas Indritz was there, also Catherine East."[59] The memo also noted that Rawalt mailed to each member of every State Commission on Status of Women about the *Life* editorial.[60]

Several NOW members addressed the *Life* editorial with comments read into the *Congressional Record*. Clarenbach and Friedan issued a joint statement: "What a shame that one of our mostly widely read magazines publishes an editorial as uniformed, misleading, and irrational as 'Unsexing the Classifieds.' Your writer wrote the editorial either without exploring the issues or with the intent of misleading the public."[61] Elizabeth Boyer, president of Women's Equity Action League wrote: "The superficial and frivolous tone of this editorial is also irritating to thinking women, and unless you make some factual presentation modifying or reversing your stand, I believe that your publication will feel the results of the resentment you have aroused, probably for a long time to come."[62] Elizabeth J. Kuck, who was an EEOC commissioner from 1968 to 1970, wrote: "Although you may 'see no need' to create a single column for most help-wanted advertisements, the Commission has concluded, after considerable public discussion and staff review, that the use of separate 'Help Wanted-male' and 'Help Wanted-female' column headings has a clear discriminatory effect. Advertisements placed under such headings permit employers virtually to pre-select their applicants by indicating an explicit sex preference, regardless of an applicant's individual ability."[63] A journalist from *Life* responded in a letter to Clarenbach: "Our argument, as presented in this editorial, was that combined help-wanted ads would be inconvenient and annoying to both employer and prospective employee."[64]

On September 29, 1968, a letter from a NOW member ran in the newspaper and addressed the issue of segregated newspaper ads. She wrote:

> Recently a significant decision was made by the EEOC: Newspapers that list "Help Wanted, Female," and "Help Wanted, Male," classified advertisements separately are doing so in violation of the Civil Rights Act. It was ascertained that segregating these ads by sex helps perpetuate the practice of offering women lower wages for essentially the same work as that being done under the guise of men's jobs. As of December 1968, any newspaper listing jobs in such categories will be violating the law intentionally, now that the EEOC has clearly stated its interpretation.[65]

Some newspapers did voluntary remove the gender designation in want ads such as the several newspapers in Wisconsin. Clarenbach received a letter from the labor department in Wisconsin on February 21, 1969:

> In the smaller weekly papers we find many of them have agreed to eliminate the heading entirely and list all ads alphabetically. The commissioners feel that this is a true mark of progress, especially when one realizes that everything we have accomplished so far has been on a purely volunteer basis and without any real authority for enforcement on our part.[66]

In addition to the media debate, there also legal action regarding the gender-segregated want ads in newspapers. The American Newspaper Publishers Association and the *Washington Star* sued the EEOC in Washington, DC, District Court. The newspaper's stand was that the EEOC lacked the authority to issue the ban again sex-segregation help wanted columns and to enforce the ban. The finding by the court cited a 1969 petition from NOW asking for the end of the segregated columns. The court ruled that the agency had the right to issue guidelines. The newspaper lost.[67]

The White House weighed in on gender equality issues on May 7, 1969. At an event, First Lady Pat Nixon spoke to a group of city and state representatives from the Commission on the Status of Women. She said: "I feel women have equal rights if they want to exercise them."[68] In the front of the White House, about one hundred women picketed, carrying signs: "Nixon Unfair to Women" and chanting: "Freedom for Women Now."[69] In response, NOW's Equal Rights Amendment Committee issued an open letter to newspapers, lawmakers and women's groups. It was addressed to President Nixon. The letter explained that "the women in this country are growing tired of second class citizenship!" Further, "the task of achieving Constitutional equality between the sexes is not completed."[70]

By 1973, the Supreme Court was addressing the question of the legality of sex-segregated want ads. The issue was over the validity of a Pittsburgh city ordinance that prohibited the practice in newspapers. The *Pittsburgh Press* filed the lawsuit seeking to have the law overturned. In a 5-to-4 decision, the court ruled for the women and against the newspaper. The decision ended the practice of sex-segregated want ads. According to the majority ruling: "By implication, at least, an advertiser whose want ad appears in the 'jobs-male interest' column is likely to discriminate against women in its hiring decisions."[71]

Another legal labor battle for NOW and other women leaders was about the requirements for flight attendants.[72] It was strictly a women's job at the time and they were required to be thin, attractive, and unmarried. One historian wrote: "They presented themselves as both photogenic representations of femininity and victims of blatant sex discrimination by their employers."[73] Complaints were filed with the EEOC and US Rep. Griffiths questioned airlines at a congressional meeting: "You point out that you are asking for a bona fide occupational exception that a stewardess be young, attractive, and single. What are you running, an airline or a whorehouse?"[74]

Fighting for a Place at the Table

Women fighting for equal rights with men was a battle fought from several perspectives—from the courtroom to the lunchroom. When Clarenbach came to the University of Wisconsin in Madison to study political science in 1937, she was not allowed to sit in the Rathskeller—a popular eatery in the Student Union. Her exclusion was based on her gender. In response, after buying her morning coffee at the Memorial Union, she would walk as slowly as she could through the Rathskeller to the Paul Bunyan Room—an area where women were permitted to study. According to an article about Clarenbach: "This quiet act of protest was a preview of Clarenbach's lifelong work, much of which played out in the background of history."[75] Excluding women from places where men gathered has a long history.

Racial discrimination at lunch counters was once a common problem, especially in the American South. Peaceful protests in the 1950s and 1960s shined a light on the practice and eventually the government stepped in. The

Civil Rights Act of 1964 banned whites-only lunch counters and discrimination in restaurants and other "places of public accommodation." Several great online projects and archives have documented the fight to racially desegregate the lunch counters. Women, on the other hand, continued to be discriminated against at eateries. Note the 1971 policy for the Gulf + Western Industries (the future Viacom Company) Luncheon Club:

> The intention of the Gulf + Western Luncheon Club is to keep it as much as possible a men's eating club. Therefore, only when having lunch with outside parties, whose group may include a female executive, will women be considered acceptable as luncheon guests. Under no circumstances are members to invite their secretaries to lunch, and only senior executives may invite their wives, when and if such a situation is absolutely necessary. There will be no exceptions to the above.[76]

Excluding women from restaurants or excluding them from sections of restaurants was a regular practice for the many places where men held lunch meetings. The thought was that men only had a limited time to eat lunch and women would gossip and eat slowly. It was assumed that no women would have a working lunch. Yet, in several cities, women began to question the discriminatory practice and took a stand. In 1968, Miami feminist and early NOW member Roxcy Bolton met with the managers of local restaurants to explain why male-only eateries were problematic. In 1969, Burdines Department Store included the restaurant, the Men's Grille. Bolton wrote letters, met with the store's management, and complained about the exclusion of women, especially when they were the main shoppers. Following the meeting, a vice president wrote a letter to Bolton indicating they were instituting a change. "We have made the decision to change the name, and the 'men only' concept, as expeditiously as possible," he explained. "We have ordered the signs to be changed, and they are to state 'Executive Grille' with no references to restrictions as to male or female usage."[77]

The practice of excluding women was being suggested in another Florida restaurant, the Tower Club at the top of the Landmark Bank building, when *Fort Lauderdale News* women's page editor Edee Greene heard about it. A longtime advocate for women, she decided to take a stand and recruited Virginia Shuman Young, the first female mayor of the city, to assist with her campaign. "When we heard it was going to be a restaurant for men," Greene said, "we told the owner that if he tried it he'd have two grandmothers picketing on the sidewalk." The male-only policy was changed.

By 1969, Friedan led a fight for women to eat lunch at the same New York restaurant. The fight to eat lunch at the Oak Room of the Plaza Hotel, which had a policy against women in the room from noon until 3:00 p.m., occurred on Abraham Lincoln's birthday. Numerous journalists covered the event, but change was not immediate. According to the *New York Times* coverage: "Three women invaded the Oak Room of the Plaza Hotel yesterday during the hours reserved for men only and succeeded in temporarily ruffling the serenity of the male haven. The women said the policy was illegal discrimination based on sex."[78]

The restaurant community has often excluded women—particularly if there was a bar involved. In February 1969, NOW proclaimed "Public Accommodations Week," and held national actions at "men-only" restaurants, bars, and public transportation—like male-only flights. The Berghoff in Chicago, for example, had long had a men's only bar. That practice ended when several members of NOW went to the bar at Berghoff and demanded service. Milwaukee members of NOW successfully fought to integrate the men's only section of Heinemann's Restaurant.

By August of 1970, New York City establishment McSorley's Old Ale House was forced to admit women—for the first time in the bar's 116-year history. It happened after Mayor Lindsay signed a bill prohibiting discrimination in public places because of gender. A *New York Times* article with a female byline noted that the women initially "drank peaceably" after being admitted. Then Lucy Komisar, a vice president of NOW, arrived. The bartender refused to accept her driver's license as proof that she was over age eighteen and demanded her birth certificate instead. The two engaged in a short wrestling match before the manager allowed her in to a chorus of "boos" from regular patrons. Later, an angry man poured his stein of ale over her head.

NOTES

1. Jean Otto, "Equal Rights: 'Wow!' and 'What's That?'" *Milwaukee Journal*, August 11, 1970.
2. Harva Hachten, Oral history, University of Wisconsin, April, 12, 2013, 7. http://minds.wisconsin.edu/handle/1793/65335
3. Ibid.
4. Wisconsin Women's Network Website, 1960s. http://www.wiwomensnetwork.org/
5. Marian McBride, *Wisconsin Women: Know Your Rights* (Milwaukee, Wisconsin: *Milwaukee Sentinel*, 1968).
6. Ibid.
7. Barbara J. Love and Nancy F. Cott, "Austin, Dorothy Witte," *Feminists Who Changed America*, 22.
8. Clarenbach, Oral history, 130–131.
9. Ibid.
10. Dorothy Austin, "New NOW Network," *Milwaukee Sentinel*, May 24, 1971.
11. Marylin Bender, "College Girl Often Sees No Future but Marriage," *New York Times*, March 26, 1962.
12. "College for Girls," *National Observer*, November 11, 1963.
13. "Tough Training Ground for Women's Minds," *Life*, December 24, 1956, 102–107.
14. Ibid.
15. David Gudelunas, *Confidential to America* (New Brunswick: Transaction Publishers, 2008), 2.

16. Eleanor Hart, "Let Daughter Go to College; She's Worth It," *Miami Herald*, January 19, 1962.
17. Ibid.
18. Glaser oral history, August 19, 1997, Penn State, 22.
19. "Hillary Clinton's 1992 Wellesley Commencement Speech Tackles Issues Relevant Decades Later," *Huffington Post*, August 3, 2013.
20. Ibid.
21. Marylin Bender, "Rusty Skills Bar Women From a Job," *New York Times*, January 5, 1962.
22. Lucinda Benzel, "Back-to-College Program for Women," *St. Louis Globe-Democrat*, September 2, 1963.
23. Frederick C. Klein, "Colleges Tempt Older Career-Minded Women to Return to Class," *Wall Street Journal*, May 7, 1964.
24. "College for Girls? An Old Argument Takes New Turns," *National Observer*, November 11, 1963.
25. Marylin Bender, "College Girl Often Sees No Future but Marriage," *New York Times*, March 26, 1962.
26. "Just the Facts: My Lady Fair," Council for the Continuing Education of Women, 1971. Papers of Marie Anderson, National Women and Media Collection, Historical Society of Missouri.
27. "CCEEW Looks at Women's Lib," Your Cue from CCEW, The Greater Miami Council for the Continuing Education of Women, August–September 1970. Papers of Marie Anderson, National Women and Media Collection, Historical Society of Missouri.
28. Ibid.
29. Paterson, *Be Somebody*, 171.
30. Nicholas Pedriana, "Help Wanted NOW: Legal Resources, the Women's Movement, and the Battles Over Sex-Segregated Job Advertisements," *Social Problems*, 2004, 184.
31. Clarenbach, Oral history, 133.
32. Pedriana, "Help Wanted NOW,"189.
33. Mills, *A Place in the News*, 149.
34. Terri Schultz-Brooks, "Getting There: Women in the Newsroom," *Columbia Journalism Review* (March/April 1984): 25–31. Jeff Pundyk, "AP's $2 Million Denial," *Washington Journalism Review* (September 1983): 13–14.
35. Kimberly Wilmot Voss, "Colleen 'Koky' Dishon: Journalism Legend," *Timeline*, July/September 2010, 2–17.
36. Lois Wille, "Women in Journalism," Washington Press Club Foundation Oral History Project, Session 3, 91.
37. Povich, *The Good Girls Revolt*, 9.
38. Nan Robertson, *Girls in the Balcony: Women, Men, and the New York Times* (New York, NY: Random House, 1992)
39. "News Guild Urges Equal Jo Status," *New York Times*, July 13, 1962.
40. Irin Carmon and Shana Knizhnik, *Notorious RBG: The Life and Times of Ruth Bader Ginsburg* (New York: Harper Collins, 2015), 58–59 and 74–75.
41. "11 Picket Times Classified Office To Protest Male-Female Labels," *New York Times*, August 31, 1967.
42. Nicholas Pedriana, "Help Wanted NOW: Legal Resources, the Women's Movement, and the Battles Over Sex-Segregated Job Advertisements," *Social Problems*, 2004, 188.
43. Pedriana, "Help Wanted NOW," 189.
44. Pedriana, "Help Wanted NOW," 182.
45. Ibid.
46. Ibid.
47. Betty Friedan letter to Clifford L. Alexander, Jr., October 25, 1967. Papers of Kathryn Clarenbach, Box 9, folder 3.
48. NOW letter to President of the United States, October 27, 1967, Papers of Kathryn Clarenbach, Box 9, folder 3.
49. Pedriana, "Help Wanted NOW,"189.

50. Monroe Karmin, "New US Commission Plans Big Push to Open More Posts to Negroes," *Wall Street Journal*, October 13, 1965.
51. "Panel Backs Separate Job Listings," *Milwaukee Journal*, September 22, 1968.
52. Jan Petrus letter to Kathryn F. Clarenbach, November 20, 1968. Papers of Kathryn Clarenbach, Box 3, folder 18.
53. Ibid.
54. Ibid.
55. Kathryn F. Clarenbach letter to Jan Petrus, September 27, 1968. Papers of Kathryn Clarenbach, Box 3, folder 18..
56. Kathryn F. Clarenbach to Commission Members, November 26, 1968. Papers of Kathryn Clarenbach, Box 3, folder 18.
57. "Unsexing the Classifieds," *Life*, December 6, 1968.
58. Catherine East note to Kathryn Clarenbach, December 13, 1968. Papers of Kathryn Clarenbach, Box 3, folder 18.
59. Marguerite Rawalt memo to NOW, "Subject: The ANPA suit in advertising guidelines," January 10, 1969. Papers of Kathryn Clarenbach, Box 3, folder 18.
60. Ibid.
61. Kathryn F. Clarenbach and Betty Friedan, "The Editor, Life Magazine," *Congressional Record*, December 10, 1968.
62. Elizabeth Boyer, "The Editor, Life Magazine," *Congressional Record*, December 10, 1968.
63. Elizabeth J. Kuck, "The Editor, Life Magazine," *Congressional Record*, December 10, 1968.
64. Linden Farrar letter to Dr. Clarenbach and Mrs. Friedan, January 21, 1969. Papers of Kathryn Clarenbach, Box 3, folder 19.
65. Gene Boyer letter to the editor: "Dear Sir," September 29, 1968. Papers of Kathryn Clarenbach, Box 3, folder 19.
66. Douglas Ajer letter to Katherine Clarenbach (sic), February 21, 1969. Papers of Kathryn Clarenbach, Box 3, folder 19.
67. American Newspaper Publishing Association vs Alexander, United States District Court, 1968.
68. Associated Press, "Women Equal, Pat Says," *Pittsburgh Post-Gazette*, May 8, 1969.
69. Ibid.
70. Jean Witter letter to President Nixon, 1969. Papers of Kathryn Clarenbach, Box 9, folder 3.
71. "Law on Sex-Labeled Job Ads is Upheld," *New York Times*, June 22, 1973.
72. Kathleen M. Barry, *Femininity in Flight: A History of Flight Attendants* (Durham, North Carolina: Duke University, 2007), 152–169.
73. Barry, *Femininity in Flight*, 130.
74. Matthew Andrew Wasniewski, *Women in Congress, 1917–2006* (Washington, D.C.: Government Printing Office, 2006), 360.
75. Jenny Price, "This Woman's Work," *On Wisconsin*, Fall 2016, 47.
76. David N. Judelson memo to executives, July 13, 1971. Papers of Betty Friedan, carton 27, folder 720. Schlesinger Library.
77. S. M. McColloch letter to Roxcy Bolton, October 13, 1969. Papers of Roxcy Bolton, Florida Memory.com.
78. "Women Crusaders Test Plaza's 'Men Only' Rule," *New York Times*, February 13, 1969.

Chapter Seven

Xilonen, the 1975 United Nations Women's Year Conference in Mexico City, and the 1977 International Women's Year Meeting in Houston

The assumption that women's page content was only soft news was a false and gendered one—it was much more complex, especially as Anderson, Jurney and Paxson's careers have shown. In addition to the more traditional content, there were stories about women's changing roles in society sprinkled throughout the women's sections.[1] It is where the foundation of the women's liberation movement can be found. Women's page material has often been overlooked as "fluff" because it was in a soft news section. In doing so, the concept of "quilted news," a mix of soft and hard news, was introduced in the women's pages.[2] As journalism historian Kay Mills wrote: "Soft news? Hard news? Where did these terms come from? The sexual implications fairly leap from the page."[3] This quilted approach reveals how race and gender roles were changing in this era. At many metropolitan newspapers in the post-World War II years, there was a change in content. Forward-thinking women's page editors were making improvements both shocking and subtle as they transformed their sections in ways that transformed their readership.

It is easy to simplify women's pages rather than examine the complexity of the material. In looking at the women's sections, there was fluff, and undoubtedly some of the material reinforced women's role in the private sphere. Yet, there were also stories of career women and community development by clubwomen. Just as Joanne Meyerowitz re-examined the original source material used to support Friedan's thesis in *The Feminine Mystique* and came to a different conclusion, women's pages should be looked at with fresh eyes. It has been shown that there were progressive women's sections throughout the 1960s, as various newspapers won Penney-Missouri Awards—the top recognition for women's pages.[4]

One of the primary sources for the women's page content came from the women's clubs. Most women's club meetings included both gossipy lunches and speakers who raised awareness about issues such as child abuse or environmental dangers. This awareness often led to fundraisers that allowed women to be politically and socially active in a behind-the-scenes way. It was easy to marginalize the work of women's clubs and the accompanying women's page coverage because it was considered simply gossip. Too often, clubwomen and the women's page reporters who worked with them were not credited for their significant work. Yet, the work was important in laying the foundation of communities from social services to buildings. Minnesota journalist Mary Ann Grossman said about the women of her city:

> In the 1960s and 1970s, the next generation of women didn't want anything to do with the women's section. I always told them that we climbed on the shoulders of our sisters who came before us; don't ever sneer at those women. And those women, through their charity balls and fundraisers, built hospitals and funded art projects. They helped make St. Paul the town it is today.[5]

International Women's Year, Mexico City, 1975

There have been several studies about the media's coverage of the 1975 International Women's Year in Mexico City. The consensus is that the media largely focused on conflict rather than the important issues that were raised at the meetings. Most visible was the photo and Associated Press story that went out on June 27, 1975. The photo featured a group of Latin American women fighting over a microphone. The caption noted that "Women fight at the UN Conference." (The captured moment was from the nongovernmental organization Tribune at the IWY.) AP reporter Peggy Simpson was asked for a follow-up to explain the conflict. She said: "There was no story but the damage was done." A researcher noted: "That proved to be the most widely used photo of the two weeks in Mexico City. The photo confirmed the stereotype—although not the reality—that women can't be in the same room together without getting into a catfight."[6] The media's use of the "the catfight" framework or women-against-women presentation that has marginalized the concept of feminism is also a part of how journalists covered the battle.

From its early days, the CSW had repeatedly requested an international women's conference be held.[7] By 1973 the CSW had identified the media portrayals as an area of concern and called for research about its impact on public opinion about gender roles.[8] The IWY Bulletin began in July 1974 to publicize UN and NGO activities related to women's status.[9] Despite the long interest, the meeting in Mexico City was not well put together. According to one study, "The NGO organizing committee operated by the seat of its pants, rushing to put together the Tribune in time."[10]

There were two concurrent meetings in Mexico City regarding women in 1975. The first, a United Nations Conference, included 1,300 delegates from 103 nations. They were instructed to contribute the official voice of their governments about the issues. The other meeting was unofficial but held at the same time as the official UN meeting, in a hall known as the Tribune. The second meeting was initially intended for members of the NGO. These were groups that had contracts to work with the UN, such as the Red Cross, the Business and Professional Women's Club, and Planned Parenthood. Paxson said that there was so much interest that the Tribune meeting was open to all who wanted to attend, resulting in more than 5,800 people attending the gathering.

There have been numerous reflections and research about the formal United Nations World Conference for International Women's Year in 1975, and the accompanying nongovernmental organizations. One academic study of the Mexico City examined the media coverage:

> Efforts to shape media coverage of IWY set in relief two critical and connected aspects of transnational feminist' roles in human rights struggles over the freedom of information. First, feminists recognized that the mass communications media powerfully informed the common sense. Second, arguments over the media turned on the question of what rightfully belonged in the "public sphere."[11]

It had become tradition that the NGOs would publish a daily newspaper during the conference. Prior to the conference, the NGO office in New York City set out to find an American woman who could edit this newspaper. One of those volunteers was from Philadelphia. She had gone to Temple University and taken a journalism class. She called the professor and asked if he had any ideas of who might be a good person to edit this newspaper. He suggested Paxson for the position. The NGO volunteer called Paxson to discuss the idea of her producing a newspaper during the event. The next day she went to her bosses at the *Philadelphia Bulletin* and asked for a leave of absence to work on the project. The metro editor and his deputy responded with excitement: "Oh, you've got to do it, Marj, you've got to do it."[12] In June 1975, she went to Mexico City to edit the newspaper without much preparation. The newspaper was written in half-Spanish and half-English. Paxson did not speak Spanish so a translator was hired. There were six reporters and a photographer who produced the newspaper. After some debate, they decided to call the newspaper *Xilonen*, named after the Aztec goddess of the tender corn.

According to Paxson, the facilities where the newspaper was produced were problematic. The pressroom of the Tribune was held in a conference center at a medical school, about three miles away from the Mexican State Department where the official conference was held. The newspaper did not even have a separate phone line; they had to share the phone lines and typewriters with all of the other reporters covering the event.

According to Paxson, the Mexican government had agreed to deliver the paper to the official conference and the major hotels in Mexico City. Yet, that did not regularly happen. For example, one day the truck that was supposed to deliver all the papers instead took off with a television crew. The impact was that the Tribune newspapers, which had been printed at 4:00 a.m., were still sitting on the dock five hours later. To solve the problem, one of the reporters hired a cab and piled some of the papers into the trunk of the cab to deliver them. Paxson said: "We fought stuff like that all the time. It was not easy." Paxson said of the experience:

> It's probably the hardest work that I ever did in my life because we'd start about ten o'clock in the morning and finish up the following morning at two. I followed the paper the whole way through from making the assignments in the morning to editing the copy to writing cutlines, writing the headlines, then stop for dinner, and then go down to the newspaper, the English-language newspaper in Mexico City, which was printing it for us, and reading type upside-down and backwards again and checking for corrections, and finally it would go to press.[13]

In her retirement from a newspaper publisher's position, Paxson said about the Mexico City newspaper: "I think that's probably the most important thing I've ever done."[14] It was, however, a challenge. She said that hopes that the *Xilonen* could remain "above the fray quickly proved to be naïve."[15] On the second day of the meeting, a group of reporters had issued a "feminist manifesto" calling for women to meet without men present in order to frame a challenge to cultural practices."[16] Feminist writer Germaine Greer responded in the second issue of the newspaper, "branding the manifesto as a phony, incoherent, and absurd preemption of any genuine exchange of ideas."[17]

Media coverage of the Mexico City event focused more on conflict than the issues the women had hoped to address. Journalist Peggy Simpson said while her bosses at the Associated Press had promised to treat the conference as a serious story, the coverage largely trivialize the meeting. She continued:

> My own opening day conference story, which was discarded, included background on the scope of women's problems throughout the world and reported Mexican President Luis Echeverria's unusually strong keynote address for equality for women everywhere. In its place, under my byline, was a flowery feature story picked up from a Mexico City paper about the sex appeal of the

Soviet woman cosmonaut who led her country's delegation to the conference."[18]

By 1973, Jurney had left Detroit to become assistant managing editor/features of the *Philadelphia Inquirer*. In a series of *Inquirer* articles in 1975, she wrote about International Women's Year, seeking to explain the issues and victories of the women's movement. She also attempted to correct the biased coverage of the women's liberation movement in other media stories.[19] She highlighted the demonstration at the earlier 1968 Miss America contest by writing, "Although no bras were burned, as alleged, members of the women's liberation groups were thereafter called 'bra burners' and the term 'women's lib' was applied by the news media to the entire women's movement."[20] She called on journalists to provide a more nuanced reporting of women's issues.

When Paxson returned to the United States, she found that her own newspaper had not included any information about her work at the conference. In response, Paxson wrote a five-part series about what had actually happened in Mexico City to contrast to the conflict-based coverage in other media. She sold the series to several newspapers although her own Philadelphia newspaper was not interested. In the first article, she described the "mob" scene in Mexico City. "In a country where talking is the favorite occupation, a new dimension was added—the voices of thousands of women from all over the world, most speaking in their native tongues."[21] Paxson quoted the wife of the Israeli prime minister, Leah Rabin. She "urged that if we can just sit down, give out our hands, and come to common understandings, this will be a small but important step."[22] Paxson also included information from Tribune chairman Mildred Persinger that explained the Tribune and the more than 190 unscheduled meetings of various interest groups: "Our main value is that we can talk frankly here and discuss things in depth. At the UN Conference, they have to sterilize everything they say."[23]

The second article in the series described the control that the Mexican official kept in its UN meeting place for the Conference—its Secretariat of Foreign Relations building. Paxson wrote: "The Mexicans maintained as tight a control as they could on the proceedings, especially those at the Tribune. During the meetings there, attended by probably 4,500 women at one time, only one double door was opened to the place."[24] In the third article, Paxson explained that the translation at the UN Conference was done in English, Spanish, French, Russian, and Chinese. The load was so great that additional translators had to be flown in from UN Headquarters. The Tribune did not have much translation support. Paxson wrote:

> Most of them wanted a share of the spotlight and a chance at a microphone. But there weren't enough spots or meetings rooms, or time—to get them all in.

> Frustration and emotion took over. The Tribune was not all chaos; it only seems that way.[25]

Paxson did address the conflict the rest of the media focused on: "Most of the vocal fireworks appeared to be spontaneous and largely emotional."[26] Yet, she also provided some context that was included in other media accounts: "One demonstration of about sixty hecklers may have been arranged. As the outburst proceeded and the noise volume rose and fell, a sharp-eyed observer noted that the changes seemed to follow hand signals from a woman in the rear of the auditorium."[27] Paxson balanced out the conflict with a quote that explained the difficulty of putting on such a big conference. The secretary-general of the Conference and an under-secretary at the United Nations delivered a "polite coup de grace" at the Tribune event said:

> I know how much you want to be involved in something which would be involved in something which would promote the interests of women. While there was great sympathy with the committee to hear people not concerned with the conference, it was felt this was a precedent which had not been set before. It is very difficult to set a precedent when we are even having difficulty hearing all those registered at the conference.[28]

In the last story of the series, Paxson wrote about the potential impact of the conference. She noted that women who attended the UN Conference received a plan of action to take back to their countries and a better understanding of women's issues: "And they took something else: The growing realization that full political representation is the best answer to achieving equality for women."[29] She also editorialized and offered her view of the conference with a mix of realism and optimism:

> Anyone who thought the women delegates would make a difference was ignoring the harsh political realities of the world. And one had only to see the male delegates taking the microphone in tricky political moments to realize this. The Conference was not without positive results. The World Plan was adopted with few changes, despite the 894 amendments which were proposed.[30]

To Form a More Perfect Union

After the Mexico City meeting, there was a call for a conference in the United States. Each state would send delegates to the national meeting to address women's issues. As the states prepared for the 1977 meeting in Houston, the State Department prepared a report to explain women's roles in society. In her retirement, Jurney worked for the National Commission on International Women's Year in Washington, DC. She was the writer and editor for portions of the commission's 1976 report to President Gerald R.

Ford, *To Form a More Perfect Union*, which set the foundation for the states' delegates. The report was a difficult assignment as Jurney had to work with fifteen committees in order to produce a report. Jurney recruited Paxson to help with editing the report; she was between journalism jobs at the time. Paxson wrote to Anderson about the challenge of the project and the conflicting personalities on the commission. Paxson noted that "one staff member's chief talent lies apparently in undercutting all the rest."[31] Several people noted the challenges of the project. According to East: "Throughout a very difficult period Dorothy was unflappable. She was tactful, helpful, considerate and constructive in her direction of the preparation of the report."[32]

Initially, Jurney was told to write short narratives for the beginning of each section in the chapters. It is a way of personalizing an issue—a journalistic style sometimes called the *"Wall Street Journal"* lead. For example, in the section about opportunities for women in sports, Jurney featured Lucy Harris—a star center for Delta State University. It was an analysis of the positives and the challenges of Title IX, which required equal educational opportunities for each gender although was most often attached to sports. Jurney used an anecdote about Harris to make her overall point about opportunity: "Basketball has opened up for Lucy opportunities that she might never have had otherwise. Such opportunities have been available to boys for decades, but they are just beginning for girls."[33]

Jurney had long been aware of gender inequities. In 1977, she organized an editorial talent search firm, the Woman's Network. She placed several women in newspaper management positions before ending the service because of funding problems. She continued to give speeches about women and newspaper content. She advised the 1977 Penney-Missouri winners that, "while progress is notable, publishers still have a long way to go, however, in meeting the needs of the staff and of their readers."[34] Jurney said in an industry speech that the roles of wife and mother in the lives of women added to their journalistic abilities—allowing them to place more of an emphasis on human concerns. She said, "These experiences do not rob an able woman journalist of traditional news concepts. Rather they add dimension. She sees news value in many areas that seldom occur to a man to be important."[35]

Also during the late 1970s, Jurney began preparing an annual report on women in news management positions that was published in *The Bulletin* of the American Society of Newspaper Editors. She explained there were few women in decision-making positions at newspapers. She continued the reports for a decade and wrote many articles for journalism industry publications about the topic. According to an ASNE history, these studies were a major stimulus for the "long-delayed and tortuous rout of women into positions of ASNE leadership."[36] Like many journalism organizations, ASNE had been not been welcoming to women, as Jurney had experienced.[37]

Paxson was also looking for a new project when she signed on to help with the details of the report, *To Form a More Perfect Union*. The staff needed somebody to help with editing, to write captions, and to work on page layout with government printing people. She was suggested for a three-month job with the Status of Women's Commission to issue a report that would lay the foundation for the 1977 meeting in Houston. For Paxson, the position was lucrative—she was paid $13,000 for the three months of work.[38] (For context, according to the US Department of Labor, that amount would be worth $57,000 in 2015.)

Part of the reason Paxson was hired was because of the challenge Jurney found herself in during the production of the report. Jurney started working at the Secretariat in October of 1975 and the report was due to the president on July 4, 1976. She said: "The whole structure was new to me. They were developing such interesting material in these hearings that I wanted to alert the newspapers to the hearings."[39] Yet, Marcy did not want the press to attend the meetings, according to Jurney. (In an oral history, Marcy does not mention the conflict and only mentioned the two women were writers and editors of the document.[40]) There were numerous committees that contributed content to the report. The media committee was headed by Pat Corbine, who did not approve of Jurney's approach to findings about the media.

According to Jurney, in the spring, they had a full meeting of the commission and the staff where she presented a draft of the final report. Jurney said she was "dumbfounded to find that there was great resentment to the way I was presenting this report. I got no support from Jill, and I was under the impression that I was doing it the way she had directed me to do it."[41] The commission meeting took a mid-day break and there was a gathering with Ruckelshaus. She addressed concerns about the way the report was written, using *The Wall Street* style. She said, "Dorothy: I direct you to do it all over and do it in a different way." Jurney was surprised as Marcy and East had seen the report and it been presented to the Government Printing Office. In response to Ruckelshaus, Jurney said: "No, I would just leave." She recalled:

> I couldn't do it. It was impossible for me to have redone the whole thing, have it ready for the Government Printing Office deadline, and get it to President Ford on July 4, 1976. It was just an impossibility. There was still an awful lot to be done.[42]

Jurney recalled:

> Jill's mouth dropped, you know, she was thinking that she was dealing with a civil service person who was dependent upon her job. It didn't make any difference to me whether I had that job or not.[43]

After the confrontation, Jurney went to the cafeteria to have lunch. Marcy and East came down and asked to join her. According to Jurney, she said: "Mildred, I would really like to stay on until this goes to the printers." And Mildred responded, "No, I want you to leave. Leave now." So, within a week or two, Jurney had left. She said in her oral history: "It very uncomfortable for me. And it had been—I had enjoyed it up to that, except it had been hard work and not enough time given to it."[44] She wrote a three-page memo in April 1976 to describe what she called a "recapitulation of the planning of the Commission's Report." She and East reflected on the experience several years later. In 1988, East wrote that Jurney's memos "brought back many unpleasant memories that I have not thought about for a longtime. I was very shocked and disappointed at the criticism of the draft report." The letter was signed, "With affection and great respect."[45]

With Jurney gone, Paxson was charged with trying put the report together by the July 4th deadline. Jurney said Paxson found so many errors in the rewritten report that she convinced Ruckelshaus and Marcy to forget the version a New York writer had drafted after Jurney had left. Instead, Jurney's original version would be published. Paxson edited the copy and got it to the government printers. Ultimately, Jurney wrote the whole front section of the report and wrote a front section for each committee, which told in everyday journalism terms what the commission was aiming at for its resolutions. In an attempt to find compromise for the report's format, Jurney recruited Glaser to write an introduction to the report. Jurney said of Glaser's writing that "it contributed a great deal." Jurney was invited to go to the White House presentation of *To Form a More Perfect Union* but was not introduced as having been the editor of the report.

The new commission under Bella Abzug's administration was getting organized and planning for Houston, when Jurney's good friend, Hilary Whittaker, was going to work for International Women's Year. Whittaker thought there needed to be more news stories in the various states for the Houston conference. Every state had its own women's conference to elect delegates. In many states, there was little newspaper coverage of the conferences. So, Jurney went back to Washington, lived with Whittaker, and worked on increasing media coverage. Jurney started getting in touch with the editors at various newspapers throughout the country. At this point, Jurney was called a consultant rather than a staff member; she was there for six months preparing for the Houston meeting.

The victories and problems of the Abzug have been written about in many publications.[46] She was known for making both friends and enemies easily. According to her obituary: "Bella Abzug was a founding feminist, and an enduring one. In the movement's giddy, sloganeering early days, Ms. Abzug was, like Betty Friedan and Gloria Steinem, an icon, the hat bobbing before the cameras at marches and rallies."[47] Abzug was certainly a formable personality. Fran Henry, who served in both state and national commissions, said of Abzug:

> She wasn't full of hatred or anything, but she just threw off her energy any time she wanted. If she didn't like what was going on and you happened to be standing in front of her, she would scream and yell at you, which she did to me at these state meetings.[48]

International Women's Year in Houston, 1977

Gloria Steinem said the IWY Conference in Houston "may take the prize as the most important event nobody knows about."[49] The meeting in November of 1977 drew more than two thousand people—including appointed commissioners, elected delegates, and volunteers to Houston. In 1975, Congress passed Public Law 94–167 that authorized funding for the conference. The following year, Congress passed an appropriations bill for five million dollars for the event. Some in Congress were suspicious of the use of federal dollars for work that promoted the ERA. The Government Accounting Office conducted an audit of the funds after several congressmen requested it; the GAO found no problems with what the commission was doing. In 1977, Senator Jesse Helms again requested action by the GAO to audit the women's conference funding. The office responded with a letter that stated the previous audit would stand. The comptroller general wrote to Helms: "We believe that many people who oppose ratification of the ERA believe—or have been led to believe—that federal law prohibits a federal agency, such as the IWY, from adopting an advocacy position."[50] Yet, he noted that the law simply stated that there had to be a mix of state and regional representation. He explained: "Nowhere in any applicable statute is there a requirement that the conference members must represent different points of view on ratification of the ERA."[51]

There was some disagreement over certain women's issues—most commonly the ERA, abortion, and homosexuality. The debate of lesbian rights in the women's movement had evolved from the creation of NOW through the 1977 meeting in Houston, as had debates over reproductive rights. Questions over birth control were clearly issues for most women. For example, when Jurney married her husband, she told him that she would have not children. Clarenbach, the mother of three children, said it took her some time to connect reproductive rights with equality issues. She said it was a presentation by Pauli Murray at the first national NOW meeting. Clarenbach said: "I hadn't thought of it as having a political implication until she pointed it out."[52] In preparation for the IWY at some state meetings, there were groups of women who also opposed rape crisis centers, peace, and equal opportunities in education. There were also votes against child abuse legislation as it interfered with family privacy and the rights of parents to discipline in the way they chose. According to Clarenbach: "They were bent on disruptive tactics and for the sake of disagreement opposed everything."[53]

There was significant push back at the platforms of the IWY—especially those items that were considered to be anti-family, such as the ERA and homosexuality. Clarenbach said: "That the whole IWY Conference might be portrayed as an attack on the American family is one of the worst misrepresentations of all. It's 180 degrees off."[54] She said to newspaper columnist Ellen Goodman:

> You know the strange thing? About ten years ago we were busily trying to persuade the world that there was a problem, that discrimination against women existed. Then, a year ago, we were trying to convince the press that the problem hadn't been solved. Now, here we are, the establishment, being attacked by the radical right.[55]

Schlafly attacked the IWY with her own speech in St. Louis, Missouri—near her hometown of Alton, Illinois. Her talk was called: "International Women's Year: A Front for Lesbians and Radicals." About 160 people attended her talk where Schlafly described the many lesbians who had attended the state meetings. She mentioned the meeting in California: "They tell me there were at least two thousand lesbians there, wearing all kinds of lesbian T-shirts."[56]

Initially, the Presiding Officer Jill Ruckelshaus was in charge of the commission. Later, several members of the commission resigned and President Carter installed a new commission. There was a paid staff, headed by Clarenbach, who went from a part-time to a full-time position, with members who handled the administrative and logistical details out of Washington, DC. When Clarenbach was named the executive director of the International Women's Year, 1977, she took a leave of absence from the university. The women's page editor of the Appleton, Wisconsin, newspaper, *The Post-Crescent,* wrote to Clarenbach about the announcement: "You have accepted a tremendous responsibility in an important year for women, and we stand behind you, personally and professionally for the public to see."[57] An article about Clarenbach ran in the newspaper, and its editorial page congratulated the IWY on its choice.[58] According to the editorial: "Dr. Clarenbach, while no less determined in the cause for women's equality, seems to represent a moderate view. She doesn't expect all the discrimination and prejudices to be wiped out immediately. She may be a strong promoter of equality of the sexes in the most practical way."[59] The initial planning was done in Washington, DC. Clarenbach spent the weekdays on the East Coast and traveled back to Madison on the weekends.

Again, Clarenbach was put in a position of peacemaker. Abzug was known for her aggressive personality and habit of yelling at people. It took a toll on East, who moved up her retirement date in order to leave the IWY. She told her daughter Betsy that she had aches and pains in her feet that got worse when she was at work. The pain immediately went away when she turned in her resignation papers and no longer had to walk into Abzug's office. East later said: "I didn't like Bella's style of administration; it was very difficult to work with her because she was volatile and did a lot of yelling and screaming."[60] Clarenbach then stepped in to be the intermediary between Abzug and the staff.

Overcoming short deadlines, predictions of disaster from the media, and a lack of concern on the part of the National IWY Commission, the committee and its allies successfully coordinated the massive project. The chair of the local Houston committee at the end of the meeting announced that a "Miracle occurred!"[61] There was also a group of women organizing for the Conference in Houston—an interesting mix of activists and clubwomen, including the League of Women Voters, NOW and the Junior League. Houston Committee member Nikki R. Van Hightower said:

> We brought in women who had been traditionally involved in sort of 'do good' activities and feminists. That was very useful, because the women that had been involved in some of those charitable activities were very skilled organizers. They knew how to train volunteers. They knew how to discipline their workers, and feminists were a lot looser in that regard.[62]

As the Houston meeting came together, an olive branch between the government women was reached. Marcy made sure that Jurney was a delegate to Houston. While Jurney was standing in the long line to register for IWY, she looked up and saw Ruckelshaus, who said, "Come with me, Dorothy, I will see you get registered right away."[63] Jurney recalled: "She was just as pleasant as she could be. So, we sort of made up."[64] Many women have written that the Houston meeting was a turning point for women's rights. All of those years after President Kennedy's commission, there had finally been a national conference with a variety of women. They came from across the country to reflect on their successes and to talk about goals for the future.

The Houston Conference included symbolism that went back to the early American fight for gender rights. Beginning on September 29, 1977, a torch was lit at Seneca Falls, New York, which was the location of the first women's rights convention more than one hundred years before. The 1977 torch was carried by a relay of runners who traveled the 2,600 miles to Houston, Texas. The torch eventually arrived the day before the conference began. Feminist and poet Maya Angelou wrote a new Declaration of Sentiments to parallel the document presented at the 1848 convention. The declaration accompanied the torch on its journey. At the opening day of the conference, the torch was presented to three American first ladies who all spoke about their lives in ways other than as political wives. They signed the new declaration and then circulated it among the delegates to sign. Many of the women at the event would be considered feminists, but about 20 percent of the attendees were against some of the issues that feminist supported such as the ERA and abortion rights. While it was a significant moment for American women, in later reflection, some saw the event as the end of that era's women's movement. Said Fran Henry:

> We thought it was just the beginning, but it ended the era of the kind of feminist activism. An awful lot of that was due to conservatives that organized around that meeting. It's not as if the women's movement died. I never felt that way. It's just that it took a different form.[65]

The final report, *The Spirit of Houston*, was sent to the president, and women's organizations pledged to implement the recommendations. The twenty-six planks in the plan of action included federally funded day care, accurate portrayals of women in the media, services for elderly and disabled women, and the elimination of violence. Also included were platforms on minority women's issues and the end of discrimination based on sexual orientation.[66]

NOTES

1. Kimberly Wilmot Voss, "Vivian Castleberry: A Case Study of How a Women's Page Editor Lived and Translated the News of a Social Movement," *Southwest Historical Quarterly*, Spring 2007, 514–532. Kimberly Wilmot Voss and Lance Speere, "A Women's Page Pioneer: Marie Anderson and Her Influence at the *Miami Herald* and Beyond," *Florida Historical Quarterly*, Spring 2007, 398–421. Kimberly Wilmot Voss, "Forgotten Feminist: Women's Page Editor Maggie Savoy and the Growth of Women's Liberation Awareness in Los Angeles," *California History*, Spring 2009, 48–64. Kimberly Wilmot Voss, "Dorothy Jurney : The 'Godmother' of Women's Page Editors," *Journalism History*, Spring 2010, 13–22. Kimberly Wilmot Voss, "Anne Rowe Goldman: Refashioning Women's News in St. Petersburg, Florida," *FCH Annals: Journal of the Florida Conference of Historians*, March 2011, 104–111.
2. Kimberly Wilmot Voss and Lance Speere, "Quilted News: Mixing Hard and Soft News to Create a New Definition for Women's News," Florida Communication Association Conference, Orlando, October 18, 2013.
3. Mills, *What Difference*, 110.
4. Kimberly Wilmot Voss, "Penney-Missouri Awards: Honoring the Best in Women's News," *Journalism History*, Spring 2006, 43–50.
5. "Mary Ann Grossman's 50 Years at the St. Paul Pioneer Press Celebrated," *St. Paul Pioneer Press*, April 11, 2011.
6. Jocelyn Olcott, "Empires of Information: Media Strategies for the 1975 International Women's Year," *Journal of Women's History*, 2012, 24.
7. Olcott, *Empires of Information*, 27.
8. Olcott, *Empires of Information*, 29.
9. Olcott, *Empires of Information*, 31.
10. Olcott, *Empires of Information*, 39.
11. Olcott, *Empires of Information*, 26.
12. Paxson, "Women in Journalism," 161.
13. Ibid.
14. Ibid.

15. Ibid.
16. Olcott, *Empires of Information*, 40.
17. Ibid.
18. Peggy A. Simpson, "1979: Covering the Women's Movement," Nieman Reports, Winter 1999–Spring 2000. Judy Klemesrud, "Scrappy, Unofficial Women's Parley Sets Pace," *New York Times*, June 29, 1975. For an analysis of coverage: Anne Cooper and Lucinda D. Davenport, "Newspaper Coverage of International Women's Decade: Feminism and Conflict," *Journal of Communication Inquiry*, 1987, 108–115.
19. Dorothy Jurney, "Women's Liberation," *Philadelphia Inquirer*, November 10, 1967.
20. Ibid.
21. Marjorie Paxson, "Day One of IWY," July 1975. Papers of Marjorie Paxson, folder 85.
22. Ibid.
23. Ibid.
24. Marjorie Paxson, "Day Two of IWY," July 1975. Papers of Marjorie Paxson, folder 85.
25. Ibid.
26. Ibid.
27. Ibid.
28. Marjorie Paxson, "Day Three of IWY," July 1975. Papers of Marjorie Paxson, folder 85.
29. Marjorie Paxson, "Day Four of IWY," July 1975. Papers of Marjorie Paxson, folder 85.
30. Ibid.
31. Marjorie Paxson letter to Marie Anderson, nd. Papers of Marie Anderson.
32. Catherine East letter to Dorothy Jurney, January 29, 1984. Papers of Dorothy Jurney.
33. "To Form a More Perfect Union…,"1976, 51.
34. Dorothy Jurney, "The Weekly People in Review," *Penney Press*, March 1977, 8.
35. Jurney, Talk at Carolina Symposium, 4.
36. Paul Alfred Pratte, *Gods Within The Machine: A History of the American Society of Newspaper Editors, 1923–1993* (Westport, Conn.: Praeger, 1995), 155.
37. Alf Pratte, "A Tortuous Route to Growing Up: The Rise of Women in the American Society of Newspaper Editors," *Journal of Women's History* (Spring 1994): 51–66.
38. Paxson, "Women in Journalism," 163.
39. Jurney, "Women in Journalism," 89.
40. Mildred Marcy, Association for Diplomatic Studies and Training Foreign Affairs Oral History Project, February 15, 1991, 36.
41. Jurney, "Women in Journalism," Session 2, 89.
42. Jurney, "Women in Journalism," Session 2, 90.
43. Ibid.
44. Jurney, "Women in Journalism," Session 2, 90–91.
45. Catherine East letter to Dorothy Jurney, September 19, 1988. Papers of Dorothy Jurney.
46. Alan H. Levy, *The Political Life of Bella Abzug, 1976–1998* (Lanham, Maryland: Lexington Books, 2013); Suzanne Braun Levine and Mary Thom, *Bella Abzug: How One Tough Broad from the Bronx Fought Jim Crow …* (New York: Farrar, Strauss & Giroux, 2008).
47. Laura Mansnerus, "Bella Abzug, 77, Congresswoman and a Founding Feminist Is Dead," *New York Times*, April 1, 1998. http://www.nytimes.com/learning/general/onthisday/bday/0724.html.
48. Fran Henry, Voices of Feminism Oral History Project, October 22 and 25, 2004, 43. Available at Smith College, Northampton, M.A.
49. Gloria Steinem, *My Life on the Road* (New York: Random House, 2015), 53.
50. Comptroller General of the United States letter to Senator Jesse Helms, August 10, 1977, General Accounting Office, B–182389.
51. Ibid.
52. Clarenbach oral history, 175.
53. UPI, "Kathryn Clarenbach Analyzes Issues at Fall Women's Conference," *Milwaukee Sentinel*, August 13, 1977.
54. Leader and Hyatt, *American Women on the Move,* 80.
55. Ellen Goodman, "Yesterday's Conservatives, Today's Radicals," *Boston Globe,* November 7, 1977.

56. "Mrs. Schlafly Attacks Women's Year Project, *St. Louis Globe-Democrat*, July 16–17, 1977, 9A.
57. Alice K. Huck letter to Kathryn Clarenbach, August 10, 1977. Papers of Kathryn Clarenbach, International Women's Year, Box 3, personal file.
58. "State Woman Named Director of IWY," *The Post-Crescent*, July 17, 1977.
59. "Clarenbach a wild choice," *The Post-Crescent*, August 3, 1977.
60. Leader and Hyatt, *American Women on the Move*, 36.
61. Ellen Pratt Fout, "A Miracle Occurred!" *The Houston Review*, Vol.1, No.1, 4.
62. Fout, "A Miracle Occurred," 5.
63. Jurney "Women in Journalism." Session 2, 90.
64. Ibid.
65. Fran Henry, "Voices of Feminism Oral History," Smith College, October 25, 2004, 47.
66. Orwin, "Labor Roots," 273.

Afterword

What Happened in the Post-Houston Years

Many of the well-behaved women who were in Houston continued to work for women's rights, although they have largely been overlooked. Another woman to fit in this category was Charlotte Curtis. She knew several of these women and interacted most often with East. Curtis was the first woman to be a top editor at the *New York Times*, beginning in 1974. She had taken a traditional path for women journalists at the time—starting in the women's pages. Curtis began at the *Times* as the fashion reporter in 1961, and four years later she became the women's page editor of the newspaper. She was known for her witty and sometimes biting columns—a combination of reporting and observation at the *Times*. She served as a social critic at her newspaper—especially about issues of social class, race and gender. A collection of her columns was published in the 1976 book, *The Rich and Other Atrocities*.[1]

Curtis' goal of improving news for women started before she came to the *Times*. Colleen "Koky" Dishon found a kindred spirit in Curtis, then the women's page editor at the cross-town rival the *Columbus Citizen*. "We competed for stories during the day and then met to discuss how we could save newspaper sections from ailing dullness and wafer-thin substance," Dishon wrote of their relationship.[2] The two agreed that women's sections could be improved with stronger writing and more news. Their goal was to "take the yardstick we used for news and move it over to the features section."[3] This was something Curtis was able to accomplish in the women's pages before being promoted. She covered the activities of NOW. In 1968, while Curtis described the members as "militants," she also described their reasonable demands of paid maternity leave, tax deductions for child care, and more local child care facilities.[4]

After several years as the Op-Ed editor, Curtis died at age fifty-eight from cancer. Her obituary in her newspaper described Curtis as the "image of Junior League elegance" with her "ladylike suits and real jewelry."[5] She would easily fit the definition of a well-behaved woman. In 1999, a biography of Curtis was published with the title, *A Woman of the Times: Journalism, Feminism and the Career of Charlotte Curtis*. A review of the book in the *Times* noted:

> Charlotte Curtis was hardly the only prominent woman to denounce feminism. Expecting her to have been a modern role model may be no more reasonable than earlier expectations that every woman should be a model housewife or have a model's figure. But this was someone who made a career of pinpointing social change and uncovering other people's self-delusions.[6]

A month after the review, a telling letter to the editor from feminist Robin Morgan was published. Morgan had been interviewed by Curtis when she covered the planned picket of the 1968 Miss American Pageant.[7] Morgan wrote about Curtis: "Actually, for a woman of her generation and prominence, Curtis was unusually supportive of women and feminist ideas and actions. She was a lady. And she was a feminist. In her, this was no contradiction."[8] Morgan recalled when Curtis interviewed her before the 1968 Miss America Pageant protest—the birth of the "bra-burning" myth. (No bras were actually burned during the protest.) Curtis had gone off the record to ask Morgan some questions:

> Did I believe they'd be effective? Might we alienate instead of persuade? Should we be more genteel, or was she being overly so? These weren't baiting questions. She was warm, curious, open; our discussion was serious. I was touched when she left saying she now understood and would try to convey the "eminently reasonable politics" behind our protest through her coverage. She did. In fact, she made us seem downright wholesome.[9]

Curtis rode along with the protesters on the bus to Atlantic City that day and remained on the boardwalk during the event. Some of the demonstrators snuck into the event that evening and were arrested. Morgan was working on collecting bail money when she learned the jailed women had been released. The cash bail had been put up earlier by "some older woman" named Charlotte Curtis. Later, Morgan called to thank Curtis. The journalist responded that the arrangement should be kept quiet as "those dreary gray guys running the *Times*" would not be approve.[10]

After the announcement of Curtis's promotion out of the women's pages, Morgan wrote to Curtis. She responded with a letter to Morgan on October 1,

1973: "How marvelous to hear from you, and I thank you for your generosity. As you might expect, I hope to have more women's voices on the Op-Ed Page, and I also you will be one of them." [11] While Curtis made strides for women, some of the feminist actions of this well-behaved woman was only known after her death. As Morgan later said of Curtis's role in the late 1960s: "She had to play both sides of the aisle." [12]

New Directions for News

In the aftermath of Houston, several of the well-behaved women studied how the media covered women. It began, in part, to better understand the role newspapers played in the defeat of the Equal Rights Amendment. The idea to study the media's coverage of women's issues had been planted a few years prior. East exchanged letters with a University of South Carolina researcher in August of 1975 about a study on readership and journalism response to news coverage of women and women's activities. Professor Severance sent her study results to East, which were later published in *Monitor: South Carolina Journalism Review*. Severance also sent East a copy of an article. The piece ran in *The State* newspaper, August 16, 1975, by Mary Terry, "USC Study: Women Criticize Press." Severance wrote to East that the reporter had asked the researcher to write a feature story about the study. Terry then rewrote the article, leaving out most of the information about journalists' views and that there should be more news concerning the women's movement published in the newspaper. Severance wrote to East:

> The article was published on the Saturday's women's pages surrounded by bridal and engagement pictures. If I hadn't been laughing so hard, I probably would have pulled my hair out. I understand, though, that the results of the study caused considerable commotion in the news rooms of both *The State* and *Record* newspapers. So maybe, just maybe, some small changes might come out of it. [13]

Jurney said that one of the most important projects during her retirement was a study of how newspapers covered particular issues related to women. In 1979, Virginia Allan, then chair of the Women's Studies Program and Policy Center at George Washington University, conceived of the research project to analyze American newspaper coverage. Jurney and East coauthored the 1983 report resulting from the research. The project studied the newspaper coverage of five other women's issues and events from 1972 to 1980 besides the ERA to increase objectivity and provide a context. The topics included were: domestic relations law; the 1977 Women's Conference at Houston, Texas; the 1980 United Nations World Conference for Women at Copenhagen, Denmark; pay equity; and the enforcement of Title IX (gender equality in education). The study analyzed 1,096 clippings from ten newspapers of various circulation sizes and geographical locations: *Arizona Daily Star, Atlanta Journal and Constitution, Cincinnati Enquirer, Dallas Times-Herald, Denver Post, Detroit Free Press, Los Angeles Times, Miami Herald, New York Times,* and *St. Louis Post-Dispatch*. The study was financed by newspapers and journalism foundations and sponsored by George Washington University.

The findings and recommendations were published in a twenty-four-page, tabloid-style report in 1983. The front page of the *New Directions for News* publication symbolized the approach that many managing editors took to the women's sections. It included a drawing of men in shirts and ties sitting in front of computers in various news departments—city news, government news, sports news, and entertainment news. The last department was the women's section and behind the desk sat a Neanderthal character in front of a manual typewriter. (Jurney persuaded the *Miami Herald* to run the cartoon in its newspaper.[14] Jurney said it was an example of a picture being worth a million words.[15])

The report's overall conclusion was that newspaper coverage of all six topics was generally inadequate or mishandled. According to the report, many editors either lacked knowledge of the topics or had no understanding of their impact on the readers.[16] The study found that of the ten newspapers examined, all except for the *St. Louis Post-Dispatch* had failed to cover the Equal Rights Amendment in a way that allowed readers to truly understand the issues. The media treated the assertions of each side equally and did not analyze the truth of the claims. In a 1976 talk to Knight-Ridder newspaper executives, Jurney addressed the false myths that the poor reporting was perpetuating such as the ERA leading to unisex bathrooms. She cited a particular article in which the reporter did not question a John Birch Society speaker about her statements against the ERA, asserting that there was no inequality. For example, Jurney said, the speaker "fails to point out that there is a discriminatory practice applied against women who want to join the military. A woman has to be a high school graduate; a man does not; a woman has to score forty points higher than a man in qualifying exams."[17] The lack of analysis allowed for a simplistic representation of the fight for and against the ERA. The study was later expanded to include coverage of education, housing, family law issues, and equal pay for comparable work.

The introduction to the study, written by Jurney, began with a quote from the American Society of Newspaper Editors' statement of principles: "The primary purpose of gathering and distributing news and opinion is to serve the general welfare by informing the people and enabling them to make judgments in the issues of the time."[18] Jurney then wrote, "If the way newspapers have covered recent issues and events of importance to women can be taken as a measure of general performance, then it would seem papers have often failed to carry out their primary purpose."[19] It was a call for action.

The findings of the study showed that the examined newspaper articles focused on conflict, even when it was not the main issue that a reporter had originally written about in his or her article. For example, reporters who had covered the International Women's Year Conference in Copenhagen complained about the revision of their stories. They had sent back stories based on issues that had been discussed. At their home newspapers, the editors would instead focus on a minor, conflict-based part of the conference, such as Israeli or Muslim women walking out.[20] Jurney stressed that the "hook of a newspaper story" did not need to be confrontational. Instead, the hook could be economical, financial or family-oriented. She wrote that reporting only on the confrontations—and a number of papers in this study did no more than that—often obscured the deeper thrust of social change. And when there was no controversy involved, the story was often neglected completely.[21]

The study pointed out the areas where newspaper editors were neglecting their responsibilities as gatekeepers. One of the main conclusions was that newspapers needed to expand their definition of what was newsworthy, particularly putting a stronger emphasis on human interest or soft news. According to the research findings: "Reporting soft news is more difficult than covering hard news because there is little action and guidelines are few. But when it is done with expertise, the rewards for the public and for the newspaper are large."[22]

In her retirement, Jurney also documented the inequities experienced by women at newspapers in numerous studies, several of which were published by the American Society of Newspaper Editors.[23] She pointed out there were few women in decision-making positions at newspapers. She continued the reports for a decade and wrote many articles for journalism industry publications about the topic. According to an ASNE history, these studies were a major stimulus for the "long-delayed and tortuous rout of women into positions of ASNE leadership."[24] Like many industry organizations, ASNE had been not been welcoming to women, as Jurney had experienced.[25] In 1986, she noted women were only 12.4 percent of editors and estimated that they would need another sixty-nine years to be represented equally at the current pace.[26]

End of Wisconsin Commission on Status of Women

Clarenbach won most political battles that she faced as a member of the Commission on the Status of Women in her home state of Wisconsin—much of it from her office on the edge of the University of Wisconsin campus. That was until she met her match in Governor Lee Dreyfus. In December 1978, Dreyfus announced to a room of journalists that he would allow the most powerful women's organization in the state "to croak." His coarse language led to significant media coverage. It began a mediated discussion about women's roles after a decade of social change. In the end, Dreyfus followed through on his threat but it was not without a fight. Clarenbach would publically take on the governor—a different style than she had used previously.

The battle over the future of the Wisconsin Commission on the Status of Women was largely fought in the press. For example, Dreyfus said in an interview, "This idea of taking everything that comes across your desk and creating a commission for it to get it out of your hair, I think is a squirrel cage operation of the first order."[27] Clarenbach's aide responded: "If Dreyfus plans to make the Women's Commission more than just a squirrel cage operation, I'm delighted."[28] A December 20, 1978 *Capital Times* editorial stated the governor would make a mistake if he eliminated the commission. The editorial noted: "We suggest that Dreyfus attend one of the commission's meetings and he might change his mind. It is a credit to the state and to Reynolds that long before equal rights became a rallying cry throughout the land, Wisconsin was one of the pioneers in establishing a body that could actively concern itself with this major issue."[29] The commission ended in 1979. (However, the Wisconsin Women's Network continued to work for women in the state.)[30]

Clarenbach would go on to co-edit the book, *The Green Stubborn Bud: Women's Culture at the Century's Close*. The title came from a line in a Robin Morgan poem; she also contributed a chapter to the book. Friedan wrote the introduction and addressed the backlash to feminism that was apparent by 1987, such as complaints by young women who said, "I'm not a feminist, but I intend to use these opportunities that feminists won to advance my career."[31] Clarenbach retired from the university in 1988 and was later named an emeritus professor of political science.

Paxson Reaches Newspaper Management

Paxson twice lost her journalism job because the women's pages she headed were transitioned into lifestyle sections. Yet, she eventually was able to rise through the ranks of newspaper management. In 1980, Paxson became the fourth female publisher in the Gannett newspaper chain. It was not an easy progression for women at the top positions at newspapers at that time. (This is not to imply there is gender equality in newspaper management today.) Numerous studies have found women journalists often faced a hostile environment as they sought management positions. An academic article, for instance, revealed a reluctance to accept women in management roles from 1925 through 1988 at ASNE.[32] A survey of newspaper mid-level managers in 1974 found when women did get hired, they were often treated differently than their male counterparts and were paid less.[33] A 1981 study showed that despite awareness about gender inequities, men dominated newspaper management positions.[34]

Like most journalists who came through the women's pages, Paxson had no training in hiring and firing employees, as well as managing a budget. For example, when Paxson was at the *Philadelphia Bulletin*, she was asked if she wanted to send a fashion reporter to Paris. Paxson said she could make a better educated decision if she knew how expensive the trip would be. Her supervisor responded: "Aren't you glad you don't have to worry your pretty head about things like that?"[35] When she arrived at Gannett in a middle-management position, she did receive training on a variety of management issues. She became the chain's fourth female publisher when she served as a publisher of the *Public Opinion* in Chambersburg, Pennsylvania, in 1978.

There were still gender-based battles ahead. On her first day of work as a new Gannett newspaper publisher in 1980, Paxson learned about the former male publisher's clothing policy: Women could not wear pants. Although Paxson said she had planned to look "every inch the lady publisher" and went shopping for skirts, she decided to wear her lone pantsuit to the office on her second day. The next morning, wearing that pantsuit, she walked into the *Muskogee Phoenix* departments. On the way to her office, she went through the pressroom, through the composing room and through the news room. By noon, the publisher's secretary came upstairs and she said, "Everybody is asking if there's been a change—if they can wear pants?" That afternoon Paxson called a meeting of the newspaper management and announced a change in the dress code—women could wear pants. She said, "I really was not going to dictate what either men or women wore, as long as they were neat, as long as they were clean, and as long as they were dressed appropriately for the job they were supposed to do for the *Phoenix*."[36]

She later learned many of the female employees went to a local store that evening. The next day, of the forty-five women working at the paper, twenty-nine wore pants. She recalled, "That story got around town very quickly."[37] Paxson remembered shopping at Sears when the clerk looked down at the name on her credit card. She looked up at Paxson: "Are you the new lady at the paper?" Paxson replied that she was, and the clerk responded: "I'm so glad you let them wear pants."[38] Pants had become a symbol of change—a challenge to the status quo in terms of gender roles. She also changed the newspaper's policy to be supportive of the Equal Rights Amendment.

Marie Anderson Leaves the *Miami Herald*

While Anderson was lauded nationally for her work in the women's pages, she became more unhappy at the *Miami Herald*. She wrote to a friend: "My fundamental trouble is that the managing editor and I don't think alike. I had thought that it didn't make any difference, but I'm about to decide it does."[39]

Anderson left the newspaper in 1972, and she became the dean of University Relations and Development at Florida International University. After five years, she retired and became active in the Miami history community. She served as the editor of *Update*, the Historical Association of Southern Florida's magazine, from 1979 until 1988. Anderson continued to travel with Jurney over the years, including trips to China, Egypt, and India.

Anderson wrote the book, *Julia's Daughter: Women in Dade's History* in 1980. (The title is a reference to Julia Tuttle, known as the "Mother of Miami.") The book focused on the important women of Miami from 1513 to 1975. There was an initial pool of several hundred nominees, and 272 women were chosen to be profiled. According to the preface written by Anderson: "My approach was to try to tell a history of Dade County that emphasized women's contributions, whatever they might be."[40] While Anderson was not included as a significant woman in her own book, she was included in the 2015 book about important Florida women.[41]

Vera Glaser

Glaser stayed in journalism. She continued her column for several more years and then went on to write for the *Washingtonian* magazine in the 1980s and later the Maturity News Network in the 1990s. She was included in the oral history project: "A Few Good Women: Advancing the Cause of Women in Government, 1969–1974" at Penn State University. Her contribution helped to better understand the complicated contribution of the Nixon Administration to gender equality.

Legacies and the Continued Fight for the Equal Rights Amendment

After East retired from the federal government, she continued to work to have the Equal Rights Amendment—endorsed by the 1970 President's Task Force on Women's Rights and Responsibilities—passed in Virginia. The Task Force's report, written by Glaser, noted: "The Supreme Court has thus far not accorded the protection of those amendments to female citizens. It has upheld or refused to review laws and practices making discriminatory distinctions based on sex." Some have argued that the ERA is not needed as the Fourteenth Amendment would include women in the Constitution. Yet, in widely quoted comments in a 2011 issue of *California Lawyer*, the late Supreme Court Justice Scalia said the equal protection clause of the Fourteenth Amendment to the Constitution does not protect against discrimination on the basis of gender. Several lawmakers responded to Scalia's remarks. For example, Rep. Gwen Moore, who was co-chair of the Congressional Women's Caucus, said: "It's a wake-up call when a sitting Supreme Court justice says there are no Constitutional protections for women. Apparently women's rights are at the whim of the Court and will remain that way without the Equal Rights Amendment."[42]

The fight for the ERA may not be over. A legal strategy to revive the ERA was created more than a decade ago. It was based on a "three-state strategy" developed after 1992, when the Twenty-Seventh Amendment to the Constitution was ratified 203 years after its passage by Congress.[43] Acceptance of this ratification period has led supporters to argue that Congress has the power to maintain the legal viability of the ERA's existing thirty-five state ratifications. Supporters also argued that the ERA's time limit is open to change because Congress already demonstrated a willingness to extend the original deadline for ratification from 1979 to 1982. This would mean that Congress could accept state ratifications that occur after 1982 and keep the existing thirty-five ratifications alive. A bill in the 108th Congress stipulates that the House of Representatives shall take any necessary action to verify ratification of the ERA when an additional three states ratify.[44]

Ratification bills continue to be introduced in the unratified states. Most of the arguments of the anti-ERA movement have proven untrue or irrelevant, and every constitution in the world written after World War II includes an ERA-like statement that men and women are equals. In the words of Supreme Court Justice Ruth Bader Ginsberg:

> The Equal Rights Amendment remains important in a symbolic sense. Every modern human rights declaration in the world, at least since 1970, contains a statement that men and women are persons of equal dignity entitled to the laws' equal respect. I would write the lawmakers of the United States in Congress and in the states to perfect the fundamental instrument of government in this regard for the sake of my daughter, my granddaughters, and all the daughters in generations yet to come. I would like to see in our Constitution this clarion statement of bedrock principle—equal rights shall not be denied or abridged on account of sex.[45]

While women are achieving more in politics and the workplace, the one cause that these women advocated for has yet to be achieved—passage of the ERA. Contemporary debate regarding the ERA began with the Kennedy Administration and the President's Commission on the Status of Women. Later, East helped create the strategy that got the legislation passed by Congress. As a publisher, Paxson changed her newspaper's editorial policy to support the ERA. Glaser and Jurney wrote about the need for the amendment in government reports. In different ways, they advocated for the ERA only to have the various tactics fail. Yet, the amendment they fought for may still be ratified.

As recently as 2011, the Constitution was read on the House floor and then several US Representatives members and leaders from women's organizations led a press conference in front of the US Capitol to remind the public what was missing from the founding federal document: women. This was good news for ERA advocates. They had been hard at work in statehouses for years, despite the widespread belief the ERA was left for dead in 1982, three states short of the thirty-eight needed for ratification. In recent years, several states have adopted their own ERA statements. The ERA's revival remains a real possibility. Today's leaders should heed the efforts of those who shouldered the burden so tirelessly and unglamorously for so long. The fact that much has been accomplished for and by women must not mask that which remains unfulfilled.

NOTES

1. Charlotte Curtis, *The Rich and Other Atrocities*, (New York: Harper & Row Publishers, 1976)
2. Voss, "A Journalism Legend," *Timeline*.
3. Ibid.
4. Charlotte Curtis, "White House Candidates Let the Women Down," *New York Times*, May 7, 1968.
5. Robert D. McFadden, "Charlotte Curtis, a Columnist for the *Times*, is Dead at 58," *New York Times*, April 17, 1987.
6. Judith Martin, "Too Much a Lady?" *New York Times*, August 29, 1999.
7. Robin Morgan, *The Word of a Woman: Feminist Dispatches, 1968–1992* (New York: W.W. Norton & Company, 1992).
8. Robin Morgan, "Letter to the editor," *New York Times*, September 26, 1999.
9. Ibid.
10. Ibid.
11. Charlotte Curtis letter to Robin Morgan, October 1, 1973. Papers of Robin Morgan, Duke University Libraries.
12. Author interview with Robin Morgan, January 15, 2016.
13. Carol Severance letter to Catherine East, August 25, 1975. Papers of Catherine East.
14. Jurney, "Women In Journalism," Session 2, 99.)
15. Ibid.
16. New Direction for News Papers, description, National Women and Media Collection, State Historical Society of Missouri.
17. Dorothy Jurney, untitled talk to Knight-Ridder newspaper executives, Point Clear, Alabama, 1976. Papers of Dorothy Jurney.
18. Virginia Allan, Catherine East and Dorothy Jurney, "New Directions for News," Women Studies Program and Policy Center of George Washington University, 1983, 2.
19. Jurney, "New Directions for News," 2.
20. Jurney, "Women in Journalism," Session 4, 129.
21. Jurney, "Women in Journalism," Session 3, 2.
22. Jurney, "Women in Journalism," Session 3, 10.
23. Dorothy Jurney, "Percentage of Women Editors Creeps Upward to 11.7—But Other Fields Continue to Progress Faster," *ASNE Bulletin* (January 1986): 8–11.
24. Pratte, *Gods Within The Machine*, 155.
25. Pratte "A Tortuous Route to Growing Up," 51–66.
26. Dorothy Jurney, "Tenth Annual Survey Reports Women Editors at 12.4 percent," *ASNE Bulletin* (November 1986): 5.
27. Mike Stamler, "Commission Shouldn't 'Croak,' 2 women officials tell Dreyfus," *Capital Times*, December 20, 1978.
28. Ibid.
29. "Dreyfus Pops Off Too Much," *Capital Times*, December 20, 1978.

30. "Beginning of the Wisconsin Women's Network," Wisconsin Women's Network, nd. http://www.wiwomensnetwork.org/history/.

31. Betty Friedan, "Introduction," in Kathryn F. Clarenbach and Edward L. Kamarck, eds., *The Green Stubborn Bud: Women's Culture at Century's Close* (Metuchen, New Jersey: Scarecrow Press, 1987).

32. Norman Lewis, "From Cheesecake to Chief: Newspapers Editors' Slow Acceptance of Women," *American Journalism* 25:2 (Spring 2008): 33–55.

33. Christine Ogan, "On Their Way to the Top? Men and Women Middle-Level Newspaper Managers," paper presented at the annual meeting of AEJMC, Houston, Texas, August 5, 1979.

34. Ardyth Broadrick Sohn, "Women in Newspaper Management: An Update," *Newspaper Research Journal* 3:1 (Fall 1981): 94–106.

35. Paxson, "Women in Journalism," Session 4, 90.

36. Paxson, "Women in Journalism," Session 4, 118.

37. Paxson, "Women in Journalism," Session 4, 118.

38. Paxson, "Women in Journalism," Session 5, 120.

39. Marie Anderson letter to Paul Myhre, March 17, 1965. Papers of Marie Anderson.

40. Marie Anderson, ed., *Julia's Daughters: Women in Dade's History* (Miami, Florida: Herstory of Florida, 1980), 9.

41. Doris Weatherford, *They Dared to Dream: Florida Women Who Shaped History* (University Press of Florida, 2015).

42. Kimberly Wilmot Voss, "Thank You, Justice Scalia, For Helping Revive the ERA," *Ms* Magazine Blog, January 10, 2011.

43. "The Equal Rights Amendment: Why the ERA Remains Legally Viable and Properly Before the States," *William & Mary Journal of Women and the Law*, Spring 1997.

44. The Equal Rights Amendments, "Frequently Asked Questions," http://www.equalrightsamendment.org/.

45. Ruth Pollack, *The Equal Rights Amendment: Unfinished Business for the Constitution*, Educational Film Center, 1998.

Bibliography

PRIMARY SOURCES

Papers of Marie Anderson, National Women and Media Collection, State Historical Society of Missouri.
Papers of Roberta Applegate, National Women and Media Collection, State Historical Society of Missouri.
Papers of Kathryn Clarenbach, University of Wisconsin Library.
Papers of Catherine East, Schlesinger Library, Radcliffe Institute for Advanced Study, Harvard University.
Papers of Vera Glaser, Heritage Center, University of Wyoming.
Papers of Martha Griffiths, Bentley Historical Library, University of Michigan.
Papers of Dorothy Jurney, National Women and Media Collection, State Historical Society of Missouri.
Papers of Marjorie Paxson, National Women and Media Collection, State Historical Society of Missouri.

SECONDARY SOURCES

"11 Picket Times Classified Office To Protest Male-Female Labels." *New York Times*, August 31, 1967.
"Anti-ERA leader Schlafly predicts Houston meeting." *Houston Chronicle*, November 3, 1977.
Anderson, Marie, ed. *Julia's Daughters: Women in Dade's History*. Miami, Florida: Herstory of Florida, 1980.
Anderson, Marie. "Too Bad Jo's Just a Girl." *Miami Herald*, July 1970.
Anderson, Marie. "Women in Journalism." Washington Press Club Foundation. http://www.wpcf.org/women-in-journalism/.
Applegate, Roberta. "Cape Canaveral: A New World." *Miami Herald*, July 3, 1960.
Applegate, Roberta. "Children at Florida Farm Colony Range from 6 to 60." *Miami Herald*, October 14, 1954.
Applegate, Roberta. "Ellie Knows Her Space Facts—From Monkeys to Catnip." *Miami Herald*, July 4, 1960.
Applegate, Roberta. "Emphasis at Florida Farm Colony Placed on Rehabilitation, Training." *Miami Herald*, October 15, 1954.

Applegate, Roberta. "Her Missile Base Work's a Huge 'Clean-Up' Chore." *Miami Herald*, July 5, 1960.
Applegate, Roberta. "June Tells Missiles Where To Go." *Miami Herald*, July 6, 1960.
Applegate, Roberta. "Ollie's a Housekeeper—for Cape Canaveral." *Miami Herald*, July 7, 1960.
Applegate, Roberta. "Women Keep Peace at Home; They Can Do It in Industry." *Miami Herald*, October 31, 1958.
Applegate, Roberta. "Dimples Don't Sway a Woman's Vote." *Miami Herald*, August 29, 1959.
Ashley, Laura, and Beth Olson. "Constructing Reality: Print Media's Framing of the Women's Movement, 1966–1986." *Journalism and Mass Communications Quarterly*, (1998): 263–277.
Associated Press, "GOP? It Means Gals' Own Party." *Miami Herald*, June 18, 1964.
Austin, Dorothy. "New NOW Network." *Milwaukee Sentinel*, May 24, 1971.
Banaszak, Lee Ann. *The Women's Movement: Inside and Outside the State*. New York: Cambridge University Press, 2010.
Barbakso, Maryann. *Governing NOW: Grassroots Activism in the National Organization for Women*. Ithaca, New York: Cornell University, 2004.
Barry, Kathleen M. *Femininity in Flight: A History of Flight Attendants*. Durham, North Carolina: Duke University, 2007.
Beale, Betty. *Power at Play: A Memoir of Parties, Politicians and the Presidents in My Bedroom*. Washington, DC: Regnery Gateway Books, 1993.
Beasley, Maurine, and Sheila Gibbons. eds. *Taking Their Place: A Documentary History of Women and Journalism*. Washington, DC: The American University Press, 1993.
Beasley, Maurine H. *Women of the Washington Press: Politics, Prejudice, and Perspective*. Evanston, Illinois: Northwestern University Press, 2012.
"Beginning of the Wisconsin Women's Network." Wisconsin Women's Network, nd. http://www.wiwomensnetwork.org/history/.
Bender, Marylin. "College Girl Often Sees No Future but Marriage." *New York Times*, March 26, 1962.
Bender, Marylin. "Rusty Skills Bar Women From a Job." *New York Times*, January 5, 1962.
Bender, Marylin. "College Girl Often Sees No Future but Marriage." *New York Times*, March 26, 1962.
Benzel, Lucinda. "Back-to-college program for women." *St. Louis Globe-Democrat*, September 2, 1963.
Bers, Trudy Haffron, and Susan Gluck Mezey. "Support for Feminist Goals among Leaders of Women's Community Groups." *Signs*, (1981): 741.
Biggs, Gloria. "To Catch a Woman." *Editorially Speaking*, Gannet Group of Newspapers, Vol. 25, 1967, 21.
Blair, Karen J. *The Clubwoman as Feminist: True Womanhood Redefined 1868–1914*. New York: Holmes & Meier Publishers, 1980.
Boyer, Elizabeth. "The Editor, Life Magazine." *Congressional Record*, December 10, 1968.
Bradley, Patricia. *Mass Media and the Shaping of American Feminism, 1963–1975*. Mississippi: University Press of Mississippi, 2003.
Broder, David. *Behind the Front Page*. New York: Simon & Schuster, 1987.
Brownmiller, Susan. *In Our Time: Memoir of a Revolution*. New York: Random House, 1999.
Callender, David. "Henry Clarenbach Dies From a Long Illness." *Capital Times*, June 20, 1987.
Carmon, Irin and Shana Knizhnik. *Notorious RBG: The Life and Times of Ruth Bader Ginsburg*. New York: Harper Collins, 2015.
Chang, Won. "Characteristics and Self Perceptions of Women's Page Editors." *Journalism Quarterly*, (1975): 61–65.
Chesler, Ellen. "Lives Well Lived: Kathryn F. Clarenbach." *New York Times*, January 1, 1995.
Chusmir, Janet. "First Female Party Chief" 'Effort, Time and Energy.'" *Miami Herald*, August 5, 1968.
"Clarenbach a wild choice." *The Post-Crescent*, August 3, 1977.
"Class for Clubwomen." *Time*, September 30, 1946.

Cohen, Marcia. *The Sisterhood: The Inside Story of the Women's Movement and the Leaders Who Made It Happen.* New Yok: Fawcett Columbine, 1988.
Cohen, Rhaina. "Who Took Care of Rosie the Riveter's Kids?" *The Atlantic,* 2015.
"College for Girls? An Old Argument Takes New Turns." *National Observer,* November 11, 1963.
Comptroller General of the United States letter to Senator Jesse Helms, August 10, 1977, General Accounting Office, B–182389.
Coontz, Stephanie. *A Strange Stirring: The Feminine Mystique and America Women at the Dawn of the 1960's.* New York: Basic Books, 2011.
Cooper, Anne and Lucinda D. Davenport. "Newspaper Coverage of International Women's Decade: Feminism and Conflict." *Journal of Communication Inquiry,* 1987, 108–115.
Cott, Nancy. *The Grounding of Modern Feminism.* New Haven, Connecticut: Yale University Press, 1987.
"Court Blocks Ruling on Age Limit, Marriage Ban for Airline Stewardesses." *Washington Post,* November 22, 1966.
Curtis, Charlotte. *The Rich and Other Atrocities.* New York: Harper & Row Publishers, 1976.
Curtis, Charlotte. "White House Candidates Let the Women Down." *New York Times,* May 7, 1968.
Davies, David. *The Postwar Decline of American Newspapers, 1945–1965.* Westport, Connecticut: Praeger Publishers, 2006.
Diamondstein, Barbaralee. *Open Secrets: 94 Women in Touch With Our Time.* New York: Viking Press, 1972.
Douglas, Susan. *Where the Girls Are: Growing Up Female With the Mass Media.* New York: Random House, 1995.
Downey, Kirstin. *The Woman Behind the New Deal.* New York: Anchor Books, 2009.
"Dreyfus Pops Off Too Much." *Capital Times,* December 20, 1978.
Duerst-Lahti, Georgia. "The Government's Role In Building the Women's Movement." *Political Science Quarterly,* 1989.
Dwyer, Florence. "Appeals to President Nixon for Equality." *Sarasota Herald-Tribune,* March 15, 1969.
East, Catherine. "Remarks for Veterans of Feminist America Meeting." May 26, 1993, 5, Veteran Feminist of America Papers, Duke University.
Edwards, Susan. *Erma Bombeck: A Life in Humor.* New York: Avon Books, 1997.
Eisenhower, Julie Nixon. *Pat Nixon: The Untold Story.* New York: Simon and Schuster, 1986.
"The Equal Rights Amendment: Why the ERA Remains Legally Viable and Properly Before the States." *William & Mary Journal of Women and the Law,* Spring 1997.
Feingold, Russ. "Kathryn Clarenbach." *Congressional Record,* Vol 140, Number 26, March 10, 1994.
"Feminist Sees Improving Climate." *Milwaukee Journal,* May 23, 1971.
Ferguson, Kennan. "Intensifying Taste, Intensifying Identity: Collectively through Community Cookbooks." *Signs* 37, no. 3 (2012): 696.
Fitzgerald, Sara, and Elly Peterson. *Mother of the Moderates.* Ann Arbor, Michigan: University of Michigan Press, 2012.
Fogel, Helen. "GM and Women Today." *Detroit Free Press,* April 1972.
Fogel, Helen. "GM Executive Looks at the Impact of Women Workers." *Detroit Free Press,* April 1972.
Fogel, Helen. "Putting New Rules into Effect," *Detroit Free Press,* April 1972.
Fogel, Helen. "US Industry, Women Head For New Era." *Detroit Free Press,* April 1972.
Fout, Ellen Pratt. "A Miracle Occurred!" *The Houston Review,* Vol.1, No.1, 4.
Freeman, Jo. *We Will Be Heard: Women's Struggles for Political Power in the United States.* Lanham, Maryland: Rowman & Littlefield, 2008.
Friedan, Betty. "Introduction." in *The Green Stubborn Bud: Women's Culture at Century's Close* Kathryn F. Clarenbach and Edward L. Kamarck, eds., Metuchen, New Jersey: Scarecrow Press, 1987.
"The Gasparilla Cookbook's 50th Edition Media Kit." www.jltampa.org/documents/17931/85667/The_Gasparilla_Cookbook_Media_Kit.pdf.

Gerbner, George and Larry Gross. "Living with Television: The Violence Profile." *Journal of Communication*, 1976, 172-199.
Gilmore, Stephanie. *Groundswell: Grassroots Activism in Postwar America.* New York: Routledge, 2013.
Gilmore, Stephanie. "Thinking about Feminist Coalitions." *Feminist Coalitions: Historical Perspectives on Second-Wave Feminism in the United States.* Urbana, Illinois: University of Illinois Press, 2008, 228–229.
Glaser, Vera. "Ballots or Bullets." *Miami Herald*, March 21, 1969.
Glaser, Vera. *Congressional Record*. E1987, March 17, 1971.
Glaser, Vera. "Elly Peterson Is Bowing Out." *Detroit Free Press*, October 17, 1970.
Glaser, Vera. "Elly Peterson Raps GOP Senator, Aide." *Miami Herald*, March 20, 1979.
Glaser, Vera. "Females Are Still 'Forgotten' in D.C." *Miami Herald*, April 30, 1969.
Glaser, Vera. "For the Female Sex, There Is No Justice." *Miami Herald*, March 20, 1969.
Glaser, Vera. "Karate School Linked to Korean Power Play." *Evening Independent (FL)*, November 19, 1976.
Glaser, Vera. "Women Discriminated Against?" *Amarillo, Texas Globe-Times*, October 16, 1963.
Glaser, Vera and Malvina Stephenson. "Far East Visitor—No Official Status." *Evening Star*, July 20, 1969.
Glaser, and Malvina Stephenson. "Jackie's Renounced Pension is Surrounded by Secrecy." *Boston Globe*, January 9, 1969.
Goodman, Ellen. "Yesterday's Conservatives, Today's Radicals." *Boston Globe*, November 7, 1977.
Gore, Emily. *Martha W. Griffiths*. Washington, DC: University Press of America, 1982.
Grimes, William. "Elly Peterson, 94, a Leader of Moderate Republicans, Is Dead." *New York Times*, June 30, 2008.
Gudelunas, David. *Confidential to America.* New Brunswick: Transaction Publishers, 2008, 2.
Guenin, Zena Beth. "Women's Pages in the 1970s." *Montana Journalism Review*, 27.
Hammel, Lisa. "They Meet in Victorian Parlor to Demand 'True Equality'—NOW." *New York Times*, November 22, 1966.
Hanlon, Pam. "Women's Rising Status Will Affect News Coverage." *Columbia Missourian*, March 17, 1967.
Harrison, Cynthia. *On Account of Sex: The Politics of Women's Issues 1945–1968.* Berkeley, California: University of California Press, 1988.
Hart, Eleanor. "Let Daughter Go to College; She's Worth It." *Miami Herald*, January 19, 1962.
Heilbrun, Carolyn G. *Writing A Woman's Life*. New York: Ballentine Books, 2002.
Hewitt, Nancy, ed. *No Permanent Waves: Recasting Histories of U.S Feminism.* New Jersey: Rutgers University Press, 2010.
"Hillary Clinton's 1992 Wellesley Commencement Speech Tackles Issues Relevant Decades Later." *Huffington Post*, August 3, 2013.
"History." National Press Club Website. http://www.press.org/about/history.
Hole, Judith, and Ellen Levine. *Rebirth of Feminism*. New York: New York Times Book, 1971.
Honan, William. "Frances Knight, 94, Director Of Passport Office for Decades." *New York Times*, September 18, 1999.
Horn, Miriam. *Rebels in White Gloves: Coming of Age with Hillary's Class – Wellesley '69.* New York: Random House, 1999.
Houck, Jeff. "50 Years Later, 'Gasparilla Cookbook' A Tasty Classic." *Tampa Tribune*, September 13, 2011.
Hoyt, Ken, and Frances Spatz Leighton. *Drunk Before Noon: The Behind-the Scenes Story of the Washington Press Corps.* Englewood Cliff, New Jersey: Prentice-Hall, 1979.
Hutchinsin, Louise. "Nixon Pledges to Seek Jobs for Women." *Chicago Tribune*, July 9, 1969.
Jurney, Dorothy. "I Was Replaced As a City Editor By An Ex-Copy Boy." *ASNE Bulletin*, November 1992, 27.
Jurney, Dorothy. "Percentage of Women Editors Creeps Upward to 11.7—But Other Fields Continue to Progress Faster." *ASNE Bulletin* (January 1986): 8–11.

Jurney, Dorothy. "Tenth Annual Survey Reports Women Editors at 12.4 percent." *ASNE Bulletin* (November 1986): 5.
Jurney, Dorothy. "Women in Journalism." Washington Press Club Foundation. http://www.wpcf.org/women-in-journalism/.
Jurney, Dorothy. "Women In Journalism." *The Bulletin*, American Society of Newspaper Editors, January 1, 1956, 5.
Jurney, Dorothy. "Women's Liberation." *Philadelphia Inquirer*, November 10, 1967.
Karmin, Monroe. "New U.S. Commission Plans Big Push to Open More Posts to Negroes." *Wall Street Journal*, October 13, 1965.
Klein, Frederick C. "Colleges Tempt Older Career-Minded Women to Return to Class." *Wall Street Journal*, May 7, 1964.
Klemesrud, Judy. "In Small Town U.S.A., Women's Liberation Is Either a Joke or a Bore." *New York Times*, March 22, 1972.
Klemerud, Judy. "International Women's Year Torch Arrives." *New York Times*, November 19, 1977.
Klemesrud, Judy. "Scrappy, Unofficial Women's Parley Sets Pace." *New York Times*, June 29, 1975.
Kotlowski, Dean J. *Nixon's Civil Rights: Politics, Principle, and Policy.* Cambridge, Massachusetts: Harvard, 2001.
Kuck, Elizabeth J. "The Editor, Life Magazine." *Congressional Record*, December 10, 1968.
"Law on Sex-Labeled Job Ads is Upheld." *New York Times*, June 22, 1973.
Leader, Shelah Gilbert, and Patricia Rusch Hyatt. *American Women on the Move: The Inside Story of the National Women's Conference, 1977.* Lanham, Maryland: Lexington Books, 2016.
Leighton, Frances Spatz. "Has Women's Lib Gone Too Far—Or Not Far Enough?" *Family Weekly*, June 9, 1976, 4.
Lerner, Gerta. "Midwestern Leaders of the Modern Women's Movement: An Oral History Project." *Wisconsin Academy Review*, Winter 1994–95, 12.
Levine, Suzzane Braun, and Mary Thom. *Bella Abzug.* New York: Farrar, Strauss and Giroux, 2007.
Levy, Alan. *The Political Life of Bella Abzug, 1976–1998.* Lanham, Maryland: Lexington Books, 2013.
Lewis, Norman. "From Cheesecake to Chief: Newspapers Editors' Slow Acceptance of Women." *American Journalism* 25:2 (Spring 2008): 33–55.
Love, Barbara J., and Nancy F. Cott. *Feminists Who Changed America 1963–1975.* Urbana, Illinois: University of Illinois Press, 2006.
Maas, Jane. *Mad Women: The Other Side of Life on Madison Avenue in the 60's and Beyond.* New York: St. Martin's Press, 2012.
MacPherson, Myra. "Wives, Silent Partners at Combined Cabinet Session." *Toledo (Ohio) Blade*, April 20, 1969.
Mandigo, Pauline. "Good Public Relations." *General Federation of Women's Clubs Newsletter*, December 1950, 12.
Mansnerus, Laura. "Bella Abzug, 77, Congresswoman and a Founding Feminist Is Dead." *New York Times*, April 1, 1998.
"Mary Ann Grossman's 50 Years at the St. Paul Pioneer Press Celebrated." *St. Paul Pioneer Press*, April 11, 2011.
Martin, Janet M. *The Presidency and the Women: Promise, Performance & Illusion.* College Station, Texas: Texas A & M University Press, 2003.
Martin, Judith. "In Defense of 'Women's Pages.'" *Washington Post*, December 12, 2014.
Martin, Judith. "Too Much a Lady?" *New York Times*, August 29, 1999.
McBride, Genevieve. *Women's Wisconsin: From Native Matriarchies to the New Millennium.* Madison, Wisconsin: Wisconsin Historical Society, 2005.
McBride, Marian. *Wisconsin Women: Know Your Rights.* Milwaukee, Wisconsin: *Milwaukee Sentinel*, 1968.
McElhaney, Jacquelyn Masur. *Pauline Periwinkle and Progressive Reform in Dallas.* College Station, Texas: Texas A & M Press, 1998.

McFadden, Robert D. "Charlotte Curtis, a Columnist for the *Times*, is Dead at 58." *New York Times*, April 17, 1987.
McLendon, Winzola. *Martha: The Life of Martha Mitchell*. New York: Balllantines, 1979.
McLendon, Winzola, and Scottie Smith. *Don't Quote Me: Washington Newswomen & the Power Society*. New York: E.P Dutton & Company, 1970.
Mills, Kay. "What Difference Do Women Journalists Make?" in Pippa Norris, ed, *Women, Media, and Politics*. New York: Oxford University Press, 1997.
Molotsky, Irvin. "Esther Peterson Dies at 91; Worked to Help Consumers." *New York Times*, December 22, 1997.
Morales, Beverly. "Candidate Use of Sex Appeal Woos Women." *Sun-Sentinel*, October 7, 1966.
Morgan, Robin. "Letter to the editor." *New York Times*, September 26, 1999.
Morgan, Robin. *The Word of a Woman: Feminist Dispatches, 1968-1992*. New York: W.W. Norton & Company, 1992.
Moyers, Bill. 1971 Penney-Missouri Magazine Awards Luncheon, November 3, 1971, New York, New York. Papers of J.C. Penney, Southern Methodist University, Dallas, Texas.
"Mrs. Schlafly Attacks Women's Year Project. *St. Louis Globe-Democrat*, July 16–17, 1977.
Mueller, Carol. *Conflict Networks and the Origins of Women's Liberation*. Edited by Enrique Larana, Hank Johnston, and Joseph Gusfied. New Social Movements. Philadelphia: Temple University Press, 1994.
Murphy, Kay. "What Makes Women's Department Tick?" A Green-Eyed Editor Named Dorothy," *Miami Herald*, April 17, 1955.
Murray, Pauli. *Song in a Weary Throat: An American Pilgrimage*. New York: Harper & Row, 1987.
National Association of Commissions for Women. *Handbook for Commissions on the Status of Women*. Madison, Wisconsin: Regents of the University of Wisconsin System, 1979.
National Commission on the Observance of International Women's Year, *To Form a More Perfect Union, Justice for American Women*, 1976.
National Organization for Women, "Honoring Our Founders and Pioneers." NOW Website. http://now.org/about/history/honoring-our-founders-pioneers/
"News Guild Urges Equal Jo Status." *New York Times*, July 13, 1962.
"Nixon's Task Force Urges US Department of Women." *Miami Herald*, April 22, 1970.
Norris, John. *Mary McGrory: The First Queen of Journalism*. New York: Viking Press, 2015.
O'Farrell, Brigid, and Joyce L. Kornbluh. *Rocking the Boat: Union Women's Voices, 1915–1975*. New Jersey: Rutgers University Press, 1996.
Ogan, Christine. "On Their Way to the Top? Men and Women Middle-Level Newspaper Managers." Paper presented at the annual meeting of AEJMC, Houston, Texas, August 5, 1979.
Olcott, Jocelyn. "Empires of Information: Media Strategies for the 1975 International Women's Year," *Journal of Women's History*, 2012, 24.
Orwin, Anne S. "Labor Roots and the Women's Movement." *Women's Studies Quarterly*, Fall 1999, 269.
Otto, Jean. "Equal Rights: 'Wow!' and 'What's That?'" *Milwaukee Journal*, August 11, 1970.
"Oveta Culp Hobby." Famous Texans. http://www.famoustexans.com/OvetaCulpHobby.htm.
"Panel Backs Separate Job Listings." *Milwaukee Journal*, September 22, 1968.
Paterson, Judith. *Be Somebody: A Biography of Marguerite Rawalt*. Austin, Texas: Eakin Press, 1986.
Paxson, Marjorie. *New Guardians of the Press: Selected Profiles of America's Women Newspaper Editors*, ed. Judith Clabes. Indianapolis: R.J. Berg & Co. Publishers, 1983, 126-129.
Paxson, Marjorie. "Where the Girls Are Going." *The Iowa Publisher*, October 1967, 13.
Paxson, Marjorie. "Women in Journalism." Washington Press Club Foundation. http://www.wpcf.org/women-in-journalism/.
Pedriana, Nicholas. "Help Wanted NOW: Legal Resources, the Women's Movement, and the Battles Over Sex-Segregated Job Advertisements." *Social Problems*, 2004, 184.
Peterson, Esther. *Restless: The Memoirs of Labor and Consumer Activist Esther Peterson*. Washington, DC: Caring Publishing, 1997.

Peterson, Esther. "Working Women." *Daedalus*, (1964), 671–699.
Pollack, Ruth. *The Equal Rights Amendment: Unfinished Business for the Constitution*. Educational Film Center, 1998.
Povich, Lynn. *The Good Girl Revolt: How the Women of Newsweek Sued Their Bosses and Changed the Workplace*. New York: Public Affairs, 2012.
Pratte, Alf. "A Tortuous Route to Growing Up: The Rise of Women in the American Society of Newspaper Editors." *Journal of Women's History* (Spring 1994): 51–66.
Pratte, Paul Alfred. *Gods Within The Machine: A History of the American Society of Newspaper Editors, 1923–1993*. Westport, Conn.: Praeger, 1995.
Price, Jenny. "This Woman's Work." *On Wisconsin*, Fall 2016, 44–49.
Pundyk, Jeff. "AP's $2 Million Denial." *Washington Journalism Review* (September 1983): 13–14.
Radcliffe, Donnie. "New Order at Press Club." *Washington Evening Star*, September 17, 1971.
Ramirez, Anthony. "Catherine East, 80, Inspiration For National Women's Group." *New York Times*, August 20, 1996.
Ritchie, Donald A. *Reporting from Washington: The History of the Washington Press Corps*. New York: Oxford University Press, 2005.
Roberson, Nellie. "The Work of Women's Organizations." *The Journal of Social Forces*, (1922): 50.
Robertson, Nan. *The Girls in the Balcony: Women, Men, and the New York Times*. New York: Random House, 1992.
Robinson, Melinda. "Irene Walczak on Betting and Arts." *Palm Beach Daily News*, January 5, 1971.
Roe, Dorothy. *The Problem With Women in Men*. New York: Prentice-Hall, 1961.
Rosen, Ruth. *The World Split Open: How the Modern Women's Movement Changed America*. New York: Viking Penguin, 2000.
Rossi, Alice S. *Feminists in Politics: A Panel Analysis of the First National Women's Conference*. New York: Harcourt Brace Jovanovich, 1982.
Rupp, Leila, and Verta Taylor. *Surviving the Doldrums: The American Women's Movement, 1945 to the 1960s*. Columbus, Ohio: Ohio State University Press, 1990.
Ryan, Aileen. "Women's World: 'Not so.'" *Once a Year*, 1961, 57.
Ryan, Barbara. *Feminism and the Women's Movement: Dynamics of Change in Social Movement Ideology and Activism*. New York: Routledge, 1992.
Sartorius, Kelly C. *Dean of Women and the Feminist Movement*. New York: Palgrave MacMillan, 2014.
Saulsbury, Marie. Associated Press Managing Editors, 1975. Papers of Marie Anderson.
Saxon, Wolfgang. "Elizabeth Koontz, 69, Dies; Led Teachers' Union." *New York Times*, January 8, 1989.
Schultz-Brooks, Terri. "Getting There: Women in the Newsroom." *Columbia Journalism Review* (March/April 1984): 25–31.
Scott, Anne Firor. *Making the Invisible Woman Visible*. Urbana, Illinois: University of Illinois Press, 1984.
"Select Committee on the Centennial History of the Indiana General Assembly: Indiana Historical Bureau." *A Biographical Directory of the Indiana General Assembly*, Vol. 2. 1980–1984.
Sherry, Dick. "Women's Page Revolt: To the Classifieds!" *Editor & Publisher*, December 26, 1964.
Siegel, Deborah. *Sisterhood Interrupted: From Radical Women to Grrls Gone Wild*. New York: Palgrave Macmillan, 2007.
Simpson, Peggy A. "1979: Covering the Women's Movement." *Nieman Reports*, Winter 1999–Spring 2000. http://niemanreports.org/articles/1979-covering-the-womens-movement.
Sinclair, Molly. "Demands Get Louder for Release Of Task Force Report on Women." *Miami Herald*, May 8, 1970.
Skow, John. "Erma in Bomburbia." *Time*, July 2, 1984, 2, 10.
Smith, Marie. "Blows Bugle for Senator But Can't Vote for Her Boss." *Washington Post*, October 24, 1958.

Sohn, Ardyth Broadrick Sohn, "Women in Newspaper Management: An Update." *Newspaper Research Journal* 3:1 (Fall 1981): 94–106.

Stamler, Mike. "Commission Shouldn't 'Croak,' 2 women officials tell Dreyfus." *Capital Times*, December 20, 1978.

"State Woman Named Director of IWY." *The Post-Crescent*, July 17, 1977.

Steinem, Gloria. *My Life on the Road*. New York: Random House, 2015.

Step by Step: Building a Feminist Movement. Wisconsin Public Television. 1998. VHS.

Stout, Lee. *A Matter of Simple Justice: The Untold Story of Barbara Hackman Franklin and a Few Good Women*. University Park, Pennsylvania: Pennsylvania State University Libraries, 2012.

Straitmatter, Rodger. "Transforming the Women's Pages." *Journalism History*, 24 (2), 1998, 72–81.

Sullivan, Patricia. "Vera Glaser, Veteran Washington Reporter, Dies at 92." *Washington Post*, January 5, 2009.

Times Wire Service, "Esther Van Wagoner Tufty, Newswoman, Dies at 89." *Los Angeles Times*, May 6, 1986.

"Tough Training Ground for Women's Minds." *Life*, December 24, 1956, 102–107.

Tuchman, Gaye. *Making News*. New York: Free Press, 1978.

Ulrich, Laurel Thatcher. *Well-Behaved Women Seldom Make History*. New York: Knopf, 2008.

"Unsexing the Classifieds." *Life*, December 6, 1968.

UPI, "Kathryn Clarenbach Analyzes Issues at Fall Women's Conference." *Milwaukee Sentinel*, August 13, 1977.

Wasniewski, Matthew Andrew. *Women in Congress, 1917–2006*. Washington, DC: Government Printing Office, 2006.

Weatherford, Doris. *They Dared to Dream: Florida Women Who Shaped History*. University Press of Florida, 2015.

Weil, Martin. "Pioneering Post Journalist Marie Sauer." *Washington Post*, October 9, 2001.

Wells, Robert Wells. *The Milwaukee Journal: An Informal Chronicle of Its First 100 Years*. Milwaukee: The Milwaukee Journal, 1981.

Werne, Jo. "Marie Anderson." *Miami Herald*, July 2, 1996.

Werne, Jo Anne. "Women Demand Fair Share." *Miami Herald*, September 19, 1969.

"What Katie Did—Use Imagination." *Miami Herald*, June 18, 1964.

Wisconsin Women's Network Website, 1960s. http://www.wiwomensnetwork.org/.

"Women Crusaders Test Plaza's 'Men Only' Rule." *New York Times*, February 13, 1969.

"Women's Bureau Anniversary 90 Years: Still Working." Women's Bureau, http://www.dol.gov/wb/90years.htm.

Women's National Press Club. *Second Helping*. Washington, DC: McIver, 1962.

Women's National Press Club. *Who Says We Can't Cook!* Washington, DC: McIver, 1955.

Voss, Kimberly Wilmot, and Lance Speere. "A Women's Page Pioneer: Marie Anderson and Her Influence at the Miami Herald and Beyond." *Florida Historical Quarterly*, Spring (2007): 398–421.

Voss, Kimberly Wilmot. "Anne Rowe Goldman: Refashioning Women's News in St. Petersburg, Florida." *FCH Annals: Journal of the Florida Conference of Historians*, March 2011, 104–111.

Voss, Kimberly Wilmot. "Colleen 'Koky' Dishon: Journalism Legend." *Timeline*, July/September 2010, 2–17.

Voss, Kimberly Wilmot. "Forgotten Feminist: Women's Page Editor Maggie Savoy and the Growth of Women's Liberation Awareness in Los Angeles." *California History*, Spring 2009, 48–64.

Voss, Kimberly Wilmot. "Marjorie Paxson: From Women's Page Editor to Publisher." *Media History Monograph*, (2008).

Voss, Kimberly Wilmot and Lance Speere. "Quilted News: Mixing Hard and Soft News to Create a New Definition for Women's News." Florida Communication Association Conference, Orlando, October 18, 2013.

Voss, Kimberly Wilmot. "Remembering the Real Pioneers of Lifestyle Journalism." *Ms* Magazine blog, November 4, 2014.

Voss, Kimberly, "Roberta Applegate: Breaking Barriers in Michigan." *Michigan History Magazine,* March/April 2008.

Voss, Kimberly Wilmot. "Thank You, Justice Scalia, For Helping Revive the ERA." *Ms* Magazine Blog, January 10, 2011.

Voss, Kimberly Wilmot. "Vera Glaser: A Journalist's Ode to Offbeat Washington Politics." Hall Institute of Public Policy, (2009).

Voss, Kimberly Wilmot, and Lance Speere. "Way Past Deadline." *Wisconsin Magazine of History,* Autumn 2008.

Voss, Kimberly. "'You Can't Hug a Newspaper': Janet Chusmir, the *Miami Herald* and Newspaper Management," *FCH Annals: Journal of the Florida Conference of Historians*, May 2012.

Zann, Cally S. "Catherine East: Gatekeeper of the Women's Movement." Graduate paper, University of Maryland, May 1987.

Index

abortion, 120
Abzug, Bella, 2, 4, 12, 119–120, 121–122
advertising, help wanted, 100, 101–105
advice columns, 36, 96
African Americans: Koontz and, 21; and women's pages, 15; *See also under* Civil Rights
Agnew, Spiro, 80
airline discrimination, 89, 105
Alexander, Clifford L., Jr., 102
Allan, Virginia, 19, 22, 84, 129
Alverno College, 12
American Civil Liberties Union Women's Rights Project, 101
American Governmental Woman in Industry Service, 38
American Society of News Editors (ASNE), 15, 117, 130, 131
American Women, 40
Anderson, John, 12
Anderson, Marie: background of, 17–18; and continuing education, 99; in later years, 133–134; and media coverage, 86; on Paxson, 52; and politics, 22; and President's Task Force report, 18, 84–85; and relationships, 8, 9–10, 17, 18, 19, 35, 134; and women's clubs, 35, 36; in WWII, 17, 31, 35
Anderson, Mary, 38
Angelo, Bonnie, 73
Angelou, Maya, 122

Applegate, Roberta, 2, 34, 36–37, 51
Ashley, Laura, 29
ASNE. *See* American Society of News Editors
Associated Press, 114
Association for Women in Communications, 16, 52–53
Austin, Dorothy Witte, 94–95

Banaszak, Lee Ann, 8
bars, segregated, 74, 107
Beale, Betty, 56
Beasley, Maurine, 30, 56–57
Beebe, Lorraine N., 40
behind-the-scenes work. *See* well-behaved women
Berger, Caruthers, 50
Biggs, Gloria, 69
birth control, 49–50, 67, 120
Black, Shirley Temple, 60
Bolton, Roxcy O'Neal, 22, 106
Bombeck, Erma, 67–68
bona fide occupational qualification, term, 102
Boyer, Elizabeth, 103
Boyer, Gene, 21–22
Boylan v. New York Times, 100
Bradlee, Ben, 57
Broder, David, 55, 81
Brownmiller, Susan, 4, 81
Buchwald, Art, 68

Burdines Department Store, 106
Burns, Arthur, 85–86
Business and Professional Women Foundation, 38, 40

Canfield, James H., 33
Carswell, G. Harrold, 56
Carter administration, 62, 121
catfight framework, 4–5, 112
Chennault, Anna Chan, 61–62
Chesler, Ellen, 6
child care, 11, 30, 31
Chusmir, Janet, 55–56
Civil Rights Act, 20–21
Civil Rights movement, as model, 40, 42, 101, 105
Clapp, Charles, 75, 84
Clarenbach, Henry, 12
Clarenbach, Kathryn "Kay", 3, 88, 93–107; and airlines, 89; background of, 12–14; and behind-the-scenes work, 5, 6; and EEOC, 100, 101; on feminism, 80; and Houston Conference, 121; and IWY, 121–122; in later years, 131–132; and NOW, 20, 42–43, 44; and press clubs, 69; and relationships, 4, 8; and reproductive rights, 120; and state commissions, 40–41, 43–44; in WWII, 12, 33
Clinton, Hillary, 1, 97
clubwomen. *See* women's clubs
Cohen, Marcia, 6, 50
college. *See* education
Collins, Mary Jean, 13
Collins, Michael, 60
community development, women's clubs and, 33
conflict: Martin on, 51; media coverage of, 4–5, 112, 114, 131; Paxson on, 116; well-behaved women and, 29
Congressional Record, 76, 88
Conroy, Catherine, 44
continuing education for women, 18, 41, 97–99
cookbooks, 69–72
Cooke, Marlow, 97
Corbine, Pat, 118
Costanza, Midge, 62
Cott, Nancy, 79–80

Craig, May, 74
Croly, Jane Cunninham, 33
culture, women's clubs and, 33
Curtis, Charlotte, 127–129

Dear Abby, 96
Declaration of Sentiments, 122
discrimination, 41; DC journalism and, 56–57; EEOC and, 43, 101–102; Glaser's work on, 61, 83, 85–87; McBride on, 94; National Press Club and, 73–75. *See also* sexism
Dishon, Colleen "Koky", 100, 127–128
Douglas, Susan, 4–5, 37
dress code, 133
Dreyfus, Lee, 131–132
driver's licences, 41
dual waves theory, 9
Dwyer, Florence, 85

East, Catherine, 2; background of, 10–12; and behind-the-scenes work, 5, 5–6; on Glaser, 6; and help-wanted ads, 103; and IWY, 122; and media coverage, 129–131; on methods, 29; and NOW, 20, 42, 47n69; and political education, 85–87; and Presidential Commission, 39–40; and President's Task Force, 84; and relationships, 8, 18–19, 19–20, 84; and State Department report, 118, 119; and Supreme Court, 1, 82–83; in WWII, 11, 32–33
East, Charles D., 11
Eastwood, Mary, 11, 42, 95
Echeverria, Luis, 115
education: Anderson on, 17; continuing education for women, 18, 41, 97–99; controversy over, 95–97; Koontz and, 21; quotas in, 85–86, 96–97
EEOC. *See* Equal Employment Opportunity Commission
Eisenhower, Dwight D., 8, 54, 56
Eisenhower, Julie Nixon, 83
Ellsworth, Bob, 59
employment, women and: airlines and, 89, 105; controversy over, 95–97; government and, 37–38; Jurney and, 62; versus marriage, 11, 17, 18; want ads and, 100, 101–105; women's pages

and, 50–51; WWII and, 30–33
Equal Employment Opportunity Commission (EEOC), 43, 87, 99–101, 101–102
Equal Rights Amendment (ERA), 12, 120, 123; Bombeck and, 67, 68; continued fight for, 134–135; media and, 129, 130

Fagan, commissioner, 103
federal government: and constraints on behavior, 42, 43, 118; East and, 11, 11–12; Hobby and, 8; journalists and, 7–8; women and, 7, 37–38, 39; Women's Bureau, Labor Department, 2, 21, 37–38, 39, 40
Feingold, Russ, 14
"Female Revolt" series, 87–89
The Feminine Mystique (Friedan), 42
feminism: backlash to, 132; Biggs on, 69; Jurney and, 14; term, 37, 68–69, 79–80
Finch, Bob, 58
Fogel, Helen, 63
Franklin, Barbara Hackman, 11, 82
Friedan, Betty: and airlines, 89; on careers, 98; and Clarenbach, 95, 132; and East, 5; and EEOC, 100; Hachten and, 94; and help-wanted ads, 102; media coverage and, 4, 5, 6; and NOW, 20, 42, 44; and restaurant integration, 106
Furness, Betty, 10

Gannett newspapers, 16, 132–133
Garth, Joseph, 76
The Gasparilla Cookbook, 70–71
Gibbons, Shelia, 30
Gilmore, Stephanie, 8–9
Ginsburg, Ruth Bader, 101, 135
girls, term, 33
Glaser, Herbert, 9
Glaser, Vera, 2, 5, 7; background of, 9–10; and behind-the-scenes work, 6–7; and discrimination, 73; and educational quotas, 96–97; "Female Revolt" series, 87–89; and journalism, 53–55, 56; in later years, 134; and media coverage, 29; and National Press Club, 75–76; and Nixon, 81–82; and political education, 85–87; and President's Task Force, 83–85; and relationships, 9–10, 18–19; and State Department report, 119; and Supreme Court, 1, 55, 82–83; and Washington Offbeat, 58–62
Goldwater, Barry, 72
Goodman, Ellen, 121
Graham, Richard, 20, 43
Greene, Edee, 106
Greer, Germaine, 114
Griffiths, Martha, 11, 12, 20–21, 42, 79, 87
Grossman, Mary Ann, 112
Guarnotta, Gloria, 30
Guenin, Zena Beth, 49
Gulf + Western Industries Luncheon Club, 105–106

Hachten, Harva, 94
Haig, Alexander, Jr., 83
Haldeman, H. R., 83
hard news, term, 111
Harris, Lucy, 117
Hart, Eleanor, 96
Heilbrun, Carolyn, 4
Helms, Jesse, 120
help-wanted ads, 100, 101–105
Henry, Fran, 120, 123
Hernandez, Aileen, 43, 61, 102
Hickey, Margaret, 43
Hills, Lee, 18
Hobby, Oveta Culp, 7–8, 54
Hobby, William P., 7
homosexuality, 120
Houston, TX. *See* National Women's Conference, Houston
Hyatt, Patricia Rusch, 113

Indritz, Phineas, 103
International Women's Year, 1–2, 12, 111–123
Interstate Association of Commissions for Women, 40

Jennie June, 33
Jennings, Clyde, Jr., 61
Johnson, Lyndon B., 10, 57, 72
Joseph, Geri, 85
journalism, 49–63; and federal government, 7–8; Glaser and, 53–55; Jurney and, 14–15; Paxson and, 15–17; press clubs for women, 69–72;

Stephenson and, 22; and Washington, DC, 56–58; women and, 2, 3, 6–7, 131; WWII and, 31–32. *See also* media coverage; women's pages
Junior League, 17, 35, 70–71, 122
Jurney, Dorothy, 2, 7; background of, 14–15; and Houston Conference, 122; and media coverage, 115, 129–131; and relationships, 8, 17, 18, 19–20, 35, 134; and reproductive rights, 120; and State Department report, 116–119; and women's clubs, 35, 36; and women's pages, 49–50, 51, 62–63; in WWII, 31–32
jury service, 94

Keating, Kenneth B., 54
Kennedy, Jackie, 59–60, 70–71
Kennedy, John F., 74
Kennedy, Teddy, 59
Kennedy administration, 58; East and, 11; and women, 39
Kerr, Robert S., 22
Keyserling, Mary, 43
Khrushchev, Nikita, 74
Klemesrud, Judy, 80
Knight, Frances, 60
Knight Newspapers, 9
KNOW, Inc., 10
Komisar, Lucy, 107
Koontz, Elizabeth Duncan "Libby", 12, 21

labor movement: Jurney and, 62; Martin and, 51; and women's movement, 2, 9, 44, 101
Laidlaw, Dorothy, 50
Landers, Ann, 36, 68, 96
Lawrence, Bill, 74
Leader, Shelah Gilbert, 113
League of Women Voters, 12, 122
Lederer, Eppie. *See* Landers, Ann
Lee, Elinor, 71
legal issues, 94; discrimination lawsuits, 100–101, 104
Lerner, Gerda, 5, 6
Lewine, Fran, 75
libraries, women's clubs and, 33
Life, 103
Lindsay, John V., 107

Livingston, Eleanor, 50
Logan Act, 61–62
Louchheim, Katie, 52
Luce, Clare Boothe, 54
Lucy, Patrick, 21
Luther, June, 50

Maas, Jane, 30
management positions, women and, 32; Jurney and, 117, 131; Paxson and, 132–133
Marcy, Mildred, 118, 119, 122
marriage: Anderson on, 17; Clarenbach and, 12; Clinton on, 97; East and, 11; Paxson on, 16
Martin, Judith, 58, 74
Martin, Marion, 51
May, Catherine, 82
McBride, Marian, 94
McClendon, Sarah, 85
McDuffie, Ann, 70
McGhee, Roy, 74
McGrory, Mary, 57
McSorley's Old Ale House, 107
media coverage, 50; Anderson and, 17; catfight framework, 4–5, 112; Clarenbach and, 93–95; and education, 95; Fogel on, 63; Glaser and, 10; as hostile, 29–30, 80–81, 103; of Houston Conference, 119; Jurney and, 62; and lawsuits, 100–101; of Mexico City Conference, 7, 112, 113, 115–116; of NOW, 44; Paxson and, 16; and political education, 85–87; recommendations for, 36; research on, 129–131; and State Department report, 118; and symbolic annihilation, 87; and well-behaved women, 3–4; and women's clubs, 34, 35–37; *Xilonen*, 113–116. *See also* journalism; Glaser, Vera
Meet the Press, 10
Mexico City Conference, 7, 112–116
Michigan, 40
Midwestern women, 5, 6. *See also* Clarenbach, Kathryn "Kay"; Wisconsin
militants: methods of, 79; relationship with well-behaved women, 99, 122; term, 43
Mills, Kay, 100, 111
Milwaukee Journal, 93–94, 102

Milwaukee Press Club, 69
Misener, Dorothy. *See* Jurney, Dorothy
Misener, Mary Hershey, 14
Miss America Pageant protest, 128
Mitchell, John, 58, 61, 82
Mitchell, Martha, 61
Moore, Gwen, 134–135
Morales, Beverly, 51
Morgan, Robin, 128–129, 132
Moyers, Bill, 68–69
Mueller, Carol, 81
Muir, Helen, 33
Murray, Pauli, 12, 120; background of, 22; and NOW, 42, 44

National Association of Commissions for Women, 41
National Commission on the Observance of International Women's Year, 15
National Conference of Governor's Commissions on the Status of Women, 40, 42–44
National Organization for Women (NOW), 3; and airlines, 89; Clarenbach and, 13, 95; East and, 20; founding of, 21, 42–44, 47n69; and help-wanted ads, 101–105; and Houston Conference, 122; media coverage and, 88; and National Press Club, 74–75; and restaurant integration, 106–107
National Press Club, 10, 73–75; Glaser and, 75–76
National Women and Media Center, 7
National Women's Conference, Houston, 1, 119, 120–123; Boyer and, 22; Clarenbach and, 13; Jurney and, 15; progress following, 127–135; report on, 123
National Women's Political Caucus, 13
New Directions for News, 15, 129–131
Newsweek, 100
New York Times, 100
Nixon, Pat, 1, 74, 82–83, 104
Nixon, Richard M., 74, 75; Glaser and, 81–82
Nixon administration: Glaser and, 10, 58, 60, 61–62, 83–84; Koontz and, 21; McGrory and, 57; and Supreme Court, 1; and women, 81–83; and Women's

Equality Day, 22
nongovernmental organizations, 112, 113
North American Newspaper Alliance, 9, 55
NOW. *See* National Organization for Women

Oak Room, Plaza Hotel, 106
O'Connor, Sandra Day, 1
O'Hanrahan, Inka, 44
Olson, Beth, 29
opposition to women's movement: issues in, 120–121; media coverage of, 29–30; men and, 33, 73, 76; women's pages and, 37
Othman, Frederick, 74
Otto, Jean, 93

Pancoast, Kay, 31, 45n14
Paxson, Marjorie, 2, 7; background of, 15–17; in later years, 132–133; and relationships, 20; and State Department report, 117, 118, 119; and Theta Sigma Phi, 16, 52–53; and women's pages, 8; in WWII, 15, 32; and *Xilonen*, 113–115
Penney-Missouri Awards, 17, 112, 117
Periwinkle, Pauline, 35
Perkins, Frances, 8
Persinger, Mildred, 115
Peterson, Elly, 55–56
Peterson, Esther, 9, 12, 13, 39, 41; background of, 20; and continuing education, 99; and cookbook, 71; and National Conference of Commissions, 43
Phillips, Pauline, 96
polite women. *See* well-behaved women
politics: and media partnership, 85–87; Paxson on, 116; women and, 22, 51, 55–56; women's pages and, 62–63
Porto, Ollie, 50–51
Potter, Charles E., 54
Povich, Lynn, 100
Powell, lewis F., 83
Poynter, Henrietta, 71
Poynter, Nelson, 71
Presidential Commission on the Status of Women, 2, 38–40, 112; East and, 11–12; Jurney and, 15; nature of, 39

President's Task Force on Women's Rights and Responsibilities, 10, 22, 83–85; report, publication of, 18, 84–85
press. *See* journalism; media coverage
press clubs, 10, 69–72, 73–76

Quayle, Dan, 97
quilted news, term, 111

Rabin, Leah, 115
race issues: Civil Rights Act, 20; and government appointments, 60–61; Jurney and, 62; Koontz and, 21; Paxson and, 15
Rattle, Eleanor, 96
Rawalt, Marguerite, 11; background of, 21; and EEOC, 100, 103; and NOW, 42, 43
Rehnquist, William, 83
Reid, Charlotte, 82
relationships among well-behaved women, 2, 3, 8, 18–20, 35; Anderson and, 17; Clarenbach and, 13; in later years, 132, 134; Paxson and, 15–16; and President's Task Force, 84
Republican Party, and women, 54, 55–56
respectable women. *See* well-behaved women
restaurants, segregated, 12, 105–107
Reston, Scotty, 57
Reynolds, John, 13
Ricker, Dorothy, 36
Rigby, Cora, 72
Roberts, Chalmers, 73
Robertson, Nan, 74, 100
Roe, Dorothy, 31, 34
Romney, George W., 55
Romney, Lenore, 86
Roosevelt, Eleanor, 22, 72
Roosevelt, Franklin, 72
Rosen, Ruth, 30, 80
Rossi, Alice S., 9
Rubin, Barbara Jo, 86
Ruckelshaus, Jill, 118, 121, 122
Rupp, Leila J., 50
Ryan, Aileen, 76

Salinger, Pierre, 55
Sauer, Marie, 57–58
Saulsbury, Marie, 37

Scalia, Antonin, 134–135
Schlafly, Phyllis, 2–3, 121
Scott, Anne Firor, 34
Seneca Falls, NY, 1, 122
Sevareid, Eric, 80–81
Severance, Carol, 129
sexism: Nixon administration and, 83; term, 80. *See also* discrimination
Shipe, Bertha Woody, 10
Shipe, Catherine. *See* East, Catherine
Shipe, Ulysses Grant, 10
shrillness, term, 4
Simpson, Peggy, 112, 114–115
skill development: cookbooks and, 70; women's clubs and, 34, 36
Smith, Howard, 20–21
Smith, Margaret Chase, 72
Snyder, Mary Jane, 52
Society for Professional Journalists, 52
soft news, 131; term, 111
Sorosis, 34
State Commissions on the Status of Women, 18, 37–38, 40–44
State Department report, 2, 16, 20, 116–120
Steinem, Gloria, 4, 120
Stephenson, Malvina, 22, 72; and Washington Offbeat, 58–62
Stevenson, Charles, 31–32
Streitmatter, Rodger, 49–50
Stuart, Lulubelle, 62
Supreme Court, 1, 55, 82–83, 101, 105
Swainson, John, 40
symbolic annihilation, 87

Taylor, Verta, 50
Terry, Mary, 129
Theta Sigma Phi, 16, 52–53
Thomas, Helen, 75
Title IX, 117
To Form a More Perfect Union, 2, 16, 20, 116–120
Tower Club, 106
Tribune, 112, 113, 115
Trump, Donald, 1
Tuchman, Gaye, 87
Tufty, Esther Van Wagoner, 74

United Nations, and IWY, 2, 111–123

Van Buren, Abigail, 96
Van Hightower, Nikki R., 122
volunteerism. *See* women's clubs
voting. *See* League of Women Voters; politics

Walczak, Irene, 61
want ads, 100, 101–105
War Department, Women's Interest Section, 8
Washington, DC, journalism on, 56–58
Washington Offbeat, 18, 19, 22, 58–62
Washington Press Club, 10; founding of, 72–73
well-behaved women, 1–23; after Houston, 127–135; documentation on, 8–9; lack of attention to, 3, 5, 50; methods of, 29, 112; militants and, 99, 122; and women's pages, 49–50
Wells, Mildred White, 72
Whittaker, Hilary, 119
widows, 2
Williams, Claire B., 51, 54
Wilson, Bess, 36
Wilson, Lori, 79
Wisconsin: Clarenbach and, 13, 93–107, 121; Governor's Commission on the Status of Women, 12–13, 21, 41, 43–44, 131–132; Milwaukee Press Club, 69
Woman's Network, 117
Women in Journalism project, 10
Women's Army Auxiliary Corps, 8

Women's Bureau, Labor Department, 2, 21, 37–38, 39, 40
women's clubs, 33–35; women's pages and, 35–37, 112; and WWII, 31
Women's Equality Day, 22
women's liberation: term, 80. *See also* feminism; militants
women's movement: foundation of, 38–39; Glaser on, 83; Henry on, 123; issues in, 99–101; methods of, 29, 79; second wave, 30–33. *See also* media coverage
Women's National Press Club: cookbook, 71–72; founding of, 72–73
women's pages, 29–30; Anderson and, 17; content of, 8, 17, 49–52, 111–112; Curtis and, 127–128; end of, 16, 57; Glaser and, 9; Paxson and, 15–16; and politics, 62–63; and women's clubs, 35–37
Women's Press Club. *See* Washington Press Club
Women's Strike for Equality, 30, 80–81
World War II: Anderson and, 17, 31, 35; Clarenbach and, 12, 33; East and, 11, 32–33; Hobby and, 8; Paxson and, 15, 32; women and, 30–33; and women's roles, 14

Xilonen, 7, 16, 113–115

Young, Virginia Shuman, 106

Ziegler, Ronald, 83

About the Author

Kimberly Wilmot Voss (PhD, Maryland) is an associate professor at the University of Central Florida in Orlando. She researches the intersection of women and mass communication in the post-World War II years through the Women's Liberation Movement era. She specializes in the women's pages of newspapers—the only place for women in journalism for decades. She is the author of *The Food Section: Newspaper Women and the Culinary Community* (2014) and a co-author of *Mad Men & Working Women: Feminist Perspectives on Historical Power, Resistance and Otherness* (2014/2016). She has published more than forty articles about women and mass communication history. She contributes to *Ms* Magazine and *We're History* blogs. Her blog is *Women's Page History*.

CPSIA information can be obtained
at www.ICGtesting.com
Printed in the USA
BVOW04*2327220317
479089BV00001B/4/P

DATE DUE

PRINTED IN U.S.A.